SPANISH
FOR
CHRISTIAN
SERVICE

BY
KARYN
SHANDER

EDITED BY MARCO LOPEZ, CINDIE MOORE, JO MORETTA, AND DAISY TOMASSINI

FOREWORD BY DENNY HEIBERG

Although we have made every attempt to list the most commonly used terms, the vocabulary used here is not necessarily the same that is used throughout all of the Hispanic countries. Please check with your intended area for possible variations.

Published by Special Publications

743 SE Fort King Street

Ocala, Florida 34471

ISBN: 978-1-892937-02-5

Printed in the United States of America

*It is my great honor to dedicate this workbook to all who
are missionaries in the field of life, in their efforts to fulfill Jesus' Great
Commission. It is my wish to equip others for their lifetime journey.*

The Great Commission

*Go and make disciples of all nations, baptizing them
in the name of the Father and of the Son and of the Holy Spirit,
teaching them to obey everything I have commanded you.*

Matthew 28: 19-20 (NIV)

Foreword

As I reflect on my first mission trip to a Spanish-speaking country, I remember how thrilled I was to have the privilege of sharing the love of Jesus with people from a culture vastly different from the one in which I was raised. This would be my first experience in fulfilling Jesus' Great Commission of making disciples in a different people group than my own. My responsibility was to be a pastor to the team of volunteers from our church and to be ready to preach and share my faith story in any of our gatherings with the Guatemalan people. It wasn't long before I realized the priceless value of being able to communicate with others in their native tongue. My inability to speak Spanish greatly restricted me in communicating the very message God had sent me to deliver.

As soon as we arrived at the airport and worked our way through customs, I wished I had known some key Spanish phrases so I could comfortably communicate with the unfamiliar faces surrounding me. Now, as I look back on that experience and subsequent visits to Spanish speaking countries, I only wish I had had the opportunity to glean the insights from the workbook you are now holding in your hands.

It has been my privilege to know Karyn Shander for over fifteen years, and I have watched her mature in her faith as a follower of Jesus. Karyn's daily mission field is located in a university hospital in Gainesville, Florida. There she shares her faith through serving young mothers and their newborn babies. However, God has given Karyn a passion to serve the body of Christ by helping us fulfill the Great Commission with a scripturally-based working knowledge of the Spanish language. While there are countless resources in helping the average person become familiar with the Spanish language, I know of none other that targets the unique needs of those who desire to share God's truth with native Spanish-speaking people.

Within the following pages you will find a goldmine of valuable phrases that enable you to communicate effectively with the people that God is sending you to serve. As Karyn reveals in her introduction, this workbook was "created out of a desire to better equip Christian workers to evangelize in the Spanish language throughout the mission field." Karyn's heart for the church to obey Christ's Great Commission is contagious. And she is using her gifts and abilities to outfit us to communicate God's missional heartbeat to the Spanish-speaking world.

From the opening pages of the Bible, God has revealed that He is a missionary God. We find the first glimpse of the Great Commission in Genesis 12:1-3 as the Lord commissions Abram to leave the comfort of his familiar surroundings and go to a land that God would later entrust to Abram and his descendants. God reveals that Abram, in his obedience, will become a blessing to every family on the planet. God would do the blessing, but Abram had to do the going.

Some two thousand years later, God Himself left the comfort of His familiar surroundings and came into our world in the person of Jesus of Nazareth. Knowing His time would be brief, Jesus devoted Himself to learning the languages of the people to whom He was sent as well as equipping a small group of men to become His disciples. They would be held responsible for reaching their world with the Good News of

God's redeeming love. Just days before Jesus returned to heaven, Jesus met with His eleven interns and echoed the commission first given to Abram. "Go and make disciples of all the nations, baptizing them in the name of the Father and the Son and the Holy Spirit. Teach these new disciples to obey all the commands I have given you."

If you are a Christ-follower, you already know God's overall plan and will for your life; you are to become a disciple-making follower of Christ, and your mission field is wherever God sends you. If you live in North America, you have come to realize that you already live within a vast mission field. You no longer have to cross a political or geographic boundary to take the Gospel to another culture or language. People who speak Spanish can be found in many of our communities; therefore, Karyn's <u>Spanish</u> <u>for</u> <u>Christian</u> <u>Service</u> can be used by any of us who wish to be better equipped to communicate the treasure of the Gospel with our Spanish-speaking neighbors and fellow workers.

I commend you for investing your time and energy in Karyn's book. The reward for your perseverance will be the joy of looking into the eyes of our Spanish-speaking friends and communicating with confidence the treasure God has entrusted into your care as a disciple of Jesus. If you diligently apply yourself to the following strategic lessons, you will be a much more effective instrument as you seek to obey our Lord's mandate to make disciples of all peoples.

Denny C. Heiberg,
Global Discipleship Ministries
The Mission Society
Gainesville, Florida

Acknowledgements

There is one thing that I learned from the very beginning when I was writing this book, and I would like to share it with you. The task of writing this book at times was extremely challenging, but I learned quickly that God had placed the right people in my life to help me to accomplish this work. Without the many hours of their devoted time and talents, this book would not have been possible.

I would like to extend my sincere appreciation to the following individuals and to share with you several accounts on how we were brought together.

Many thanks go out to Cindie Moore for her diligence and patience with editing my work. We met one morning at a church service, when I felt compelled to sit beside her and to introduce myself. I quickly learned that her past experiences as editor and author, as well as her Spanish linguistic expertise would become a great asset to our common passion for outreach to the Hispanic population. We both believe that our chance meeting that morning was a divine placement by God. She motivated me, guided me and gave me sound advice in this new world of publishing.

I would also like to extend my thanks to Jo Moretta, who willingly poured her time and energy into editing. I know that this was not an easy undertaking. Our friendship was cultivated over the course of many years through travel time together to church retreats. When deciding to have her on my team, it was an easy decision, based on her additional talents as an English instructor.

My gratitude also is given to Marco Lopez, who diligently served as my Spanish advisor. He patiently endured many hours of editing my work and explaining many cultural variances to me.

Daisy Tomassini served as an additional support editor. I appreciate the expertise of her native Spanish language in combination with her fresh and practical ideas. This is a much better book because of her.

My appreciation also goes to Denny Heiberg, my pastor at Grace at Fort Clarke Church in Gainesville, Florida. He served as my source of inspiration and support over the years, leading the way for me to become a disciple of Jesus Christ in my own unique way. I am grateful for his big vision as well as for his agreeing to write the foreword to this book. I am honored to have him on my team.

I would like to thank the local Hispanic community of Gainesville and Ocala for their technical and spiritual support. There were many moments in writing this book when I felt that the brick walls that stood before me had become open doors through their prayers. They stood as my intercessors before our awesome God in helping to accomplish His will.

I am so deeply grateful to Sandra Graham, my beloved friend and confidant, for her time and efforts in this book. She has a special talent in knowing exactly when to arrive at the right moment to lift me up in prayer or to help facilitate tasks.

I also would like to express my deep appreciation to my husband, Rob Epperson. He showed tremendous patience and support while I spent thousands upon thousands of hours at my computer composing this book.

Special thanks to Tim Broom and Jeremiah Kilgore at the New Horizons Computer Learning Center in Gainesville for their technical support. They were able to speak the language of my great beast computer, for which I am forever grateful. Whenever I had a program glitch that I could not resolve, they were there to assist me in "taming the beast."

I would also like to thank my publisher, Alex Martínez, as well as his staff, who agreed to take on the enormous responsibility of turning my years of work into a finished book.

—Karyn Shander

Introduction

While working in a high risk tertiary care hospital, I have learned to recognize the importance of good communication. Health care workers who cannot convey crucial health concepts to patients who do not speak their primary language are limited in the ability to treat their patients effectively. In a likewise manner, a Christian worker is limited in the ability to communicate spiritual health concerns with someone who does not speak their language. For instance, how effectively can they speak about God and salvation through mere hand gestures and facial expressions? How well can they draw God on a piece of paper and convey the concept of Him to an unbeliever? Hand motions and facial expressions may be subject to cultural misinterpretations. Therefore, speaking in the listener's primary language is the key to effective communication.

There is an earnest passion for many Christians to journey to a Latin American country for mission work. I commend them for their highly valued and dedicated calling. However, what may hinder some from more effectively serving in any kind of mission capacity is the language barrier of these missionaries. Many may have acquired knowledge of a few phrases that were taught in school, but these were most likely phrases that were secular in nature. Their language curriculum may have lacked in the terminology related to spiritual matters. This book was created out of a desire to better equip Christian workers to evangelize in the Spanish language throughout the mission field.

Several years ago, I felt passionate about teaching a Spanish class at my church. Upon researching the textbooks that were available online, I found a serious need for Christian-related Spanish teaching material. This discovery led to my creation of learning tools that I compiled in the form of a workbook. In addition, I incorporated fun supplemental materials into the classroom learning environment in order to provide the students with a variety of activities. I would like to share some of my ideas here for starting a Christian Spanish class at any church, or for independent learners to create their own study program before going abroad.

In addition to this workbook, a bilingual bible is invaluable. Each page of a bilingual bible is aligned with parallel passages, both in English and in Spanish. Many English speaking students may already be familiar with popular bible passages, and may even have memorized a few. Study these same scriptural passages in Spanish. Because the scripture verses are aligned side by side on the same pages in a bilingual bible, it will be easier for the student to compare the English verse with the Spanish verse. The student would be less likely to lose his train of thought by periodically having to look up unfamiliar words in a dictionary. I have incorporated various exercises throughout this book that would benefit the student in the addition of a bilingual bible. There are also common scriptural verses located in chapter five.

I like to include simple Spanish religious tracts into the daily lesson. These may be located through online sources. These tracts will provide a good application for such words as *God, Jesus, salvation, love, heaven*, etc. Grammatical sentence structures can be studied as well. Students can practice reading these tracts out loud and identifying words that they learned in their workbook lessons.

Located in the back of the workbook, I have added a Pathway to Salvation prayer card, which may be laminated and carried in a pocket on a mission trip.

In the classroom setting, I would like to suggest popular contemporary Spanish songs as an invaluable learning tool, especially if the students are already familiar with the English version. Look for song tracts that include a printable copy of the verses. Play the songs out loud, and provide the words on paper. Review the words for pronunciation and meaning, and then replay the song. Encourage the students to sing along in Spanish.

Children's coloring books written in Spanish are also useful for classroom learning, as well for evangelism. These coloring books can be found with Christian themes for Christmas and Easter. These are great learning tools, especially when using the text material for studying grammar applications or vocabulary. I encourage the learner to read any captions out loud, as well as to share the coloring pages with their children for quality time. These Spanish words can be taught to children also.

In addition to these ideas, invite a native Hispanic as a guest speaker. Encourage conversational interactions as well as cultural sharing. Students who complete the class envisioned by this book may be encouraged to volunteer in a local community-based ministry where they may practice their Spanish in a practical, everyday application.

In the Great Commission of Matthew 28:19-20, Jesus instructed His followers to go and make disciples of all nations. One does not have to travel far to fulfill this commission: it can start on a local level. I challenge you today to seek out those in your outlying areas, to share the good news of salvation in practical and imaginative ways.

—Karyn Shander

Table of Contents

Chapter 3 55

Chapter 4 77

Chapter 5 115

Tables

List of Abbreviations Used in this Book

adj.	adjective
adv.	adverb
fam.	familiar
fem.	feminine
form.	formal
ind.	indirect
masc.	masculine
n.	noun
neg.	negative
neut.	neutral
pl.	plural
sing.	singular
ud.	usted
uds.	ustedes
v.	verb

Chapter 1

- **The Spanish Alphabet**
- **Pronunciation of Vowels**
- **Pronunciation of Consonants**
- **Word Stress and Use of the Written Accent**
- **Nouns**
- **The Plural Form of Nouns**
- **Definite Articles**
- **Conversation**
- **Adjectives**
- **Adjective Placement**
- **Vocabulary: God, Heaven, Salvation and their Attributes**
- **Scripture Passages**
- **Bonus Phrases**
- **Names of the Holy Trinity**

The Spanish Alphabet

In 2010, the 22 member countries belonging to the Association of Spanish Language Academies agreed to change the Spanish alphabet as follows:[1] the letters **ch** and **ll** are now "formally" removed from the Spanish alphabet, leaving it with 27 letters (the letter **ñ** plus the 26 letters of the English alphabet). The letter **w**, as of the year 2010, is officially called **uve doble** (even though in the past it had been also called **doble uve**, **doble ve**, and **doble u**). The letter **y** (traditionally called **i griega**) is now officially called **ye**.[2] These official uses are recommendations, not requirements. The letters **ch**, **ll**, and **rr** are included as separate letters in Spanish dictionaries that are published prior to 1994.[3]

Some of the letters will still have a variety of names depending upon the Hispanic regions. Listed below are the official principal changes to the letters found in the Spanish alphabet and their current names. The letter **n** will sometimes be used as **ñ**, and will follow its listing in the dictionary after the letter **n**.[4] The letters of the alphabet are considered feminine and will take the word "la" before them, for example, **la efe** *(the f)*, and **la uve doble** *(the w)*.[5]

TABLE 1.1—Letters used in the Spanish alphabet[6]

Letter	Name	Sound	Letter	Name	Sound	Letter	Name	Sound
a	a	ah	j	jota	HOH-tah	r	erre	EH-ray
b	be	bay	k	ka	kah	s	ese	EH-say
c	ce	ceh	l	ele	E-le	t	te	tay
d	de	deh	m	eme	E-me	u	u	oo
e	e	eh	n	ene	E-ne	v	uve	OO-vay
f	efe	efe	ñ	eñe	E-nyay	w	uve doble	OO-vay DOH-blay
g	ge	geh	o	o	oh	x	equis	AA-kees
h	hache	AH-chay	p	pe	peh	y	ye	yay
i	i	ee	q	cu	coo	z	zeta	SAY-tah

Pronunciation of Vowels

a: pronounced "**ah**"
- **a**la**b**anza—*praise*
- **a**lma—*soul*
- **a**mar—*to love*
- gr**a**ci**a**—*grace*
- m**a**nd**a**r—*to command*
- p**a**g**a**no—*pagan*
- p**a**z—*peace*
- s**a**gr**a**do—*holy*
- s**a**nto—*holy, saint*

e: pronounced "**eh**"
- b**e**nd**e**cir—*to bless*
- **e**terno—*eternal*
- f**e**—*faith*
- h**e**r**e**ncia—*inheritance*
- l**ee**r—*to read*
- cr**ee**r—*to believe*

i: pronounced "**ee**"
- Ant**i**cr**i**sto—*antichrist*
- d**i**sc**i**plina—*discipline*
- **i**ra—*anger*
- m**i**sa—*mass*
- Tr**i**n**i**dad—*Trinity*
- v**i**c**i**o—*vice*

o: pronounced "**oh**"
- ap**ó**st**o**l—*apostle*
- c**o**r**o**—*chorus*
- d**o**lor—*pain, grief*
- g**o**z**o**—*joy*
- íd**o**l**o**—*idol*
- r**o**str**o**—*face*
- tr**o**n**o**—*throne*

u: pronounced "**oo**"*
- cr**u**z—*cross*
- c**u**lpa—*blame*
- c**u**lto—*worship*
- Jes**ú**s—*Jesus*
- sep**u**lt**u**ra—*grave*
- **u**nidad—*unity*
- **u**nir—*to unite*

*Each vowel is usually pronounced, with the exception of "**u**." When "**u**" comes after "**g**" or "**q**," and then followed by "**i**" or "**e**," it is normally not pronounced (eg. sig**u**ió—*he followed,* g**u**erra—*war,* q**u**e—*what*), unless it looks like this: **ü** (eg. verg**ü**enza—*shame, embarrassment).* In this case, it is pronounced like a **w**.[7]

Pronunciation of Consonants

Here is an overview of how the consonants are pronounced. Please note that there may be minor regional variances in pronunciation.

b and v:[8]
- At the beginning of a word → they are pronounced alike.
  - examples: **b**endición—*blessing*
    - **b**ienestar—*well-being*
    - **b**autizo—*baptism*
    - **B**iblia—*Bible*
    - **b**oda—*wedding*
    - **v**erdad—*truth*
    - **v**ersículo—*verse*

- In the middle of a word → they are pronounced more softly.
  - examples: ser**v**icio—*service*
    - escla**v**o—*slave*
    - con**v**erso—*convert*

C:
- When followed by **e** or **i** → pronounced as an **s**
  - examples: sa**c**erdote—*priest (Catholic)*
    - profe**c**ía—*prophecy*
    - ora**c**ión—*prayer*
    - sacrifi**c**io—*sacrifice*
    - **c**elos—*jealousy*

- When followed by **a**, **o**, or **u** → pronounced as a hard **c**
  - examples: **c**ulpable—*guilty*
    - **c**aridad—*charity*
    - **c**onverso—*convert*
    - predi**c**ador—*preacher*
    - pe**c**ados—*sins*
    - **c**ató**c**o—*catholic*

ch:

- Pronounced as it is in the English word "church"
  - examples: mu**ch**o—*much*
    - **ch**ico—*boy*
    - di**ch**oso—*blessed*
    - desdi**ch**a—*misfortune*

d:

- At the beginning of a word → pronounced as it is in English
  - examples: **d**isciplina—*discipline*
    - **d**ifunto—*deceased, dead*
    - **d**octrina—*doctrine*
    - **d**iablo—*devil*
    - **D**ios—*God*

- Between two vowels → pronounced softer, almost like "**th**"
  - examples: fi**d**eli**d**ad—*faithfulness*
    - Re**d**entor—*Redeemer*

f:

- Same sound as in English[9]
  - examples: **f**e—*faith*
    - **f**ondo—*fund*
    - edi**f**icio—*building*

g:

- Before an **e** or **i** → pronounced as an **h**
  - examples: prodi**g**io—*miracle*
    - reli**g**ioso—*religious*
    - án**g**el—*angel*
    - un**g**ido—*anointed*
    - evan**g**elio—*gospel*
    - ele**g**ido—*chosen one*
    - elo**g**io—*eulogy*

- Followed by an **a**, **o**, or **u** → **g** is pronounced as a hard **g**
  - examples: re**g**alo—*gift*
    - a**g**uantar—*to tolerate, hold*
    - testi**g**o—*witness*

- In order to retain the hard **g** sound before **e**, or **i** → the **g** changes to **gu**. (Important with verbs when changing tenses.)
  examples: lle**g**ar *(to arrive)*—lle**gu**é/lle**g**aste/lle**g**ó
  ne**g**ar *(to deny)*—ne**gu**é/ne**g**aste/ne**g**ó

h:

- Is completely silent
  examples: **h**onra—*honor*
  hora—*hour*
  himno—*hymn*
  hambre—*hunger*
  hombre—*man*
  humildad—*humility*
  Abra**h**am—*Abraham*

j:

- Pronounced as an exaggerated **h** in English
  examples: **j**unto—*together*
  juvenil—*juvenile*
  le**j**os—*far away*
  Jesús—*Jesus*

k:

- Used in foreign words and is pronounced the same in English
  examples: **k**ilo—*kilo*

l:

- Same sound as in English
  examples: **l**adrón—*thief*
  a**l**ma—*soul*
  asi**l**o—*asylum*
  cárce**l**—*prison*

ll:

- Can have two different sounds
- It may be pronounced like the **y** in English, while in other regions it can be pronounced like "**dj**".[10]

   examples: **ll**enar—*to fill*

   capi**ll**a—*chapel*

   cape**ll**án—*chaplain*

   llorar—*to cry*

   llamar—*to call*

   fa**ll**ecido—*deceased*

m, n, and p:

- Same sound as in English

   examples: a**m**or—*love*

   paz—*peace*

   novia—*girlfriend*

   pacto—*covenant*

   maldad—*evil*

   Mesías—*Messiah*

ñ:

- Pronounced as "**ny**", like in "onion" or "canyon"

   examples: Se**ñ**or—*Mr. / Lord*

   cari**ñ**osa—*affectionate*

   se**ñ**ales—*signs*

   enga**ñ**ar—*to deceive*

q:

- Pronounced as "**k**" in English

   examples: e**q**uipo—*team*

   quemar—*to burn*

   quejarse—*to complain*

r:

- When it begins a word → it has a trilling sound [11]

   examples: **r**obar—*to rob, steal*

   romper—*to break*

   redimir—*to redeem*

   rendirse—*to submit*

- When it is before a consonant or at the end of a word → it sounds like **rr**
  - examples: carta—*card*
    - perdón—*pardon*
    - hablar—*to speak*

- When in the middle of a word, it has a weaker trilling sound
  - examples: varón—*male*
    - dinero—*money*
    - desastre—*disaster*

rr:
- It is pronounced as a long, trilling sound, like an airplane engine[12]
  - examples: arrepentimiento—*repentance*
    - corrupto—*corrupt*
    - socorro—*help, assistance*

s and t:
- Pronounced the same as in English[13]
  - examples: **s**antuario—*sanctuary*
    - **S**alvador—*Savior*
    - **s**acramento—*sacrament*
    - **t**entar—*to tempt*

v:
- Pronounced the same as the letter **b**, but some countries pronounce it like the English **v** [14]
  - examples: **v**oluntario—*volunteer*
    - **v**irtud—*virtue*
    - ni**v**el—*standard, level*
    - ser**v**icio—*service*
    - **v**iudo—*widower*

w:
- Found in foreign words, it has the same sound as in English[15]
  - examples: **w**hisky—*whiskey*
    - **w**indsurf—*windsurf*

x:

- Before a consonant→ pronounced as an English **ks** (although in words like "México" and "Texas," it can be pronounced like the English **h**).[16,17]

    examples: ex**pl**icar—*to explain*
    ex**c**elente—*excellent*
    exa**m**en—*exam*
    ex**ig**ir—*to demand*
    ex**il**io—*exile*
    ex**or**cista—*exorcist*

y:

- It may be pronounced in some regions as an English **j**
- In many countries it is pronounced as the **y** in "you" [18]

    examples: **yu**go—*yoke*
    yo—*I*
    cre**y**ente—*believer*
    a**y**uno—*fast*
    apo**y**o—*support*

z:

- Pronounced as an **s**
- In some parts of Spain, it is pronounced as a "**th**" sound[19]

    examples: cru**z**—*cross*
    go**z**o—*joy*
    esperan**z**a—*hope*
    die**z**mo—*tithing*
    amena**z**a—*threat*
    triste**z**a—*sadness*
    confian**z**a—*confidence*

Word Stress and Use of the Written Accent

Most words that end:

- in a **vowel**, or **n** or **s** → stress is on the **next to the last** syllable (stressed syllables shown in bold print)[20]

    examples: ala**ban**za—*praise*
    hablan—*they speak*
    or**a**mos—*we pray*

- in a **consonant**, except **n** or **s** → stress is on the **last** syllable

    examples: humil**dad**—*humility*
    pas**tor**—*pastor*
    adulter**ar**—*to adulterate*
    espiritu**al**—*spiritual*

Words that are not pronounced according to the above rules have an accent mark placed on the stressed syllable

    examples: religi**ón**—*religion*
    ver**sí**culo—*verse*
    Je**sús**—*Jesus*
    ángel—*angel*
    hu**ér**fano—*orphan*
    Jeho**vá**—*Jehovah*

Nouns

All nouns are considered either masculine or feminine, even if they refer to things that are non-living (eg: **milagro**—*the miracle*, **promesa**—*the promise*). Here are a few simple rules that will help you to determine which gender a noun is:[21]

- Most nouns that end in **–o** or refer to male beings are considered masculine.
    examples: ciel**o**—*heaven*
                diabl**o**—*devil*
                pact**o**—*covenant*
                diácon**o**—*deacon*
                testimoni**o**—*testimony*

- Most nouns that end in **–a** or refer to female beings are considered feminine.
    examples: iglesi**a**—*church*
                doctrin**a**—*doctrine*
                ayud**a**—*help*
                ofrend**a**—*offering*
                promes**a**—*promise*

- A few nouns have the same form for both genders.[22]
    examples: creyente—*believer* (masc.)
                creyente—*believer* (fem.)

- Nouns that end in **-ción, -d, -dad, -sión, -umbre,** and **-z** are usually feminine.[23]
    examples: santi**dad**—*holiness*
                pa**z**—*peace*
                invita**ción**—*invitation*
                interce**sión**—*intercession*
                cost**umbre**—*custom*
                lealta**d**—*loyalty, faithfulness*
                eterni**dad**—*eternity*

- Nouns that end in **-o, -l, -r, -ma, -pa** are usually masculine.[24]
    - examples: hono**r**—*honor*
        - amo**r**—*love*
        - bienesta**r**—*well-being*
        - apósto**l**—*apostle*
        - dolo**r**—*pain, grief*
        - pasto**r**—*pastor*
        - alta**r**—*altar*
        - nive**l**—*level, standard*
        - carácte**r**—*character*
        - progra**ma**—*program*
        - idio**ma**—*language*
        - ma**pa**—*map*
        - siste**ma**—*system*
        - caris**ma**—*charisma*
        - estig**ma**—*stigma*

There are many Spanish nouns where it is not easy to determine the gender based on the word-ending clues. A good Spanish dictionary will help to determine the gender. It is important to learn which nouns are feminine or masculine because in later lessons the forms of the articles and adjectives are affected by the gender of the noun.

Ejercicio A (Exercise A)

Indicate below whether these nouns are feminine (F), masculine (M), or both (B). The first one is given to you.

1. Biblia	F	6. paz		11. altar	
2. iglesia		7. invitación		12. pastor	
3. diácono		8. pacto		13. programa	
4. ayuda		9. lealtad		14. creyente	
5. cielo		10. amor		15. eternidad	

The Plural Form of Nouns

To create the plural form, if the noun ends:

- in a vowel → add "**s**" to the singular form[25]
  examples: escritur**a**—*scripture*
  escritur**as**—*scriptures*

  discípul**o**—*disciple*
  discípul**os**—*disciples*

- in a consonant → add "**es**"
  examples: pasto**r**—*pastor*
  pasto**res**—*pastors*

  oració**n**—*prayer*
  oracio**nes**—*prayers*

  comunida**d**—*community*
  comunida**des**—*communities*

- with a "**z**" → change the **z** to "**ces**"[26]
  examples: cru**z**—*cross*
  cru**ces**—*crosses*

  lu**z**—*light*
  lu**ces**—*lights*

Definite Articles

Several Spanish words are definite articles and are translated as "*the.*" The article usually comes before the noun and must agree with both its gender (masculine or feminine) and number (singular or plural).[27]

	Singular	Plural
Masculine	el	los
Feminine	la	las

examples: **el** templo—*the temple*   **los** templos—*the temples*
                 el testigo—*the witness*   **los** testigos—*the witnesses*
                 la obra—*the work*   **las** obras—*the works*
                 la viuda—*the widow*   **las** viudas—*the widows*

TABLE 1.2—Exceptions regarding gender of nouns

NOTE: There are some exceptions to the above rules. A good dictionary will usually indicate the gender of the noun. Here are a few exceptions:

el d**í**a—*day (masc.)*
el agu**a**—*water (fem.)*—also note article "el"*
el alm**a**—*soul, spirit (fem.)*—also note article "el"*

* Any noun that that begins with an "a" and takes the stress of the word will use "el" as its article, instead of "la." The noun is still considered feminine, and in its plural form it will still use "las" (eg: *las almas, las aguas*).

This is done to make it more pleasant sounding.[28]

Definite articles are also to be used:
- with abstract nouns
  - **la** salvación—*the salvation*
  - **la** fuerza—*the strength*
  - **el** sufrimiento—*the suffering*
- before titles when talking about a person
  - **la** señora López—*Mrs. Lopez*
  - **el** pastor Marco—*Pastor Mark*
- before the name of a language[29]
  - **El** español es un idioma muy bonito.
  - *Spanish is a beautiful language.*

Do not use the definite article:

   • before a language if used immediately after **hablar** or after **en** or **de**.

La señora Martínez no **habla** español.

Mrs. Martinez does not speak Spanish.

La Biblia está escrita **en** inglés.

The Bible is written in English.

   • before an unmodified noun indicating occupation[30]

Es pastor.

He is a pastor.

Es misionero.

He is a missionary.

Ejercicio B

Insert the correct definite article before the nouns listed below in the first column, according to the following examples. In the second column, change to the plural form.

el	regalo
la	alabanza
	voluntario
	edificio
	muchacha
	himno
	virtud
	Biblia
	pacto
	elogio
	doctrina
	cruz
	sacramento
	equipo
	servicio

los	regalos
las	alabanzas

Conversation

Practice using this dialogue in a conversation to introduce yourself to someone. The English translation follows.

A: Buenos días (Buenas tardes*).
B: Buenos días (Buenas tardes*), Señorita *(miss)*/Señora *(Mrs.)*/Señor *(Sir)*.

A: ¿Cómo se llama usted?
B: Me llamo _____ . Y usted, ¿cómo se llama?
A: Me llamo _____ . Mucho gusto.

A: Good day (good afternoon).
B: Good day (good afternoon), Miss/Mrs./Sir.

A: What is your name?
B: My name is _____ . And you, What is your name?
A: My name is _____ . Much pleasure.

*Use *buenas tardes* starting at noon and until 7 PM, then use *buenas noches*.

Adjectives

Adjectives are used in both English and Spanish to describe nouns. For example, a house can be described as brick or wood, brown or white, small or large. Nouns may also be modified by referring to quantities or numbers, such as "two women" or "several women." When using adjectives in Spanish, the adjective must be in agreement with the modified noun in both number and gender. [31]

For adjectives that end in **-o** (the masculine form), use four different forms **(-o, -a, -os, -as)** to modify the noun (see **Table 1.3**). Adjectives ending in consonants only use two forms, a singular and a plural form. In this case, add the endings **-s** or **-es**.[32]

When using an adjective ending in a consonant that describes a nationality, add **-a**, **-as** to make its feminine form. If masculine, add **-es** to its singular form. If the masculine singular nationality ending is **-és**, then drop the accent mark when used in its other forms, as shown in **TABLE 1.3**. [33,34]

TABLE 1.3—Forms of Adjective

Singular		Plural	
Masculine	**Feminine**	**Masculine**	**Feminine**
nuevo	nueva	nuevos	nuevas
mucho	mucha	muchos	muchas
azul	azul	azules	azules
joven	joven	jovenes	jovenes
español	española	españoles	españolas
inglés	inglesa	ingleses	inglesas

Ejercicio C

Pluralize the following phrases as shown in the example.

1	la Biblia azul	*las Bibilias azules*
2	la iglesia vieja	
3	el estudio bíblico	
4	la invitación nueva	
5	el servicio voluntario	
6	el pastor bueno	
7	el testigo falso	
8	la doctrina cristiana	
9	la ofrenda grande	
10	la mujer religiosa	

Adjective Placement

When working with adjectives, the placement will depend upon several factors. For instance, adjectives that describe a quality or condition will usually follow the modified noun.

la muchacha rica......................*the rich girl*
el programa nuevo.................*the new program*

Adjectives that describe a quantity generally precede the noun.

los cuatro meses.......................*the four months*
muchos creyentes....................*many believers*

Adjectives that indicate nationality will follow the noun.

la boda española ....*the Spanish wedding*
el estudiante cubano ....*the Cuban student*

When the expression is literal, the adjective will follow the modified noun. If it is figurative in meaning, the adjective will usually precede the noun.[35]

la pobre mujer...........................*the poor (i.e., unfortunate) woman*
la mujer pobre...........................*the poor (i.e., penniless) woman*

Ejercicio D

Translate the following phrases into Spanish, as shown in the example. Use the vocabulary located in the appendix to assist you.

1	the Baptist church	*la iglesia Bautista*
2	the Spanish missions	
3	the four angels	
4	the new prayer	
5	the Spanish community	
6	the Catholic mass	

Vocabulary
God, Heaven, Salvation and Their Attributes

These words do not all appear in the previous lesson. However, you should learn them because they may be used as active vocabulary later.

adoration—la adoración .... **to adore**—adorar
alleluia—aleluya
almighty—todopoderoso
angel(s)—el ángel/ los ángeles
anointed—ungido,-a .... **to anoint**—ungir
blessed—*(a thing or place)* bendito,-a/,   **to bless**—bendecir
           (a person) bendecido,-a
blessing—la bendición ....
chance—la oportunidad
chosen—elegido
coming of Christ—el advenimiento
confession— la confesión .... **to confess**—confesar
conversion—la conversión .... **to convert**—convertir
creator—el/la creador,-a .... **to create**—crear
cross—la cruz
crucified—crucificado,-a .... **to crucify**—crucificar
crucifix—el crucifijo
crucifixion—la crucifixión
eternal—eterno,-a
eternity—la eternidad
faithful—fiel, leal
faithfully—fielmente/ lealmente
faithfulness—la fidelidad/ la lealtad
fulfillment—el cumplimiento .... **to fulfill**—cumplir
giver—dador,-a .... **to give**—dar
glory—la gloria .... **to glorify**—glorificar, alabar
God—Dios
goodness/kindness—la bondad
gospel—el evangelio
grace—la gracia
                          .... **to grant**—conceder

---

heaven—el cielo
Heavenly Father—el Padre celestial
holiness—la santidad
holy—santo,-a, sagrado,-a
Holy Spirit—El Espíritu Santo
honor—el honor/ la honra .... **to honor**—honrar
humility—la humildad
immortal—inmortal
inheritance—la herencia ....**to inherit**—heredar
Jehovah—Jehová
Jesus—Jesús
Jesus Christ—Jesucristo, Cristo Jesús
kingdom—el reino
Lord—el Señor
Lord Jesus—el Señor Jesús
love—el amor
loving—amoroso,-a ....**to love** (*someone*)—amar
majesty—la majestad
merciful—misericordioso,-a
mercy—la misericordia
Messiah—el Mesías
miracles—los milagros ....**to work miracles**—hacer milagros
Most High—Altísimo,-a
mystery—el misterio
name—el nombre
offering—la ofrenda
omnipotent—omnipotente/
            todopoderoso,-a
omnipresent—omnipresente
omniscient—omnisciente
only begotten—unigénito,-a
peace—la paz
praising God—alabando a Dios ....**to praise**—alabar
promises—las promesas ....**to promise**—prometer
provision—la provisión ....**to provide**—proveer
Redeemer—el Redentor
redemption—la redención ....**to redeem**—redimir
repentance—el arrepentimiento ....**to repent**—arrepentirse de

resurrection—la resurrección
Revelation—Apocalipsis
salvation—la salvación
Savior—el Salvador ....**to save**—salvar
Scriptures—las Escrituras
signs & wonders—señales y maravillas
spiritual—espiritual
strength—la fuerza ....**to strengthen**—fortalecer
soul—el alma *(fem.-note gender)* / el
        ánimo
sovereign—soberano,-a
suffering—el sufrimiento .... **to suffer**—sufrir, padecer
tabernacle—el tabernáculo
temple—el templo
throne of God—el trono de Dios
Trinity—la Trinidad
will of God—la voluntad de Dios
wisdom—la sabiduría
witness—el testigo
Word (*of God*)—el Verbo *(de Dios)*
worship—el culto ....**to worship**—adorar, venerar *(venerar
                                                    is more often used in the Catholic faith)*

Scripture Passages

Here are two NIV/NVI scripture verses[36] that may be familiar to you. Increase your vocabulary by inserting the corresponding words that may be found in the vocabulary from this chapter.

A) ...That God the Father and Christ Jesus our Lord grant you grace, mercy and peace. **2 Timothy 1:2**	...Que _____ el Padre y _____ _____ nuestro _____ te concedan _____, _____ y _____. **2 Timoteo 1:2**

| **B)** Holy, holy, holy is the Lord God Almighty, who was and is and is to come.

Revelation 4:8 | _____, _____, _____
es el _____ _____
_____, el que era y que es y que ha de venir.

Apocalipsis 4:8 |

Bonus Phrases

go with God—vaya con Dios

rapture of the church—el rapto de la iglesia

kingdom of heaven—el reino del cielo

God will provide—Dios proveerá

to give your life to Jesus—rendir su vida a Jesús

the gift of His love—el regalo de Su amor

to hand over your concerns to the Lord—entregarle sus preocupaciones al Señor

the grace of God—la gracia de Dios

to have confidence in the promises of God—tener confianza en las promesas de Dios

the gift of salvation—el regalo de la salvación

the Son of God died for our sins—el Hijo de Dios murió por nuestros pecados

God bless you—que Dios le bendiga

I am faithful—soy fiel

God willing—si Dios quiere

the gospel of salvation—el evangelio de salvación

the forgiveness of sins—el perdón de pecados

marked with the seal of the Holy Spirit—marcado con el sello del Espíritu Santo

by grace you have been saved—por gracia ustedes han sido salvados

to die on the cross—morir en la cruz

the blood of Jesus Christ—la sangre de Jesucristo

Names of the Holy Trinity

Using the given clues, fill in the groups of blanks below with Spanish words. When you are finished, the first letter of each answer will form a name that pertains to God. The first answer is given to you. Use the vocabulary in the appendix to assist you.

1. J e s ú s .... the Son of God
    _ _ _ _ _ _ .... chosen
    _ _ _ _ _ .... honor
    _ _ _ _ _ _ _ .... prayer
    _ _ _ _ _ _ .... truth
    _ _ _ _ _ .... angel

2. _ _ _ _ _ _ _ _ .... religion
    _ _ _ _ _ _ .... eternal
    _ _ _ _ .... God
    _ _ _ _ _ _ _ _ _ .... gospel
    _ _ _ _ _ _ .... name
    _ _ _ _ _ .... throne
    _ _ _ _ _ _ _ .... offering
    _ _ _ _ _ _ .... gift

3. _ _ _ _ .... cross
    _ _ _ _ _ _ _ _ _ _ _ _ _ ..... resurrection
    _ _ _ _ _ _ _ _ _ .... immortal
    _ _ _ _ _ _ .... holy
    _ _ _ _ _ _ _ .... temple
    _ _ _ _ _ _ _ _ _ _ _ .... opportunity

4.

_ _ _ _ _ _ _ _ _ .... scripture

_ _ _ _ _ _ _ .... holy

_ _ _ .... peace

_ _ _ _ _ .... idol

_ _ _ _ _ .... kingdom

_ _ _ _ _ _ _ .... church

_ _ _ _ _ _ _ _ .... trinity

_ _ _ _ _ _ _ .... anointed

_ _ _ _ _ _ _ _ .... priest

_ _ _ _ .... soul

_ _ _ _ _ _ .... name

_ _ _ _ _ _ _ .... witness

_ _ _ _ _ _ _ .... offering

5.

_ _ _ _ _ _ _ .... miracle

_ _ _ _ _ _ _ _ _ .... eternity

_ _ _ _ _ _ _ _ .... savior

_ _ _ _ _ .... idol

_ _ _ _ _ _ _ _ .... praise

_ _ _ _ _ .... holy

Chapter 2

- **Subject Pronouns**
- **Infinitive Verbs**
- **Present Tense of Regular Verbs**
- **Present Tense of Irregular Verbs** *querer*, *saber* **and** *venir*
- **Present Tense of Irregular Verbs** *dar, decir, tener* **and** *ir*
- **Word Scrambles**
- **Forming Questions and Negative Sentences**
- *Ser* **and** *estar*
- **Indefinite Articles**
- **Present Tense of Irregular Verbs**
- **Prepositions and Contractions**
- **Demonstrative Adjectives**
- **Vocabulary—Virtues and Gifts of the Believer**
- **Conversation**
- **Adverbs**
- *Hay*
- *Hay* **+ Noun**
- **Bonus Phrases**
- **Words of Discernment**
- **Virtues and Gifts of the Believer Puzzle**
- **Scripture Passage**

Subject Pronouns

Subject pronouns are used to talk about people. If the pronoun is used to designate the one who is doing the action, it is called the subject pronoun. Below is a list of these pronouns:

TABLE 2.1—Subject Pronouns

Singular		Plural	
I	**yo**	*we*	**nosotros** *(masc.)* **nosotras** *(fem.)*
you (familiar)	**tú**	*you (familiar)*	**vosotros** *(masc.)* **vosotras** *(fem.)*
he	**él**	*they (masc.)*	**ellos**
she	**ella**	*they (fem.)*	**ellas**
you (polite)	**usted (ud.)**	*you (polite)*	**ustedes (uds.)**

In the table above, the familiar **tú** form is used with children and family, as well as friends. The polite or formal forms (**usted** and **ustedes**) are used in all other situations, or until the listener tells you to use the **tú** form. The **vosotros,-as** form is used in Spain, not in Latin America, and it will not be included in our lessons.

Infinitive Verbs

In English, infinitive verbs are formed by placing *to* in front of the verb. In Spanish, however, the infinitive verb form consists of (1) a stem, and (2) an ending. The clue that a word is usually an infinitive verb is that it ends in **-ar, -er,** or **-ir**. Some examples of infinitive verbs are **amar** *(to love)*, **beber** *(to drink)*, and **compartir** *(to share)*. The verb stem part of these examples are **am-, beb-,** and **compart-**, respectively. Their respective endings, **-ar, -er,** and **-ir**, will determine how a verb will be conjugated. When verbs are conjugated, there are special endings that are attached to the verb stem. These endings help to determine the subject and whether the action occurs in the present, past, or future.[1]

Present Tense of Regular Verbs

In order to form the present tense, remove the **-ar**, **-er**, or **-ir** ending from the infinitive verb. Next, add the personal endings to the stem, based upon whether it is an **-ar**, **-er**, or **-ir** verb, using the following table. The stress will always fall on the stem part, except in the *nosotros,-as* form.

Every one of these endings represents the action of a specific person or persons. The subject pronouns may be omitted in the sentence once you learn the endings. However, sometimes the pronoun is retained in order to clarify which person is meant. [2] For example, **él**, **ella**, and **usted** will all use the third person singular verb form, but may refer to **he**, **she**, or **you**, respectively. The endings are listed below, followed by examples of how to conjugate regular **-ar**, **-er**, and **-ir** verbs.

TABLE 2.2—Present Tense Endings of Regular **-ar**, **-er** and **-ir** Verbs

	-ar	-er	-ir
yo	-o	-o	-o
tú	-as	-es	-es
él/ella	-a	-e	-e
usted	-a	-e	-e
nosotros, -as	-amos	-emos	-imos
ellos/ellas	-an	-en	-en
ustedes	-an	-en	-en

TABLE 2.3—Examples of Present Tense Regular **-ar**, **-er** and **-ir** Verbs

	am**ar** *(to love)*	beb**er** *(to drink)*	compart**ir** *(to share)*
yo	am**o**	beb**o**	compart**o**
tú	am**as**	beb**es**	compart**es**
él/ella	am**a**	beb**e**	compart**e**
usted	am**a**	beb**e**	compart**e**
nosotros, -as	am**amos**	beb**emos**	compart**imos**
ellos/ellas	am**an**	beb**en**	compart**en**
ustedes	am**an**	beb**en**	compart**en**

When to use the Present Tense:

Spanish has no equivalent for the English *am* (is, are) or *do* (does) in the present tense. Use this tense to describe something that is happening at the present time.[3] Here are some examples:

Yo amo. *I love/ I am loving/ I do love.*
Tú amas. *You love/ You are loving/ You do love.*
Él ama. *He loves/ He is loving/He does love.*

Nosotros bebemos. *We drink/ We are drinking/We do drink.*
Ellas beben. *They (fem.) drink/ They are drinking/ They do drink.*

Ella comparte. *She shares/She is sharing/She does share.*
Usted comparte. *You (formal) share/You are sharing/You do share.*

Ejercicio A

Complete the following sentences according to the clues.

1. *(prometer)* Yo prometo venir mañana. *(I promise to come tomorrow).*
Tú _____
Ella _____
María y yo _____
El pastor _____

2. *(creer)* Él cree en Jesucristo. *(He believes in Jesus Christ).*
Yo _____
Nosotros _____
Los niños _____
Tú _____

3. *(orar)* La creyente ora en la·iglesia. *(The believer prays in the church).*
Usted _____
Ella _____
Nosotros _____
Juan y Miguel _____

Present Tense of Irregular Verbs *Querer, Saber* and *Venir*

There are many irregular verbs in the present tense. Here are a few of the more commonly used verbs. Note that there are some changes from the stem vowel **e** to **ie** in certain forms of the present tense (**quiere, viene**, etc.). This change does not happen in the **nosotros** form.[4]

Also note the irregular **yo** forms for both **saber** and **venir**: **sé, vengo**.

TABLE 2.4—Present Tense of *querer, saber* and *venir*

	querer (to want)	**saber** (to know)	**venir** (to come)
yo	quiero	sé	vengo
tú	quieres	sabes	vienes
él/ella	quiere	sabe	viene
usted	quiere	sabe	viene
nosotros, -as	queremos	sabemos	venimos
ellos/ellas	quieren	saben	vienen
ustedes	quieren	saben	vienen

Present Tense of Irregular Verbs *Dar, Decir, Tener* and *Ir*

On the next page there are more of the present tense irregular verbs that are commonly used. Many of these will just have to be memorized. Frequent practice of the verbs will help you to remember the correct form to use.

TABLE 2.5—Present Tense of *dar, decir, tener* and *ir*[5]

	dar *(to give)*	**decir** *(to say, tell)*	**tener** *(to have)*	**ir** *(to go)*
yo	doy	digo	tengo	voy
tú	das	dices	tienes	vas
él/ella	da	dice	tiene	va
usted	da	dice	tiene	va
nosotros, -as	damos	decimos	tenemos	vamos
ellos/ellas	dan	dicen	tienen	van
ustedes	dan	dicen	tienen	van

Ejercicio B

Change the following irregular verbs into their correct present tense form, according to the example given.

1	querer *(to want)*	2	saber *(to know)*
	yo **quiero**		ella
	nosotras		yo
	usted		María y yo

3	venir *(to come)*	4	dar *(to give)*
	él		ustedes
	ellos		yo
	nosotros		tú
	yo		Jesús

5	decir *(to say)*	6	tener *(to have)*
	yo		usted
	tú		ella
	Pedro y Mario		yo
7	ir *(to go)*		tú
	Dios		
	nosotros		
	el pastor		

Unscamble the Spanish words below, using the given clues in English. The first scramble has been done for you.

	Scramble	Clue	Answer
1	ZRUC	CROSS	CRUZ
2	GZOO	JOY	
3	ABDO	WEDDING	
4	GÁNLE	ANGEL	
5	ABDILO	DEVIL	
6	MAAL	SOUL	
7	ABBLI	BIBLE	
8	ROOC	CHORUS	
9	OONRT	THRONE	
10	CAAIGR	GRACE	
11	HOUMC	MUCH	
12	HOMIN	HYMN	
13	YOUNA	FAST	
14	BORATAJ	WORK	
15	NOTAS	HOLY	

Forming Questions and Negative Sentences

Questions have a different sentence structure in Spanish. The subject is placed directly after the verb when forming a question. An upside down question mark begins the sentence, and a regular question mark ends it. Also, there are no Spanish equivalents for the English words **do** or **does**.[6]

¿Recibe Mario la invitación?	*Does Mario receive the invitation?*
¿No lee él la lección bíblica?	*Doesn't he read the Bible lesson?*

Interrogative words introduce the question, and they precede the verb. These words have written accents. Here are the most common[7]:

¿Quién? *Who?*	¿A quién? *To whom?*
¿Quiénes? *Who (pl.)?*	¿De quién? *Whose?*
¿Cuál? *Which?*	¿Dónde? *Where?*
¿Cuáles? *Which ones?*	¿Cuándo? *When?*
¿Qué? *What?*	¿Cuánto/-a? *How much?*
¿Cómo? *How? What?*	¿Cuántos/-as? *How many?*
¿Por qué? *Why?*	¿Para qué? *For what?*
	(i.e., goal, purpose)

¿**Cómo** se llama usted?	*What is your name?*
¿**Qué** hora es?	*What time is it?*
¿**Quién** es el pastor?	*Who is the pastor?*
¿**Dónde** está la iglesia?	*Where is the church?*
¿**Quién** enseña la clase de español?	*Who teaches the Spanish class?*

To form a negative sentence, place **no** or other negative words before the verb. Spanish sentences will sometimes contain double negatives that are added for emphasis. Some of the negatives that may be used are **nada** *(nothing)*, **nadie** *(no one)*, and **nunca** *(never)*.[8,9]

Ella **no** necesita regresar a la iglesia.	*She does not need to return to the church.*
Ellos **no** comprenden el artículo.	*They do not understand the article.*
No, **nunca** estudio.	*No, I never study.*
No canta **nadie** en el servicio.	*No one sings in the service.*

Ejercicio C

Change the following sentences into questions, then answer the questions negatively, according to the example below.

1. La congregación sabe la doctrina. <u>¿Sabe la congregación la doctrina?</u> <u>No, la congregación no sabe la doctrina.</u>

2. María tiene el regalo. ¿_____?
_____.

3. Ustedes dicen la bendición. ¿_____?
_____.

4. María quiere leer la Biblia. ¿_____?
_____.

Ser and Estar

In Spanish, there are two verbs that both mean "to be." These verbs are both irregular, and the present tense conjugation of each is listed below.

TABLE 2.6—Present Tense of *ser* and *estar*

	Ser	Estar
yo	soy *(I am)*	estoy *(I am)*
tú	eres *(you are)*	estás *(you are)*
él/ella	es *(he/she is)*	está *(he/she is)*
usted	es *(you are)*	está *(you are)*
nosotros, -as	somos *(we are)*	estamos *(we are)*
ellos/ellas/ustedes	son *(they are)*	están *(they are)*

Here is a table that will help you to decide whether to use **ser** or **estar** in a sentence:

TABLE 2.7—Using *ser* and *estar*[10,11]

Ser	Estar
It is used to tell:	It is used to indicate:
• **Who is the subject** *Ella es bautista.* She is Baptist.	• **Location, whether temporary or permanent** *Denny está en la iglesia.* Denny is in the church.
• **Nationality or origin** *El misionero es de México.* The missionary is from Mexico.	• **Condition of persons or objects that may be temporary, variable or the result of change.** *Ella está triste.* She is sad.
• **Occupation or profession** *Yo soy pastor.* I am a pastor.	
• **Characteristics of a subject or object** *Pablo es apóstol de Jesucristo.* Paul is an apostle of Jesus Christ.	• **an idiomatic expression** *Los misioneros están de visita en Perú.* The missionaries are visiting Peru.
• **Time or dates** *Es la una.* It is one o´clock. *Es domingo.* It is Sunday.	*El pastor está de vacaciones en los Estados Unidos.* The pastor is on vacation in the United States.
• **Possession** *La Biblia es de ella.* The Bible is hers.	
• **Expressions that are impersonal** *Es importante estudiar las escrituras.* It is important to study the scriptures.	

Ejercicio D

Complete each sentence using the correct form of **ser** or **estar**. The first has been completed for you.

1. Él _____es_____ pastor.

2. Nosotros _____ de Cuba.

3. Carlota _____ madre.

4. ¿Dónde _____ la iglesia?

5. Ellas _____ misioneras.

6. ¿ _____ en casa Luisa y Miguel?

7. El libro _____ de él.

8. La niña _____ triste.

9. Los creyentes _____ en la iglesia.

10. _____ necesario leer las escrituras.

Indefinite Articles

These words refer to nouns that have not been previously identified. Their use implies that the item mentioned is non-specific. These articles agree in both number and gender with the introduced noun.[12]

TABLE 2.8—Indefinite Articles

	Singular		Plural	
Masculine	**un** regalo **un** ángel	*a gift* *an angel*	**unos** regalos **unos** ángeles	*some gifts* *some angels*
Feminine	**una** iglesia **una** oración	*a church* *a prayer*	**unas** iglesias **unas** oraciones	*some churches* *some prayers*

Un and **una** correspond to the words "**a**" and "**an**," as well as the number **one**.[13]

> Tengo **un** regalo.
> *I have a gift.*
> *I have one gift.*

The plural forms **unos** and **unas** mean "**some**," "**several**," or "**a few**."

> Tengo **unos** regalos.
> *I have some gifts.*

Algunos/as, **varios/as**, **unos/as** and **pocos/as** are other words that may also be used to indicate "**some**," "**several**," or "**a few**."

> Tengo **algunos** regalos. *I have some gifts.*
> Tengo **varios** regalos. *I have several gifts.*
> Tengo **unos** pocos regalos. *I have a few gifts.*

When to omit the indefinite article:

After questions with certain verbs, such as **necesitar** *(to need)* and **tener** *(to have).* When the idea of **a**, **an**, or **one** is not emphasized, it may be omitted. In English, the words **some** or **any** is used.[14]

> ¿Tienes regalos?
> *Do you have (some/any) gifts?*
>
> La iglesia tiene Biblias.
> *The church has (some) Bibles.*
>
> Necesito dinero.
> *I need (some) money.*

Ejercicio E

Add the following indefinite articles as given in the examples below:

1	*un*	trono	*unos*	tronos
2		profecía		profecías
3		oración		oraciones
4		sacrificio		sacrificios
5		caridad		caridades
6		pecado		pecados
7		servicio		servicios
8		boda		bodas
9		Biblia		Biblias
10		doctrina		doctrinas

Present Tense of Irregular Verbs

Many of the irregular verbs change vowels in the stem form of the verb. However, note that the ***nosotros/nosotras*** forms have no change in the stem forms. These verbs can usually be categorized in one of these three changes:

TABLE 2.9-1—Present Tense of Irregular Verbs (e→i)[15]

	servir *(to serve)*	Other examples of **e → i** verb changes:	
yo **tú** **él/ella** **usted** **nosotros, -as** **ellos/ellas** **ustedes**	sirvo sirves sirve sirve servimos sirven sirven	pedir *(to ask)* repetir *(to repeat)* rendir *(to surrender)*	decir *(to say)* seguir *(to follow, continue)* perseguir *(to follow)*

TABLE 2.9-2—Present Tense of Irregular Verbs (e→ie)[16]

	mentir *(to lie)*	Other examples of **e → ie** verb changes:	
yo **tú** **él/ella** **usted** **nosotros, -as** **ellos/ellas** **ustedes**	miento mientes miente miente mentimos mienten mienten	arrepentirse *(to repent)* comenzar *(to begin)* entender *(to understand)* pensar *(to think)* perder *(to lose)*	sentir *(to feel)* confesar *(to confess)* convertir *(to convert)* enterrar *(to bury)* querer *(to want)* empezar *(to begin)*

TABLE 2.9-3—Present Tense of Irregular Verbs (o→ue)[17]

	recordar *(to remember)*	Other examples of **o → ue** verb changes:	
yo **tú** **él/ella** **usted** **nosotros, -as** **ellos/ellas** **ustedes**	recuerdo recuerdas recuerda recuerda recordamos recuerdan recuerdan	dormir *(to sleep)* mover *(to move)* morir *(to die)* poder *(to be able to)*	encontrar *(to find)* volver *(to turn, go back)* devolver *(to return or to give back)*

Ejercicio F

Change the following irregular verbs into their correct form, according to the examples given.

	pedir *(to ask)*			confesar *(to confess)*
	yo **pido**			el **confiesa**
1	tú		2	Miguel y yo
	nosotros			usted
	ustedes			ellas
	dormir *(to sleep)*			morir *(to die)*
	Juan **duerme**			ella **muere**
3	tú		4	nosotros
	yo			Juan y José
	nosotros			él

Prepositions and Contractions

Prepositions are placed in front of pronouns or nouns and are used to establish relationships with the remaining parts of the sentence.

The preposition **de** is used to show origin or possession. Note that when it indicates possession, the apostrophe is not used as in English. **Del (de+el)** is a contraction that is used when the preposition **de** comes before the masculine singular definite article **el.**[18,19]

Llegamos temprano de la iglesia. *We arrive early from the church.*
Es el evangelio de Juan. *It is the gospel of John.*
La Biblia es de Eric. *The Bible is Eric's.*
Es el rostro de un ángel. *It is the face of an angel.*
Es el trabajo del Espíritu Santo. *It is the work of the Holy Spirit.*

The preposition **a** is used to show direction or destination like the English word *to*. The preposition **a** is needed before a verb of motion *(coming, going, etc.)*[20]

Vamos a la boda. *We go to the wedding.*

Al is a contraction of **a+el**, and is used when the preposition **a** comes before the masculine singular definite article **el**.[21,22]

Voy al servicio. *I go to the service.*

There are some verbs of movement, such as **regresar** and **llegar**, that take the preposition **de** before a noun to express the departure point, equivalent to the English *from*.[23]

Él regresa de Guatemala. *He is returning from Guatemala.*

Ejercicio G

Complete the following sentences by supplying the correct preposition (**a, de, al** or **del**).

1. Yo soy _____ Chicago.

2. Voy _____ la iglesia y después _____ bautizo.

3. Los libros son _____ Pastor Denny.

Demonstrative Adjectives

To point out a referred object, a demonstrative adjective is used. It agrees with the noun in both gender and number, as do other adjectives.[24]

If the item is close to the person who is speaking, use either **esta**, **estas**, **este** or **estos**, as shown in **TABLE 2.10**. Note that the singular masculine form ends with the letter **-e**, while the masculine plural form ends with **-os.** The English equivalent is **this** or **these**.

If the item is close to the listener, the speaker should use **esa**, **esas**, **ese** or **esos**. Also note that the singular masculine form ends with the letter **-e**, while the masculine plural form ends in **-os**. The English equivalent is **that** or **those**.

If the speaker wishes to indicate remoteness, **aquel, aquella (aquellos, aquellas)** should be used.[25]

TABLE 2.10—Demonstrative Adjectives

	Masculine	**Feminine**
this	este	esta
these	estos	estas
that (nearby) (distant)	ese aquel	esa aquella
those (nearby) (distant)	esos aquellos	esas aquellas

este libro *this book*
estos libros *these books*

ese libro *that (nearby) book*
esos libros *those (nearby) books*

aquel libro *that (distant) book*
aquellos libros *those (distant) books*

esta Biblia *this Bible*
estas Biblias *these Bibles*

esa Biblia *that (nearby)Bible*
esas Biblias *those (nearby) Bibles*

aquella Biblia *that (distant) Bible*
aquellas Biblias *those (distant) Bibles*

Ejercicio H

Substitute the nouns in parentheses for the noun underlined to form new sentences.

1. Miguel va a abrir esa <u>iglesia</u>. (puertas, libro, capilla)

_____

_____

_____

2. Nosotros conocemos bien aquella <u>calle</u>. (edificios, comunidad)

_____

_____

3. Yo quiero esta <u>Biblia</u>. (himno, plumas, versículos)

_____

_____

_____

Bendecir is an irregular verb. It would be beneficial to learn its present tense forms:

TABLE 2.11—Present Tense of *Bendecir*

Bendecir *(to bless, consecrate)*			
yo	bendigo	**nosotros,-as**	bendecimos
tú	bendices		
él/ella/usted	bendice	**ellos/ellas/ustedes**	bendicen

Vocabulary
Virtues and Gifts of the Believer

These words do not all appear in the previous lesson. However, you should learn them because they may be used as active vocabulary later.

believer—el/la creyente .... **to believe**—creer
blessed—bendito,-a / dichoso,-a .... **to give the blessing**—dar la bendición
blessing—la bendición ....**to bless**—bendecir
charity—la caridad, la organización
      benéfica
Christian—cristiano,-a
Christianity—el cristianismo
comfort—el confort, el consuelo ....**to comfort**—confortar
conviction—la convicción
deeds—las acciones, las obras
devout—devoto,-a, piadoso,-a
discipline—la disciplina
encouragement—el ánimo ....**to encourage**—animar
evangelism—el evangelismo ....**to evangelize**—evangelizar
faith—la fe
faithfulness—la fidelidad
forgiveness—el perdón ....**to forgive**—perdonar
freedom—la libertad
Fruit of the Spirit—el fruto del Espíritu
gentleness—la ternura
gift—el regalo/ el don
gift of tongues—el don de lenguas
gifted—dotado,-a
gifts of the Spirit—los dones espirituales
goodness—la bondad
grace—la gracia
holiness—la santidad
holy—sagrado,-a
hope—la esperanza .... **to hope, expect**—esperar
humility—la humildad
integrity—la integridad
intercession—la intercesión ....**to intercede**—interceder
invitation—la invitación ....**to invite**—invitar

joy—la alegría/ el gozo
kindness—la bondad
knowledge—el conocimiento
love—el amor ....**to love each other**—amarse
meek—manso,-a, paciente
meekness—la mansedumbre
mercy—la misericordia
miracle—el milagro, el prodigio ....**to work wonders**—hacer prodigios
patience—la paciencia
peace—la paz
perseverance—la perseverancia ....**to persevere**—perseverar
persistence—la persistencia ....**to persist**—persistir
praise—la alabanza ....**to praise**—alabar
prophecy—la profecía ....**to prophesy**—profetizar
pure—puro, -a
purity—la pureza
purpose—el propósito
righteousness—la rectitud
self-control—dominio propio
submission—la sumisión ....**to submit**—someter a, rendirse
tender—tierno,-a
thankful—agradecido,-a ....**to thank**—agradecer a
the chosen few—los elegidos
to give—dar
tolerant—tolerante ....**to tolerate**—aguantar, soportar
trust—la confianza.....................................**to trust**—confiar en
truth—la verdad
unity—la unidad ....**to unite**—unirse/ juntarse
virtue—la virtud
volunteer—voluntario,-a
well-being—el bienestar
wisdom—la sabiduría
wise—sabio,-a
witness—el/la testigo

Conversation

Maria and Jose are on a date at a local coffee shop. As they become better acquainted, they discuss their family situations.

MARIA: How many brothers and sisters do you have in your family?

JOSE: I have two brothers and three sisters, but all of them still live in Mexico.

MARIA: What about your parents, are they still alive?

JOSE: Yes, they are. My youngest sister lives with them. Maria, what about your family?

MARIA: My parents have been divorced for six years now. I have not seen my father for almost two years, and my mother is remarried. I have three brothers and two sisters. They all live in different parts of California.

MARÍA: ¿Cuántos hermanos y hermanas tienes en la familia?

JOSÉ: Yo tengo dos hermanos y tres hermanas, pero todo ellos aún viven en México.

MARÍA: ¿Qué tal tus padres, aún viven?

JOSÉ: Sí, mi hermana menor vive con ellos. María, ¿qué de tu familia?

MARÍA: Hace seis años se divorciaron mis padres. No he visto a mi padre por casi dos años, y mi madre se casó de nuevo. Tengo tres hermanos y dos hermanas. Todos viven en diferentes partes de California.

aún—still

casarse—to marry

divorciarse—to divorce

hermanas—sisters

hermanos—brothers

menor—younger

vivir—to live

Adverbs

There are several purposes for adverbs. They can be used to modify a verb, adjective, or another adverb. In Spanish, some adverbs are formed by adding the ending **-mente** to the adjective's feminine form. This would be the English equivalent of adding **-ly**[26]

lenta *(slow)*.................................... lentamente *(slowly)*
alegre *(joyful)*................................. alegremente *(joyfully)*
veloz *(swift)* .... velozmente *(swiftly)*
rápida *(rapid)*................................. rápidamente *(rapidly)*

Él trabaja lentamente. *He works slowly.*
Los niños comen rápidamente. *The children eat rapidly.*
El Señor viene rápidamente. *The Lord comes rapidly.*

Several adverbs are not created according to this formula. Here are some adverbs that are often used.

bien ....*well*   despacio...................*slowly*
pronto............*soon*   tarde ....*late*
mal..................*badly, not well*

Los misioneros hablan español muy bien. *The missionaries speak Spanish very well.*
Llega pronto. *He arrives soon.*
La misa empieza tarde. *The mass begins late.*

Hay

The Spanish word **hay** is used to mean **there is** and **there are.** The form **hay** does not express a subject.[27]

Hay un milagro en este sitio. *There is a miracle in this place.*
Hay una boda en la iglesia. *There is a wedding in the church.*
¿Hay unas Biblias y unos himnarios? *Are there some Bibles and some hymn books?*
Donde no hay fe, no hay esperanza. *Where there isn't faith, there isn't hope.*

Hay + Noun

Hay may also be used in visible, observed weather conditions.[28]

Hay nieve en Chicago. *There is snow in Chicago.*
Hay lluvia en Guatemala. *There is rain in Guatemala.*
Hay lodo después del huracán. *There is mud after the hurricane.*

Ejercicio I

Translate the following sentences, as shown in the example.

1. There is rain in Chicago.
   Hay lluvia en Chicago.

2. There is praise here.
   _____

3. The Antichrist is very bad.
   _____

4. There is love in this place.
   _____

5. There is freedom in the United States.
   _____

6. The children speak slowly.
   _____

7. The service is beginning late.
   _____

8. There are Christians here.
   _____

9. There is wisdom in the scriptures.
   _____

10. Jesus and the apostles arrive slowly.
    _____

Bonus Phrases

to be blessed—ser bendito,-a (s)/ ser bendecido,-a (s)
God bless you—Dios te bendiga
to do one's good deed for the day—hacer su obra buena diaria
by the grace of God—por la gracia de Dios
meditate on these things—medita en estas cosas
a person of good character—una persona de buena reputación
to speak in tongues—hablar en lenguas
it's against my beliefs to do that—es contra mis creencias hacer eso

Words of Discernment

Three of the four words in each group are related. Find the word that does not belong and note what the remaining words have in common. The first example is given.

_D_ 1.   A. Dios   B. el Espíritu Santo   C. Jesús   D. la escritura

_____*names of the Holy Trinity*_____

____ 2.   A. la fuerza   B. los ángeles   C. el cielo   D. el trono de Dios

_____

____ 3.   A. soberano   B. omnipresente   C. santo   D. creyente

_____

Virtues and Gifts of the Believer Puzzle

Fill in the blanks from the vocabulary previously presented. Then match each number beneath the letters to the corresponding boxes. You will then obtain a related scriptural passage. The first clue is given for you. <u>Hint</u>: Some letters and numbers are used more than once, and can also help you with the answers to the remaining clues.

A. The encouragement/ spirit

E L   Á N I M O
1 2   3 4 5 6 7

B. The pardon/forgiveness

— —   — — — — — —
8 9   10 11 12 13 14 15

C. The truth

— —   — — — — — —
16 17   18 19 20 21 22 13

D. Humility

— —   — — — — — — — —
23 24   25 26 27 5 28 13 29 21

E. The praise

— —   — — — — — — — —
30 31   32 33 34   35 36 37 38

F. Peace

— —   — — —
39 40   41 42 37

G. The believer

E L   — — — — — — — —
     44 45 46 47 48 4 49 50

H. The test

— —   — — — — — —
51 2   46 52 53 6 1 15

I. The faith

— —   — —
2 38   54 43

J. Holy

— —   — — — —
55 53   20 17 13 14

1 Corintios 13:13 *(1 Corinthians 13:13)*

Scripture Passage

Here is an NIV/NVI scripture verse that may be familiar to you.[29] Increase your vocabulary by inserting the corresponding words that may be found in the vocabulary from this chapter.

| The fruit of the Spirit is love, joy, peace, patience, kindness, goodness, faithfulness, gentleness and self-control. **Galatians 5:22** | El _____ del _____ es _____, _____, _____, _____, _____, _____, _____, _____, y _____ _____, **Gálatas 5:22** |

Chapter 3

- **Elements of Time**
- **Past Tense of Regular Verbs**
- **Past Tense of Irregular Verbs** *dar*, *ir* **and** *ser*
- **Match Up**
- **Imperfect Tense of Regular Verbs**
- **Imperfect Tense of Irregular Verbs** *ver*, *ir*, **and** *ser*
- **Contrasting Past and Imperfect Tenses**
- **Possessive Adjectives**
- **Vocabulary: The Church and its Related Works**
- **Verb Combinations**
- **Special Uses of** *tener*
- **Scripture Passage**
- **Crossword Puzzle**
- **Conversation**
- **Bonus Phrases**

Elements of Time

Note in **TABLE 3.1** that the days of the week and the months of the year are not capitalized as in the English language. Months of the year are masculine. When referring to the days of the week, the definite article **el** is used before the day and can be translated in English as the word **on.**[1,2]

Tengo la clase de español el viernes. *I have the Spanish class on Friday.*
El domingo es el día de descansar. *Sunday is the day of rest.*

To pluralize the days of the week that end in **-s,** simply use **los** with the day. This conveys the idea of repeated occurrence. If the days of the week end in a vowel, simply add an **-s.**[3,4]

Tengo la clase de español los viernes. *I have the Spanish class on Fridays.*
Visitamos los sábados y los domingos. *We visit on Saturdays and Sundays.*

TABLE 3.1—Expressing Time

Days of the Week		Months of the Year	
Monday	lunes	January	enero
Tuesday	martes	February	febrero
Wednesday	miércoles	March	marzo
Thursday	jueves	April	abril
Friday	viernes	May	mayo
Saturday	sábado	June	junio
Sunday	domingo	July	julio
		August	agosto
		September	septiembre
		October	octubre
		November	noviembre
		December	diciembre

Here are some additional expressions that are used to indicate a specific period of time:[5]

afternoon	*la tarde*	**summer**	*el verano*
day	*el día*	**today**	*hoy*
fall	*el otoño*	**tomorrow**	*mañana*
last night	*anoche*	**tonight**	*esta noche*
month	*el mes*	**week**	*la semana*
morning	*la mañana*	**winter**	*el invierno*
night	*la noche*	**year**	*el año*
spring	*la primavera*	**yesterday**	*ayer*
noon	*el mediodía*	**midnight**	*la medianoche*

every week .... *todas las semanas*
weekend .... *el fin de semana*
last year/month .... *el año/mes pasado*
next Tuesday/week .... *el martes/la semana que viene* **or**
la semana próxima
next year/month .... *el próximo año/ mes*
tomorrow morning .... *mañana por la mañana*
yesterday morning .... *ayer por la mañana*

Ejercicio A

Fill in each blank with the correct expression of time.

1. yesterday _____

2. last year _____

3. last night _____

4. today _____

5. last month _____

6. tomorrow _____

7. Sunday _____

8. September _____

9. tomorrow morning _____
_____

10. next year _____

Visit us at www.SpanishForChristianService.com

Past (Preterit) Tense of Regular Verbs

This tense corresponds to the English past tense. It can also correspond to the emphatic form that means *did: example* **amé** *I did love, I loved;* **bebimos**, *we did drink, we drank;* **compartieron**, *they did share, they shared.* The past tense is formed by adding endings to the stem form of the verb, according to the chart that follows, and is used to express an action that began and ended at a definite time in the past.[6]

Note that the **nosotros/nosotras** form in the **-ar, -ir** past tense is the same as the present tense. By studying the context of the sentence, the time in which an event happened can be clarified.

TABLE 3.2—Past Tense of Regular *-ar, -er* and *-ir* Verbs

	-ar	-er	-ir
yo	-é	-í	-í
tú	-aste	-iste	-iste
él/ella	-ó	-ió	-ió
usted	-ó	-ió	-ió
nosotros, -as	-amos	-imos	-imos
ellos/ellas	-aron	-ieron	-ieron
ustedes	-aron	-ieron	-ieron

TABLE 3.3—Examples of Past Tense Regular *-ar, -er* and *-ir* Verbs

	-ar	-er	-ir
yo	am**é**	beb**í**	compart**í**
tú	am**aste**	beb**iste**	compart**iste**
él/ella	am**ó**	beb**ió**	compart**ió**
usted	am**ó**	beb**ió**	compart**ió**
nosotros, -as	am**amos**	beb**imos**	compart**imos**
ellos/ellas	am**aron**	beb**ieron**	compart**ieron**
ustedes	am**aron**	beb**ieron**	compart**ieron**

Ejercicio B

Complete each blank by changing the verb into the correct past tense form. Follow the example given.

1. (comer)

   Yo _____ *comí* _____
   La novia _____
   Miguel _____
   Ustedes _____

2. (adorar)

   Ella _____
   Nosotros _____
   Tú _____
   Los ángeles _____

3. (crear)

   El hombre _____
   Mario y Luís _____
   Tú _____
   Dios _____

4. (prometer)

   Yo _____
   Jesús _____
   Mis amigos _____
   El creyente _____

5. (compartir)

   Mis padres _____
   El estudiante _____
   Mi pastor y yo _____
   Yo _____

Past Tense of Irregular Verbs *Dar*, *Ir* and *Ser*

There are many verbs that are irregular in the past tense. Below are a few of the ones that may be more commonly used. Note that even though **dar** is an **–ar** verb, in the past tense it has the endings of the **–er** and **–ir** verbs, but without the accents. Also note that the verbs **ir** and **ser** have the same past tense forms. Because of this similarity, it is best to use the context of the sentence to make its meaning clear.[7]

TABLE 3.4—Past Tense of *dar, ir* and *ser*

	dar (to give)	ir (to go)	ser (to be)
yo	di	fui	fui
tú	diste	fuiste	fuiste
él/ella	dio	fue	fue
usted	dio	fue	fue
nosotros, -as	dimos	fuimos	fuimos
ellos/ellas	dieron	fueron	fueron
ustedes	dieron	fueron	fueron

Ejercicio C

Complete each blank by changing the verb into the correct past tense form. Follow the example given.

1. (dar)
   Yo _____ *di* _____
   Mi hermano _____
   José y yo _____
   Ustedes _____

2. (ir)
   Nosotros _____
   El pastor _____
   Jesús _____
   Tú _____

3. (ser)
   Ellos _____
   Él _____
   Mario y Miguel _____

Match Up!

Use the tables of "Irregular Verbs and Their Tenses" (located in the appendix of this book). Match the irregular infinitive verb with a form of its correctly conjugated past tense verb. Some choices will be used more than once.

		Infinitive		Past Tense
	1	conocer	a	creyó
	2	decir	b	dieron
	3	saber	c	dije
	4	tener	d	conocieron
	5	querer	e	diste
	6	hacer	f	supimos
	7	creer	g	tuvo
	8	dar	h	fui
	9	estar	i	quiso
	10	ir	j	hizo
	11	poder	k	vi
	12	poner	l	estuvimos
	13	ser	m	pudieron
	14	venir	n	pusieron
	15	ver	o	vino

Imperfect Tense of Regular Verbs

The imperfect tense is formed by adding the following endings to the stem form of the infinitive verb. Note that in this tense, the first and third person singular are identical. Subject pronouns are usually included more often in this tense for clarification.[8]

Use this tense to describe events that *used to happen*, or for *repeated or habitual events in the past*. The imperfect tense may also be used to set the scene or to describe past actions in progress. If there is no reference to when the action or condition started or ended, the imperfect tense may also be used. The translation of this tense in English depends upon the context.

Example: **yo amaba** means *I used to love, I was loving.*

Stem changing verbs (discussed previously in chapter 2) will not change in the root forms in this tense.[9]   Examples: m**entir** *(to lie)* yo m**entía*
r**endir** *(to submit)* yo r**endía*
r**ecordar** *(to remember)* yo r**ecordaba*

TABLE 3.5—Imperfect Tense of Regular *-ar, -er* and *-ir* Verbs

	-ar	-er	-ir
yo	-aba	ía	ía
tú	-abas	ías	ías
él/ella	-aba	ía	ía
usted	-aba	ía	ía
nosotros, -as	-ábamos	íamos	íamos
ellos/ellas	-aban	ían	ían
ustedes	-aban	ían	ían

TABLE 3.6—Examples of Imperfect Tense Regular *-ar, -er* and *-ir* Verbs

	amar	beber	compartir
yo	amaba	bebía	compartía
tú	amabas	bebías	compartías
él/ella	amaba	bebía	compartía
usted	amaba	bebía	compartía
nosotros, -as	amábamos	bebíamos	compartíamos
ellos/ellas	amaban	bebían	compartían
ustedes	amaban	bebían	compartían

Imperfect Tense of Irregular Verbs *Ver, Ir* and *Ser*

These are the only Spanish verbs that are irregular in the imperfect tense. Note that the only accent marks for **ir** and **ser** are in the **nosotros,-as** forms **íbamos** and **éramos**.[10]

TABLE 3.7—Imperfect Tense of *ver, ir* and *ser*

	ver *(to see)*	**ir** *(to go)*	**ser** *(to be)*
yo	veía	iba	era
tú	veías	ibas	eras
él/ella	veía	iba	era
usted	veía	iba	era
nosotros, -as	veíamos	íbamos	éramos
ellos/ellas	veían	iban	eran
ustedes	veían	iban	eran

Examples of these verbs:

yo **iba**   *I used to go, I was going, I went*
yo **era**   *I used to be, I was*
yo **veía**   *I used to see, I saw, I was seeing*

Ejercicio D

Complete each blank by changing the verb into the correct imperfect tense form. Follow the example given.

1. (perdonar)
   Tú _____perdonabas_____
   El Mesías _____
   Los señores _____
   Ana y yo _____

2. (sufrir)
   Ellos _____
   Usted _____
   Ustedes _____
   Yo _____

3. (evangelizar)
   Yo _____
   El pastor _____
   Las metodistas _____
   Nosotros _____

4. (ir)
   El apóstol _____
   Mi hermana y yo _____
   Usted _____
   Tú _____

Contrasting Past and Imperfect Tenses

Certain situations dictate whether the past tense or the imperfect tense should be used in a sentence.

TABLE 3.8—Contrasting Uses of Past and Imperfect Tenses [11]

Past Tense For:	Imperfect Tense For:
Past actions that occurred and ended at a specific time: **El año pasado trabajé en México y asistí a la iglesia Metodista.** *Last year I worked in Mexico, and I attended the Methodist church.*	Past actions that unfolded: **Mientras yo trabajaba en México, asistía a la iglesia Metodista.** *While I worked in Mexico, I used to attend the Methodist church.*
Actions that happened within a defined time period: **El verano pasado ellas estudiaron mucho sus Biblias.** *Last summer they studied their Bibles a lot.*	Actions that had progressed within a specified time period: **El verano pasado ellas estudiaban mucho sus Biblias.** *Last summer they used to study their Bibles a lot.*
A series of actions that were completed, one following another: **Anoche salí con mi clase de español. Cenamos en un restaurante mexicano, fuimos al cine, y vimos una película muy buena.** *Last night I went out with my Spanish class. We ate in a Mexican restaurant, went to the theater, and saw a good movie.*	Habitual or repeated actions in the past: **Todas las semanas, salía con mi clase de español. Cenábamos en un restaurante mexicano, íbamos al cine, y veíamos buenas películas.** *Every week, I used to go out with my Spanish class. We used to eat in a Mexican restaurant, go to the theaters and see good movies.*
Sentences that contain adverbs indicating a specific time period: **ayer,** *yesterday;* **anoche,** *last night;* **esta tarde,** *this afternoon;* **un día,** one day, etc. **Ayer yo salí de la iglesia temprano.** *Yesterday I left the church early.*	Sentences that contain adverbs that express habitual or repeated events: **todos los días,** *every day;* **todas las semanas,** *every week;* **generalmente,** *generally;* **de vez en cuando,** *once in a while, etc.* **Todas las semanas yo salía de la iglesia temprano.** *Every week I used to leave the church early.*

Possessive Adjectives

Possessive adjectives reflect ownership and in English are words like *my*, *your*, *his*, *her*, etc. These adjectives must agree with the possessed item and not with the owner. They agree both in number and gender and are placed before the item modified. Note that the **mi**, **tu** and **su** forms are used for both masculine and feminine nouns and add an **-s** for the plural forms. The adjective *our* has four forms of **nuestro**, depending upon whether the noun it modifies is masculine or feminine, as well as singular or plural.[12]

TABLE 3.9—Possessive Adjectives

	Singular	Plural
my	mi	mis
your (familiar)	tu	tus
his, her, its, your (formal)	su	sus
our	nuestro, -a	nuestros, -as
their, your (plural)	su	sus

mi lección, *mis* lecciones .... *my lesson, my lessons*
su diezmo .... *his, her, your, their tithe*
la religion y *sus* doctrinas .... *the religion and its doctrines*
nuestra oración, *nuestras* oraciones .... *our prayer, our prayers*
Ella cena con *sus* hermanas .... *She has dinner with her sisters.*

Ejercicio E

Answer the following questions in a positive manner, following the example. Be sure to change the possessive adjective as necessary.

1. ¿Preparas tu lección de la Biblia? *Sí, preparo mi lección de la Biblia.*
2. ¿Leyeron ustedes mi carta? _____

   _____

3. ¿Necesitan ustedes mi apoyo? _____

   _____

4. ¿Contesta Dios nuestras oraciones? _____

   _____

5. ¿Recibió usted mi invitación de boda? _____

   _____

Vocabulary
The Church and Its Related Works

These words do not all appear in the previous lesson. However, you should learn them because they may be used as active vocabulary later.

.... **to accompany**—acompañar
adoption—la adopción .... **to adopt**—adoptar
Advent—el Adviento
altar—el altar
apostle—el apóstol
Apostle's Creed—el credo apóstolico
attendance—la asistencia .... **to attend**—asistir a
baptism—el bautizo .... **to baptize**—bautizar
Baptist—el, la bautista
believer—el, la creyente .... **to believe**—creer
Bible—la Biblia
Bible studies—estudios bíblicos
bride—la novia
bridesmaid—la dama de boda
building—el edificio .... **to build**—construir
building fund—el fondo para la construcción
care—el cuidado .... **to care for** *(someone)*—cuidar a
Catholic—católico,-a
chapel—la capilla
chaperone—el/la chaperón .... **to chaperone**—acompañar
chaplain—el capellán
chapter—el capítulo
choir—el coro
Christian—cristiano,-a
Christmas—la Navidad
church—la iglesia
church bulletin—el boletín de la iglesia
city—la ciudad
commandments—los mandamientos .... **to command**—mandar
communion—la comunión
community *(local)*—el vecindario/
                          la comunidad
confession—la confesión .... **to confess**—confesar
congregation—la congregación

convert—converso,-a ....**to convert**—convertir

covenant—el pacto

customs—las costumbres

deacon—el diácono

deceased—difunto,-a/ fallecido,-a

devotion—la devoción

disciple—discípulo,-a

doctrine—la doctrina

donation—la donación ....**to donate**—hacer una donación / donar

Easter—la Pascua

elder—anciano,-a

elect—los elegidos

emotion—la emoción

emotionally moving—conmovedor,-a

escort—acompañante ....**to escort**—acompañar, escortar

eulogy—el elogio ....**to eulogize**—elogiar

family counselors—los consejeros familiares

fast—el ayuno ....**to fast**—ayunar

fast and prayer—ayuno y oración

feeling—el sentimiento

fellowship—el compañerismo

financing—financiamiento

follower—seguidor,-dora

fundraising—el levantar fondos

funds available—fondos disponibles

funeral service—el servicio funerario ....**to bury**—enterrar, sepultar

godchild—ahijado,-a

godfather—el padrino

godmother—la madrina

Good Friday—el Viernes Santo

gospel—el evangelio

grave—la sepultura

grief—la pena, el dolor ....**to grieve**—apenar

groom—el novio

growth—el crecimiento ....**to grow**—crecer

help—la ayuda/ el socorro

helper—el/la ayudante ....**to help**—ayudar

Holy Week—la Semana Santa

homeless—los sin techo/sin hogar/sin
            vivienda

homeless shelter—la casa de refugio

hymn—el himno

hymn book—el himnario

---

immigrant community—la comunidad de inmigrantes

interpretation—la interpretación ....**to interpret**—interpretar

interpreter—el/la intérprete

invitation—la invitación

lack—la falta

leadership team—el equipo de líderes

Lord's prayer—el Padrenuestro

lost—perdido,-a ....**to lose**—perder

marriage—el casamiento ....**to marry**—casarse con

married *(person)*—casado,-a

mass—la misa

materials—los materiales

matrimony—el matrimonio

member *(of the church)*—el, la miembro,-a *(de la iglesia)*

Methodist—el, la metodista

minister—el/la pastor,-a, *or* el/la ministro,-a

ministry—el ministerio

mission—la misión

missionary—misionero,-a

need—la necesidad ....**to need**—necesitar

neglect—la negligencia/ el descuido ....**to neglect**—descuidar

offering—la ofrenda

orientation—la orientación

orphan—huérfano,-a

orphanage—el orfanato

Palm Sunday—Domingo de Ramos

pastor—el pastor

poor—los pobres

prayer—la oración ....**to pray**—orar

prayer team—el equipo de oración

preacher—el/la predicador,-a ....**to preach**—predicar

priest *(Catholic)*—el sacerdote

privilege—el privilegio

prophecy—la profecía ....**to prophesy**—-profetizar

rapture *(of the church)*—el rapto *(de la iglesia)*

related—relacionado,-a

relationship—la relación ....**to relate**—relacionar

relative—pariente,-a

religion—la religión

religious—religioso,-a

repentance—el arrepentimiento ....to repent—arrepentirse de
restoration—la restauración ....to restore—-restaurar
retreat—el retiro
reverend—el/la reverendo,-a
Sabbath—el sábado
sacrament—el sacramento
sacrifice—el sacrificio ....to sacrifice—sacrificar
saint—santo,-a
sanctification—la santificación ....to sanctify—santificar
sanctuary—el santuario
Savior—el Salvador ....to save—salvar
schedule of services—el horario de servicios
scripture—la escritura
seeker—el/la buscador,-a ....to seek—buscar
servant—el/la siervo,-a ....to serve—servir
service—el servicio
share—la parte ....to share—compartir
shelter—el refugio ....to shelter—refugiar
single (person)—soltero,-a
soul-searching—el examen de conciencia
sponsor—patrocinador,-a ....to sponsor—patrocinar
spouse—marido,-a, esposo,-a
standard—el nivel
starvation—el hambre ....to starve—privar de comida
Sunday school—Escuela Dominical
support—el apoyo ....to support—apoyar
team—el equipo
testimony—el testimonio ....to testify—dar testimonio
Thanksgiving—el día de Acción de Gracias...to thank—agradecer a
therapist—el/la terapeuta
therapy—la terapia
tithing—el diezmo ....to tithe—diezmar
together—junto,-a
verse—el versículo
volunteer—voluntario,-a ....to volunteer—ofrecerse para
wedding—la boda ....to wed—casarse con
welcome—bienvenido,-a ....to welcome—darle la bienvenida a
widow—la viuda
widower—el viudo
worship—la adoración
worshipper—el/la adorador,-a ....to worship—adorar, venerar (more often
youth group—el grupo de jóvenes   used used in the Catholic faith)

Verb Combinations

There are some verbs that can be used in combination with other words as building blocks to help create statements, questions and commands. A few of these combinations are listed here.

necesitar + infinitive[13]
Necesitamos ir al aeropuerto. *We need to go to the airport.*
Necesito comprar jabón. *I need to buy soap.*
Necesitaban construir la iglesia. *They needed to build the church.*
Necesito descansar. *I need to rest.*

necesitar + noun[14]
Necesito agua. *I need water.*
Necesito una toalla. *I need a towel.*
¿Necesitas dinero? *Do you need money?*
Necesito un intérprete. *I need an interpreter.*

querer + infinitive[15]
Quiero comer. *I want to eat.*
¿Quieres dar la bendición? *Do you want to give the blessing?*
Queremos orar. *We want to pray.*

querer + noun[16]
¿Quieres direcciones? *Do you want directions?*
Quiero mi biblia. *I want my bible.*
Quieren un taxi. *They want a taxi.*

ir + a + infinitive *(future/intention)*[17]
No van a tener dinero. *They are not going to have money.*
Vamos a trabajar en la calle. *We are going to work in the street.*
Voy a acompañarlos. *I am going to accompany them.*

ir + a + noun *(destination)*[18]
Voy a la farmacia. *I am going to the pharmacy.*
Vamos a la clínica. *We are going to the clinic.*
¿Van ellas al orfanato? *Are they going to the orphanage?*

poder + infinitive[19]
Puedo ayudar mañana. *I am able to help tomorrow.*
Él pudo predicar. *He was able to preach.*
Puedo ir. *I am able to go.*

tener + que + infinitive *(obligation)*[20]
Ella tiene que esperar. *She has to wait.*
La niña tiene que mendigar. *The girl has to beg.*
Tengo que comer. *I have to eat.*
Marco tuvo que comprar un mapa. *Marco had to buy a map.*
Tienen que dar la vuelta. *They have to turn around.*

deber + infinitive[21]
Debemos cuidar a nuestra madre. *We must care for our mother.*
María debe ir a la iglesia. *Maria must go to the church.*
Él debe construir un refugio. *He must construct a shelter.*

Special Uses of *Tener*

The Spanish verb **tener** may be used with certain emotions or other expressions. Review the following list[22] for examples.

tener alergias	*to have allergies*	**tener miedo de**	*to be afraid of*
tener _ años	*to be _ years old*	**tener prisa**	*to be in a hurry*
tener calor	*to be hot*	**tener razón**	*to be right*
tener cuidado	*to be careful*	**tener sed**	*to be thirsty*
tener frío	*to be cold*	**tener sueño**	*to be sleepy*
tener ganas de	*to feel like*	**tener suerte**	*to be lucky*
tener hambre	*to be hungry*		

Ejercicio F

Match the following sentences in the first column with the expression form of **tener** in the second column as in the example. Each choice should be used only once.

	1	Mi padre gana la lotería porque ...	a	tiene miedo de
	2	En invierno generalmente yo ...	b	tengo calor
	3	José _____ morir.	c	tiene sed
	4	El niño tuvo un accidente porque no...	d	tiene suerte
	5	Mi padre es muy viejo porque ...	e	tengo ganas de
	6	En verano generalmente yo ...	f	tengo frío
	7	Los muchachos van a comer porque...	g	tuvo cuidado
	8	María necesita agua, porque ...	h	tienen razón
	9	Ella corre porque ...	i	tienen hambre
	10	_____ aprender la lección.	j	tiene prisa
	11	Voy a dormir porque ...	k	tiene ochenta años
	12	Ustedes _____ porque esta clase es difícil.	l	tengo sueño

Scripture Passage

Here is an NIV/NVI scripture verse that may be familiar to you.[23] Increase your vocabulary by inserting the corresponding words that may be found in the vocabulary from this chapter.

Christ did not send me to baptize, but to preach the gospel. **1 Corinthians 1:17**	_____ no me envió a _____ sino a _____ el _____. **1 Corintos 1:17**

CROSS WORD PUZZLE

See how many words you know in Spanish by filling in the squares.

ACROSS	DOWN
1. Our Father	1. to sin
5. God	2. two
7. Savior	3. he uses
12. like, as	4. deacon
13. believer	6. he submits
16. priests	8. repentance
18. to bless	9. _____ con Dios
20. Ruth	10. give us
21. three	11. to say
23. tender (masc.)	14. scriptures
25. gold	15. Jesus Christ
26. Matthew	17. Lord
27. to be	19. Christian (masc.)
28. peace	22. Bible studies (two words)
30. that one (fem.)	24. to hear
32. grace	29. prayer
33. negative	31. throne
34. homeless (3 words)	33. Christmas
38. anger	35. cross
39. a fast	36. the devil
40. baptism	37. yesterday
43. heavenly being	41. church
45. child (masc.)	42. offering
47. chosen one (masc.)	44. in
49. creator	46. choir
51. forgiveness	48. a thought
52. to praise	50. he loved

Conversation

Juan and Carlos are walking together on their way to attending a retreat. They are sharing this time together to talk about their past experiences with religion.

JUAN: Were you raised in a Christian family?

CARLOS: Yes, I was. Both my parents are Catholic, and every week they would take my two sisters and me to church. We used to go to Sunday school afterward. How about you?

JUAN: My mother is a devout Baptist, and my father never went to church. She would encourage us to read the Bible every day and say prayers before we went to bed every night.

>< >< ><

JUAN: ¿Fuiste educado en una familia Cristiana?

CARLOS: Sí, lo fui. Mis padres, ambos son católicos y todas las semanas nos llevaban a mis hermanas y a mí a la iglesia. Luego íbamos a la escuela dominical. ¿Y tú?

JUAN: Mi madre es una bautista devota, y mi padre nunca iba a la iglesia. Ella nos motivaba a leer la Biblia todos los días y a orar antes de acostarnos cada noche.

ambos—*both*
devota—*devout*
educar—*to bring up, educate*

luego—*later, afterwards*
motivar—*to motivate, encourage*
padres—*parents*

Bonus Phrases

Welcome to our church—bienvenido(s) a nuestra iglesia
I believe in God—yo creo en Dios
This is the gospel according to ... —éste es el evangelio según...
Let us say grace—vamos a orar por la comida/bendecimos la mesa/vamos a dar gracia
to have a church wedding—tener una boda en la iglesia
to attend funerals—asistir a los funerales
to make a donation—hacer una donación
disaster relief fund—el fondo de asistencia a los necesitados
to welcome *(someone)*—dar la bienvenida a ...
to take refuge—refugiarse/tomar refugiado
old people's home—asilo de ancianos
support group—el grupo de apoyo
to be at a loss for what to do—no saber qué hacer

Chapter 4

- Future Tense of Regular Verbs
- The Beatitudes
- Future Action Words
- Conditional Tense of Regular Verbs
- Conversation
- Irregular Verbs in the Future and Conditional Tenses
- Fill in the Blanks
- Words of Discernment
- Demonstrative Pronouns
- Location Adverbs
- Command Mood of Regular Verbs
- Command Mood of Irregular Verbs
- More Irregular Commands
- The Ten Commandments
- Subjunctive Mood
- Irregular Subjunctive Verbs
- Direct Object Pronouns
- Indirect Object Pronouns
- Pronouns as Objects of a Preposition
- Reflexive Pronouns
- Reflexive Verbs
- Vocabulary
- Match Up
- *Crucigrama* (Crossword Puzzle)
- Bonus Phrases
- Scripture Passage
- Conversation

Future Tense of Regular Verbs

Use this tense to describe actions in the future that use *shall* and *will* in English. To form the future tense of regular verbs, add the following endings to the infinitive verb.

Note that all of the tenses have accent marks except the first person plural form of **nosotros.**[1]

TABLE 4.1—Future Tense of Regular *-ar, -er* and *-ir* Verbs

	-ar	-er	-ir
yo	-é	-é	-é
tú	-ás	-ás	-ás
él/ella	-á	-á	-á
usted	-á	-á	-á
nosotros, -as	-emos	-emos	-emos
ellos/ellas	-án	-án	-án
ustedes	-án	-án	-án

TABLE 4.2—Examples of Future Tense Regular *-ar, -er* and *-ir* Verbs

	amar	**beber**	**compartir**
yo	amar**é**	beber**é**	compartir**é**
tú	amar**ás**	beber**ás**	compartir**ás**
él/ella	amar**á**	beber**á**	compartir**á**
usted	amar**á**	beber**á**	compartir**á**
nosotros, -as	amar**emos**	beber**emos**	compartir**emos**
ellos/ellas	amar**án**	beber**án**	compartir**án**
ustedes	amar**án**	beber**án**	compartir**án**

Nosotros compartiremos el evangelio de Jesucristo.
We will share the gospel of Jesus Christ.

Miguel irá a la iglesia de Jorge.
Miguel will go to Jorge's church.

The Beatitudes (Las Bienaventuranzas)

This passage from Matthew 5:3-10 is a familiar passage to many.[2,3] In Spanish, the Beatitudes are called *las Bienaventuranzas*. Search these scriptures and underline the future tense verbs in it; then above it, identify the infinitive form and what it means in English. The English translation is given to help you. The first infinitive is located for you.

3 Dichosos los pobres en espíritu, porque el reino de los cielos le pertenece.	3 *Blessed are the poor in spirit, for theirs is the kingdom of heaven.*
4 Dichosos los que lloran, ser-to be porque <u>serán</u> consolados.	4 *Blessed are those who mourn, for they will be comforted.*
5 Dichosos los humildes, porque recibirán la tierra como herencia.	5 *Blessed are the meek, for they will inherit the earth.*
6 Dichosos los que tienen hambre y sed de justicia, porque serán saciados.	6 *Blessed are those who hunger and thirst for righteousness, for they will be filled.*

7 Dichosos los compasivos, porque serán tratados con compasión.	**7** *Blessed are the merciful, for they will be shown mercy.*
8 Dichosos los de corazón limpio, porque ellos verán a Dios.	**8** *Blessed are the pure in heart, for they will see God.*
9 Dichosos los que trabajan por la paz, porque serán llamados hijos de Dios.	**9** *Blessed are the peacemakers, for they will be called sons of God.*
10 Dichosos los perseguidos por causa de la justicia, porque el reino de los cielos les pertenece.	**10** *Blessed are those who are persecuted because of righteousness, for theirs is the kingdom of heaven.*

Ejercicio A

Substitute the future tense verbs in the sentences below.

1. *Alberto* **irá** a la comunidad de inmigrantes.
   Yo
   Nosotros
   Mi pastor

2. *María y Miguel* **llegarán** después del bautizo.
   Usted
   Tú
   Nosotros

3. *Yo* **serviré** con su predicador.
   Nosotros
   Ellos
   Ustedes

Future Action Words

Here are some common time phrases that will help to identify future action:[4]

mañana .... *tomorrow*
pasado mañana .... *the day after tomorrow*
la semana próxima .... *next week*
la semana que viene .... *next week*
la semana siguiente .... *next week*
el mes/año próximo .... *next month/year*
después .... *after, later*

Conditional Tense of Regular Verbs

This tense expresses an idea that is *dependent on a condition* which is either expressed or understood. It conveys the idea of what would happen if certain conditions were met.[5] Use this tense to express the English equivalent of *would* or *should*.[6,7] (Ex: *yo amaría* means *I would love* or *I should love.*)

These endings are added to the ending of the infinitive verb form. Note the accents on all seven endings in **TABLE 4.3**. Since the endings are the same for the subject pronouns **yo**, **él, ella** and **usted**, use the context of the sentence to help clarify the meaning if these pronouns are not included in the sentence.

TABLE 4.3—Conditional Tense of Regular *-ar, -er* and *-ir* Verbs

	-ar	-er	-ir
yo	-ía	-ía	-ía
tú	-ías	-ías	-ías
él/ella	-ía	-ía	-ía
usted	-ía	-ía	-ía
nosotros, -as	-íamos	-íamos	-íamos
ellos/ellas	-ían	-ían	-ían
ustedes	-ían	-ían	-ían

TABLE 4.4—Examples of Conditional Tense of Regular *-ar, -er* and *-ir* Verbs

	amar	**beber**	**compartir**
yo	amaría	bebería	compartiría
tú	amarías	beberías	compartirías
él/ella	amaría	bebería	compartiría
usted	amaría	bebería	compartiría
nosotros, -as	amaríamos	beberíamos	compartiríamos
ellos/ellas	amarían	beberían	compartirían
ustedes	amarían	beberían	compartirían

Yo comería la comida. *I should eat the food.*
Ella iría a la iglesia Metodista. *She should go to the Methodist Church.*
Él buscaría mi apoyo. *He should seek my support.*
Juan dijo que llegaría mañana. *John said that he would arrive tomorrow.*

Ejercicio B

Substitute the conditional tense verbs in the sentences below.

1. *Mi hermano* **buscaría** *a Jesús.*   *Los niños* _____...

   El pecador _____...   *Nosotros* _____...

2. *Nuestro pastor* **enseñaría** *los estudios bíblicos.*

   Miguel y yo _____...   *Usted* _____...

   Los Señores Rodríguez _____...

3. *Tú* **creerías** *en las Escrituras.*   *Usted y yo* _____...

   El apóstol _____...   *Los ángeles* _____...

Conversation

Mario is a youth minister at the church. He is mentoring Lucas and wants to know about his spiritual growth.

MARIO: Lucas, in order to set up a program for you, I would like to know a little more about you. Do you have a Bible? How often do you read it?

LUCAS: Yes, I read my Bible about once a week, usually on Sundays.

MARIO: Do you attend church with your parents?

LUCAS: Yes, and afterwards I sometimes go to Sunday school. However, I would like to get acquainted with other kids my age in a bible study sometime during the week, maybe after school.

MARIO: That is a great idea. I know of a teen bible study about the book of Matthew that will soon start on Wednesday afternoons. You are welcome to join us if you are interested.

LUCAS: Great!

MARIO: Lucas, para organizar un programa contigo, me gustaría saber un poco más sobre ti. ¿Tienes una biblia? ¿Cuán frecuente lees tu Biblia?

LUCAS: Sí, tengo biblia y la leo más o menos una vez a la semana, usualmente los domingos.

MARIO: ¿Asistes a la iglesia con tus padres?

LUCAS: Sí, y después a veces voy a la escuela dominical. Sin embargo, me gustaría conocer otros chicos de mi edad en un estudio bíblico durante la semana, quizás después de la escuela.

MARIO: Eso es una gran idea. Sé de un estudio bíblico para jóvenes sobre el libro de Mateo que pronto comenzará los miércoles por las tardes. Estás invitado, si te interesa.

LUCAS: ¡Fantástico!

contigo	*with you*	**Mateo**	*Matthew*
domingo	*Sunday*	**miércoles**	*Wednesday*
invitar	*to invite*	**organizar**	*to organize*
jóvenes	*youth (plural)*	**programa**	*program*
más o menos	*more or less*	**semana**	*week*

Irregular Verbs in the Future and Conditional Tenses

Future tense verbs that have an irregular stem will have the same irregular stem in the conditional tense. Note the three categories of irregular verbs in **TABLE 4.5**, and that these categories are grouped according to the type of stem form changes that occur.

TABLE 4.5—Future and Conditional Tenses of Irregular Verbs[8,9]

	Infinitive	Stem	Conditional	Future
Group A	hacer—*to do*	har–	haría, etc.	haré, etc.
	decir—*to say*	dir–	diría, etc.	diré, etc.
Group B	venir—*to come*	vendr–	vendría, etc.	vendré, etc.
	tener—*to have*	tendr–	tendría, etc.	tendré, etc.
	salir—*to leave*	saldr–	saldría, etc.	saldré, etc.
	poner—*to put*	pondr–	pondría, etc.	pondré, etc.
Group C	poder—*to be able*	podr–	podría, etc.	podré, etc.
	saber—*to know*	sabr–	sabría, etc.	sabré, etc.
	querer—*to want*	querr–	querría, etc.	querré, etc.
	haber—*to have*	habr–	habría, etc.	habré, etc.

Ejercicio C

Substitute the future or conditional tense verbs in the sentences below.

1. *Los misioneros* **vendrán** *esta noche.*
   La madrina
   Nosotros
   Anna

2. *Ustedes* **podrían** *visitar el orfanato.*
   El diácono
   Usted y yo
   Yo

Complete the sentences below by filling in the blanks with the most appropriate word from the column on the right. The first example is given. All answers are used only once.

F	1	¿Quién será el pastor?	a	al
	2	María _____ leer la Biblia.	b	quiere
	3	_____ dirían la bendición.	c	Ellos
	4	Los misioneros _____ de Guatemala.	d	pluma
	5	Él tendrá _____ regalos.	e	La
	6	Yo querré la _____.	f	¿Quién
	7	_____ Biblia es de Eric.	g	unos
	8	Iré _____ servicio.	h	son
	9	La iglesia _____ Biblias.	i	dinero
	10	Necesito _____.	j	tendría

Words of Discernment

Three of the four words in each group are related. Find the word that does not belong and note what the remaining words have in common. The first example is given.

__D__ 1. A. el Salvador   B. el Señor   C. el Mesías   D. la sabiduria

_____names of Christ_____

____ 2. A. el tabernáculo   B. el templo   C. el cuidado   D. el altar

_____

____ 3. A. la paz   B. el amor   C. la alegría   D. la biblia

_____

Demonstrative Pronouns

The demonstrative pronouns have similar forms as the demonstrative adjectives that were discussed in chapter two. The difference is that the demonstrative pronouns have written accents and they replace the noun. Demonstrative pronouns agree in number and gender with the nouns that they replace.[10]

TABLE 4.6—Demonstrative Pronouns

	Masculine	**Feminine**
this (one)	éste	ésta
these (ones)	éstos	éstas
that (one)	ése aquél	ésa aquélla
those (ones)	ésos aquéllos	ésas aquéllas

Miguel interpretó esta escritura, y ésa.
Michael interpreted this scripture, and that one.

Ella visitó este orfanato, no aquéllos.
She visited this orphanage, not those.

There are also neutral forms of the demonstrative pronouns (**esto**, **eso** and **aquello**), and they are used when referring to a general idea, something abstract or something not identified in the sentence. The word that is used will depend upon the location of the item in reference to the speaker's location. Note that the neutral forms do not have accent marks.[11]

¿Qué es eso? *What is that?*
Prefiero aquellos. *I prefer those.*

Ejercicio D

In each sentence below, replace the demonstrative adjective + noun with the demonstrative pronoun. The first sentence is done for you.

1. Entraron en aquel edificio.

   <u>*Entraron en aquél*</u>.

2. El patrocinador prefiere esta caridad.

   _____.

3. No quiero leer ese versículo.

   _____.

4. El pastor entraba en aquellos refugios.

   _____.

5. Mañana sabré estos mandamientos.

   _____.

6. ¿Dónde estaba aquella Biblia?

   _____.

Location Adverbs

The following adverbs are useful for describing where things are located:[12,13]

aquí......................... *here*   **allí**....................... *there*
acá.......................... *around here*   **allá**....................... *over there*

Prefiero el himnario que está aquí. *I prefer the hymn book that is here.*
Prefiero el himnario que está acá. *I prefer the hymn book that is around here.*
Prefiero el himnario que está allí. *I prefer the hymn book that is there.*
Prefiero el himnario que está allá. *I prefer the hymn book that is over there.*

Command Mood of Regular Verbs

Use this form to give instruction or to tell someone to do something. Note that there are no commands given in the first person tense (**yo**), because one does not give oneself an order. The person who receives the command is always *you.* However, note that there is more than one form of *you* in Spanish. These forms include the singular informal **tú**, the singular formal **usted** and the plural formal **ustedes**. Each of these uses a different verb command form.[14]

The command verb endings for the second person tense (**tú**) will differ, depending upon whether or not the command is negative or positive. If it is positive, the command tense takes on the ending for the third person tense. If negative, the command tense takes on the ending for the second person, but switches the ending of the other verb form (i.e., **-ar** verbs will end in the **-er** and **-ir** verb endings, and the **-er** or **-ir** verbs will end in the **-ar** verb endings). [15]

To create the singular formal **usted** command , add the ending **-e** to the stem of the **-ar** verbs, and **-a** to the stem of the **-er** and **-ir** verbs. Verbs that are stem changing follow the same rule.[16]

To create the plural formal **ustedes** command, add an **-n** to the singular formal commands. See **TABLE 4.7** for a summary of the changes. In Spanish, the subject pronouns may be included to be more emphatic or more polite. The subject pronouns, if included in the sentence, are placed after the command verb.

TABLE 4.7—Command Forms of Regular *-ar, -er* and *-ir* Verbs

	-ar	-er	-ir
tú	-a no —es	-e no —as	-e no —as
usted	-e	-a	-a
ustedes	-en	-an	-an

TABLE 4.8—Examples of Command Forms of Regular Verbs

	amar	**beber**	**compartir**
tú	ama no am**es**	bebe no beb**as**	comparte no compart**as**
usted	ame	beb**a**	compart**a**
ustedes	am**en**	beb**an**	compart**an**

No comas tú en ese restaurante, come en éste aquí. *Don't eat in that restaurant, eat in this one.*

Comparta usted su opinión con la clase. *Share your opinion with the class.*

Command Mood of Irregular Verbs

There are some irregular verbs that do not follow the normal rules for conjugation. Some of these verbs have stem form changes (as discussed previously in chapter 2.) **TABLE 4.9** lists a few of the more commonly found irregular verbs in the *usted* and *ustedes* command form.

TABLE 4.9—Irregular Verb Stems for Command Mood[17,18]

Infinitive	Stem	Singular	Plural
decir-*say*	dig-	diga ud.	digan uds.
hacer- *do*	hag-	haga ud.	hagan uds.
ofrecer-*offer*	ofrezc-	ofrezca ud.	ofrezcan uds.
pensar-*think*	piens-	piense ud.	piensen uds.
poner-*put*	pong-	ponga ud.	pongan uds.
salir-*leave*	salg-	salga ud.	salgan uds.
tener-*have*	teng-	tenga ud.	tengan uds.
traer-*bring*	traig-	traiga ud.	traigan uds.
venir-*come*	veng-	venga ud.	vengan uds.
volver-*return*	vuelv-	vuelva ud.	vuelvan uds.

Here are a few more examples of sentences that contain commands:

No tomes esta medicina. *Do not take this medicine.*
Digan ustedes la verdad. *Tell the truth.*
Pedro, ofrezca su ayuda. *Peter, offer your help.*
Salga usted temprano. *Leave early.*
Abran ustedes sus Biblias. *Open your Bibles.*
María, traiga su pastor. *María, bring your pastor.*
Haga esto. *Do this.*

Ejercicio E

Change the following statements to a singular and a plural formal command, as shown in the example.

1. Lucas invita a los misioneros.
   Lucas, invite usted a los misioneros.
   Inviten ustedes a los misioneros.

2. Rita lleva el himnario.
   _____
   _____

3. Ana abre la Biblia.
   _____
   _____

4. Lupe viene al grupo de apoyo de matrimonios.
   _____
   _____

5. María hace una donación.
   _____
   _____

More Irregular Commands

Here are a few more irregular formal commands that have special forms and do not follow the normal rules.

TABLE 4.10—Irregular Command Moods[19]

Infinitive	Singular	Plural
dar—*give*	dé ud.	den uds.
estar—*be*	esté ud.	estén uds.
ir—*go*	vaya ud.	vayan uds.
oír—*hear*	oiga ud.	oigan uds.
saber—*know*	sepa ud.	sepan uds.
ser—*be*	sea ud.	sean uds.

Den ustedes gracias a Dios en toda situación. *Give thanks to God in all situations.*
Vaya usted con Dios. *Go with God.*
Sepa usted los versículos. *Know the verses.*

The Ten Commandments

The Ten Commandments are *los Diez Mandamientos* in Spanish. Underline the command verbs found in each of the ten commandments.[20] Above each verb, write the infinitive verb and its meaning, as shown in the first commandment. The infinitive verbs are listed at the bottom of the page to help you.

Tener-to have
1. No <u>tengas</u> otros dioses además de mí.

2. No hagas ningún ídolo.

3. No pronuncies el nombre del Señor tu Dios a la ligera.

4. Observa el día sábado, y conságraselo al Señor tu Dios.

5. Honra a tu padre y a tu madre.

6. No mates.

7. No cometas adulterio.

8. No robes.

9. No des testimonio falso en contra de tu prójimo.

10. No codicies la mujer de tu prójimo, ni nada que le pertenezca.

codiciar	cometer	consagrar
dar	hacer	honrar
matar	observar	pronunciar
robar	tener	

Subjunctive Mood

Use this form when you want to express *possibility, uncertainty or feelings* concerning an action or state. Many times it is translated as *may*. The subjunctive may be used to express doubt or when a contrary-to-fact statement is made. Note the endings for the regular verbs in **TABLE 4.11**. These endings are added to the stem form of the infinitive verb.[21,22]

TABLE 4.11—Subjunctive Mood for Regular *-ar, -er* and *-ir* Verbs

	-ar	**-er**	**-ir**
yo	-e	-a	-a
tú	-es	-as	-as
él/ella	-e	-a	-a
usted	-e	-a	-a
nosotros,-as	-emos	-amos	-amos
ellos/ellas	-en	-an	-an
ustedes	-en	-an	-an

TABLE 4.12—Examples of Subjunctive Mood for Regular *-ar, -er* and *-ir* Verbs

	amar	**beber**	**compartir**
yo	ame	beba	comparta
tú	ames	bebas	compartas
él/ella	ame	beba	comparta
usted	ame	beba	comparta
nosotros,-as	amemos	bebamos	compartamos
ellos/ellas	amen	beban	compartan
ustedes	amen	beban	compartan

Él prefiere que yo coma en este restaurante. *He prefers that I (may) eat in this restaurant.*

Es triste que él no pueda venir. *It is sad that he could not come.*

Dudo que ella hable inglés. *I doubt that she speaks English.*

Quiero que tú compartas con tu hermano. *I want that you (may) share with your brother.*

Mi padre no quiere que María vea ese programa. *My father doesn't want Maria to see (seeing) that program.*

Ejercicio F

Substitute the subjunctive mood in the sentences below, as shown in the example.

1. Quiero que usted ore con Juan.
   (leer las noticias, hablar con ellos, estudiar la Biblia)

   Quiero que usted lea las noticias.
   Quiero que usted hable con ellos.
   Quiero que usted estudie la Biblia.

2. Mi padrino prefiere que yo *visite a* mi pastor.
   (conversar con, ayudar, viajar con)

   _____

   _____

   _____

3. El misionero necesita un pastor que *hable español.*
   (leer la Biblia, visitar las viudas, interpretar)

   _____

   _____

   _____

Irregular Subjunctive Verbs

Many irregular verbs change vowels in the stem form of the verb, as previously discussed in chapter 2. Note, however, that **-ir** verbs that change **e→i** and **o→u** will also change in the **nosotros** form of the subjunctive tense. These verbs can usually be categorized in one of these three changes:

TABLE 4.13-1—Subjunctive Mood of Irregular Verbs (**e→i**)[23]

	pedir (to ask)	Other examples of **e→i** verb changes:	
yo	pida	rendir *(to surrender)*	seguir *(to follow, continue)*
tú	pidas	repetir *(to repeat)*	
él/ella	pida	servir *(to serve)*	
usted	pida	perseguir *(to follow)*	
nosotros,-as	pidamos		
ellos/ellas	pidan		
ustedes	pidan		

TABLE 4.13-2—Subjunctive Mood of Irregular Verbs (e→ie)

	pensar (to think)	Other examples of e→ie verb changes:	
yo	piense	comenzar (to begin)	confesar (to confess)
tú	pienses	entender (to understand)	convertir (to convert)
él/ella	piense	mentir (to lie)	enterrar (to bury)
usted	piense	perder (to lose)	querer (to want)
nosotros,-as	pensemos	sentir (to feel)	
ellos/ellas	piensen	arrepentirse (to repent)	
ustedes	piensen		

TABLE 4.13-3—Subjunctive Mood of Irregular Verbs (o→ue)

	recordar (to remember)	Other examples of o→ue verb changes:	
yo	recuerde	doler (to hurt)	encontrar (to find)
tú	recuerdes	mover (to move)	volver (to turn, go back)
él/ella	recuerde	morir (to die)	devolver (to return or to give back)
usted	recuerde	poder (to be able to)	
nosotros,-as	recordemos		
ellos/ellas	recuerden		
ustedes	recuerden		

Here is another group of common irregular verbs in the subjunctive form. These are given here as a reference list. To review more, please refer to the appendix in the back of this book.

TABLE 4.14—Subjunctive Mood of Irregular Verbs[24,25,26]

	ir	estar	ser	haber	dar
yo	vaya	esté	sea	haya	dé
tú	vayas	estés	seas	hayas	des
él/ella	vaya	esté	sea	haya	dé
usted	vaya	esté	sea	haya	dé
nosotros,-as	vayamos	estemos	seamos	hayamos	demos
ellos/ellas	vayan	estén	sean	hayan	den
ustedes	vayan	estén	sean	hayan	den

Direct Object Pronouns

Direct object pronouns receive the action of the verb directly.[27] These pronouns can replace nouns and are listed in the table below.

TABLE 4.15—Direct Object Pronouns[28]

SINGULAR	PLURAL
me *(me)* te *(you—familiar)* lo *(him, it, you—formal masc.)* la *(her, it, you—formal fem.)*	nos *(us—masc./fem.)* — — los *(them, you—formal masc.)* las *(them, you—formal fem.)*

Place the object pronouns immediately before the verb, as in the following examples.
Tú lo leíste. *You read it.*
Juan me ve. *John sees me.*
Nosotros los vemos. *We see them.*

The direct object pronouns in the third person (**lo, la, los, las**) must agree in number, person and gender with the replaced noun, as shown in the following examples:

María lee el capítulo. *Maria reads the chapter.*
María lo lee. *Maria reads it.*

Tengo los boletines de la iglesia. *I have the church bulletins.*
Los tengo. *I have them.*

El padre dio el dinero ayer. *The father gave the money yesterday.*
El padre lo dio ayer. *The father gave it yesterday.*

La mujer abre la puerta. *The woman opens the door.*
La mujer la abre. *The woman opens it.*

Pablo escribió las escrituras. *Paul wrote the scriptures.*
Pablo las escribió. *Paul wrote them.*

Ejercicio G

Substitute the correct direct object pronoun for each noun and modifiers, as shown below.

1. Mis amigos escuchan música Cristiana.
   Mis amigos la escuchan.

2. Luis y yo aceptamos la invitación.
   _____

3. Yo no conocí a las señoras.
   _____

4. Usted obedece los mandamientos.
   _____

5. Tomás escribe el boletín de la iglesia.
   _____

6. ¿Quién ayudó a los misioneros de México?
   _____

7. El pecador necesita la salvación de Cristo.
   _____

8. El apóstol Juan escribió el libro de Apocalipsis.
   _____

9. El maestro predica el evangelio de Jesucristo.
   _____

10. La niña oraba el Padrenuestro.
    _____

Indirect Object Pronouns

The indirect object pronoun indicates the person *to, for* or *from whom* anything is given, sent, told, etc. Note that the indirect object pronouns, unlike the direct object pronouns, are not masculine or feminine oriented, as indicated in **TABLE 4.16.** Indirect object pronouns are placed before the verb, with a few exceptions that will be discussed later.[29]

The pronouns **me, te** and **nos** are the same for both the indirect and direct object pronouns. However, the third person singular and plural forms **le** and **les** are different.[30]

TABLE 4.16—Indirect Object Pronouns[31,32]

SINGULAR	PLURAL
me *(to me)*	nos *(to us)*
te *(to you—familiar)*	— —
le *(to him, her, it)*	les *(to them)*
le *(to you—formal)*	les *(to you—formal)*

Ella te compraba una Biblia. *She bought you a Bible.*
Yo le hablo en inglés. *I speak to him (to her) in English.*
Les dieron el regalo las semana pasada. *They gave them the present last week.*

To understand this concept of direct and indirect objects better, consider the following sentence:

The deacon gave a Bible to the boy.

To determine which object directly receives the action of the verb (ie, the boy or the Bible), ask yourself what the deacon gave—the boy or the Bible? He didn't give the boy away, he gave the Bible. Therefore, the <u>direct object</u> of the sentence above is the Bible. The one who indirectly receives the action is the <u>indirect object</u> (in this case, the boy).[33]

It may also be helpful to remember that if you can add to___, for___, or from ___, the pronoun is probably an indirect object.

Sometimes, a direct and an indirect object may both be included in the same sentence. When this occurs, the indirect object pronoun always comes first:

indirect + direct

Te   lo   pagaré mañana.
I will pay you for it tomorrow.

If the infinitive verb is the main verb, attach one or both object pronouns to the ending of the infinitive.[34] In Spanish, the indirect object pronoun comes first, and an accent mark is placed over the final syllable of the verb:

indirect+direct

Quiero enseñártelo. *I want to show it to you.*

indirect+direct

El secretario quiere mandártelo por correo electrónico.
The secretary wants to send it to you by email.

Verbs that use an indirect object when referring to someone include **decir, enseñar, escribir, leer, mandar** and **preguntar.**

When both pronouns are in the third person, **se** replaces the indirect object pronoun **le** or **les**. To clarify the sentence, the preposition **a él**, **a ella**, **a usted,** etc. are often added:[35]

indirect+direct

Jonas **se   lo** entrega **a ella**. *Jonas handed it to her.*

Ejercicio H

Read the following sentences aloud and indicate whether the italicized pronoun is a direct or an indirect object pronoun.

1. La maestra *les* enseña unas películas evangélicas.

2. Yo *le* digo que *la* quiero.

3. Miguel *le* da una donación y el pastor *lo* acepta.

4. Mi madrina *me* llama mucho.

5. ¿A qué hora *te* espero en la iglesia?

6. La Señora Johnson *nos* enseña la lección.

Pronouns as Objects of a Preposition

Prepositional pronouns are identical to the forms used with subject pronouns, with the exception of the first and second person singular (**mí** and **ti**). Also note that there is an accent mark on **mí,** which helps to differentiate this word from the possessive adjective **mi** (*my*).[36,37]

TABLE 4.17—Pronouns as Objects of a Preposition[38]

Singular		Plural	
mí*	*me*	**nosotros/as**	*us*
ti*	*you (familiar)*	—	—
usted	*you (formal)*	**ustedes**	*you (formal)*
él	*him*	**ellos**	*them*
ella	*her*	**ellas**	*them*

These pronouns are used in Spanish for emphasis, contrast, or clarification, particularly with the preposition **a** *(to)*. They may also be used to replace the noun in a sentence.

Él me habló a mí; no le habló a usted.
He spoke to me; he didn't speak to you.

Los patrocinadores le dieron el dinero a ella.
The sponsors gave the money to her.

There are other prepositions that may be used with these pronouns. Some of them are **en** *(in)*, **para/por** *(for)*, **de** *(of)*, and **con** *(with)*.

Yo confio en él.
I confide in him.

Esas Biblias son para mí.
Those Bibles are for me.

La gracia es para ustedes.
Grace is for you.

NOTE: The preposition **con** combines with **mí** and **ti** to form the special words **conmigo** (*with me)* and **contigo** (*with you*).[39]

El pastor va conmigo; no va contigo.
The pastor is going with me; he is not going with you.

El Señor está contigo.
The Lord is with you.

Ejercicio I

Fill in the blanks with an object of preposition pronoun.

1. La clase _____ (of hers) tiene un examen diario.

2. Lleva la licencia de casamiento _____ (with you, *sing.—fam.*).

3. María caminaba _____ (with me).

4. La Biblia es _____ (for you, *sing.—fam.*). No es _____ (for them, *fem.*).

Ejercicio I (continued)

5. ¿Quieres ir _____ (with me), o quieres ir _____ (with him)?

6. Ayer fuí a la capilla _____ (with them, masc.), y despues fuí _____ (with her) al cuarto de los niños.

7. Le dí mi Biblia _____ (to her).

8. Pedro se la dio _____ (to him).

9. No quiere hablar _____ (with me).

10. Los huérfanos visitaban _____ (with us, *masc.*).

Reflexive Pronouns

The reflexive pronouns have the same forms (**me, te** and **nos**) as direct and indirect object pronouns, except for the third person form of **se**.

TABLE 4.18—Reflexive Pronouns [40]

Singular		Plural	
me	*myself*	**nos**	*ourselves*
te	*yourself*	—	—
se	*himself, herself, itself, yourself (formal)*	**se**	*themselves, yourselves (formal)*

Me siento. *I sit (myself) down.*

Te amas. *You love (yourself).*

Desayunamos a las nueve y luego nos preparamos para la clase de profecía. *We eat breakfast at nine and then we prepare ourselves for the prophecy class.*

Reflexive Verbs

Reflexive verbs have the same subject and pronoun, and the subject acts upon itself. In other words, the verb's subject is the same person or thing as the object of the verb. A reflexive verb can be shown by the pronoun **se** attached to the infinitive verb form. Here are a few reflexive verbs in their infinitive form:[41,42]

acostarse	*to go to bed*	**sentarse**	*to sit*
despertarse	*to awaken*	**casarse**	*to marry*
llamarse	*to call*	**amarse**	*to love*
afeitarse	*to shave*	**unirse**	*to unite*
prepararse	*to prepare*	**juntarse**	*to unite*
bañarse	*to bathe*		

Many verbs in the Spanish language can be used both as reflexive verbs and as regular verbs.

Me lavo. *I wash myself.* (Reflexive)
Yo lavo la ropa. *I wash the clothes.* (Not reflexive)

Esta mañana José se vió (en el espejo). *This morning José saw himself (in the mirror).* (Reflexive)
Esta mañana José vió a su pastor. *This morning José saw his pastor.* (Not reflexive)

Ejercicio J

Note whether the following sentences are reflexive or not reflexive:

1. Me llamo Marco.

2. Mario se acuesta a las diez.

3. Nosotros nos despertamos temprano y nos levantamos.

4. Dios te ama.

5. Me siente en este banco.

6. Jorge me dio un regalo.

Ejercicio K

Using the given reflexive words, complete the following sentences in the present tense:

1. *(llamarse)* Se _____ el pastor Ricardo.

2. *(amarse)* Me _____.

3. *(bañarse)* Mi madre se _____.

4. *(afeitarse)* El hombre se _____.

Vocabulary

These words do not all appear in the previous lesson. However, you should learn them because they may be used as active vocabulary later.

abomination—la abominación
abortion—el aborto ....**to have an abortion**—abortar
abuse—el abuso ....**to abuse**—maltratar/abusar de
abyss—el abismo
accusation—la acusación ....**to accuse**—acusar
addict—adicto,-a
addiction—la adicción
addictive—que crea dependencia
adultery—el adulterio ....**to commit adultery**—adulterar
adversity—la adversidad
affliction—la aflicción ....**to afflict**—afligir
alcoholic—alcohólico,-a
alcoholism—el alcoholismo
altercation—el altercado/ la disputa
anger—la ira ....**to anger**—enojar
Antichrist— el Anticristo
atheist—ateo,-a
bad—mal/ malo,-a
bitterness—la amargura ....**to embitter**—amargar
blasphemous words—las palabras blasfemas
blasphemy—la blasfemia ....**to blaspheme**—blasfemar
boasting—la jactancia ....**to boast**—jactarse
broken (*home*)—una familia divida ....**to break**—romper, quebrantar
       (*object*)—roto, quebrado
       (*person*) destrozado, deshecho
brute—la fiera, la bestia
burn—la quemadura ....**to burn**—quemar
character—el carácter
complaint—la queja ....**to complain**—quejarse
corrupt—corrupto,-a/ corrompido,-a
corruption—la corrupción ....**to corrupt**—corromper
crime—el crimen
curse—la maldición ....**to curse**—maldecir
death—la muerte/ el fallecimiento (*formal*) ...**to die**—morir/ fallecer
debt—la deuda ....**to run up debt**—contraer deudas,
                                         endeudarse
deception—el engaño ....**to deceive**—engañar

destruction—la destrucción ....**to destroy**—destruir, destrozar
devil—el diablo
disaster—el desastre
disobedience—la desobediencia ....**to disobey**—desobedecer
enemy—enemigo,-a
envy—(n.) la envidia ....**to envy**—envidiar/codiciar
evil—(adj.) malo,-a
evil—(n.) la maldad, el mal
evil spirits—los espíritus malos
exile—(n.) el exilio
exorcist— el, la exorcista
false prophet— el/la profeta falso,-a
false witnesses—los testígos falsos
fear—el miedo ....**to fear**—temer por
fool—tonto,-a/ necio,-a ....**to fool**—engañar
gambling—el juego con apuestas ....**to gamble**—apostar
gambling debts—las deudas de juego
gossip—el chisme ....**to gossip**—chismear
greed—la codicia
greedy—codicioso,-a
grief—la pena ....**to grieve**—apenar/ dar pena
guilt—la culpa
guilty—culpable
hell—el infierno
heresy—la herejía
homosexual—el,la homosexual
homosexuality—la homosexualidad
human nature—la naturaleza humana
hypocrisy—la hipocresía
hypocrite—el/la hipócrita
idolatry—la idolatría
idol—el ídolo
jealousy—los celos
judgment—la sentencia ....**to judge**—juzgar
killer—asesino,-a ....**to kill**—matar
lie—la mentira ....**to lie**—mentir
loss—la pérdida ....**to lose**—perder
lost—perdido,-a
lust—la lujuria/ansia ....**to lust**—lujuriar
luxury—el lujo
magic—la magia
materialism—el materialismo
misfortune—la desdicha/ la desgracia

murder—el asesinato/ el homicidio ....**to murder**—asesinar, matar
oath— el juramento
pagan—pagano,-a
pain—el dolor ....**to hurt**—doler
persecution—la persecución ....**to persecute**—perseguir
perverse—perverso,-a
poverty—la pobreza
prison officer—carcelero,-a
prison—la cárcel
problem—el problema
prostitute— la prostituta
prostitution—la prostitución ....**to prostitute**—prostituirse
rape—la violación ....**to rape**—violar
rapist—violador,-a
robber— ladrón,-ona ....**to rob**—robar
sadness—la tristeza
satanic—satánico,-a
satan—satán/ satanás
shame—la vergüenza ....**to shame**—avergonzar
sickness—la enfermedad
sinner—pecador,-a
sins—los pecados ....**to sin**—pecar
slave—esclavo,-a ....**to enslave**—esclavizar
sorcerer—el mago/ el brujo
sorceress—la bruja
sorcery—la brujería
sorrow—la tristeza
spiritual warfare—la guerra spiritual
suffering—el sufrimiento ....**to suffer**—sufrir
suicide—el suicidio ....**to commit suicide**—suicidarse
temptation—la tentación ....**to tempt**—tentar
thief—ladrón,-a ....**to steal**—robar
threat—la amenaza ....**to threaten**—amenazar
trials—las aflicciones
tribulation—la tribulación
unbeliever—incrédulo,-a
vice—el vicio, la mala costumbre
victim—la víctima
violent—violento
weak—débil
weakness—la debilidad
wickedness—la maldad
worldliness—la mundanería

Match the Spanish word in the left column with the English word on the right, as shown in the first example.

		Spanish		English
G	1	el abuso	a	lie
	2	la mentira	b	deception
	3	la violación	c	rape
	4	la envidia	d	envy
	5	el engaño	e	lust
	6	el alcoholismo	f	murder
	7	la lujuria	g	abuse
	8	la blasfemia	h	alcoholism
	9	el homicidio	i	blaspheme
	10	la jactancia	j	boasting

CROSS PUZZLE (CRUCIGRAMA)

See how many words you know in Spanish by filling in the squares.

ACROSS	DOWN
1. words that blaspheme *(2 words)*	1. persecution, pursuit
6. anger	2. lust
8. oath	3. abomination
13. to read	4. male slave
15. idol	5. addiction
16. one addicted to alcohol	7. year
17. feminine article	9. bad, evil
18. vice	10. fools
21. to hurt	11. lost *(masc.)*
22. hypocrite *(fem.)*	12. homosexuality
24. enemies	14. he robs
28. reflexive pronoun	17. personal pronoun *(neut.)*
30. a lie	19. exorcist
31. Antichrist	20. anger
32. to afflict	23. even
33. you afflict	24. to anger
35. false witness *(2 words)*	25. that *(fem.)*
36. he boasts *(se _____)*	26. a lie
37. nothing	27. brute
	29. children
	30. evil
	32. opposite of hatred
	34. without

Bonus Phrases

wrath of God—la furia/ira de Dios
lust of the flesh—los deseos de la carne
dead in your sins—muerto(s) en sus pecados
to have a violent temper—ser de temperamento violento
to hurt someone's feelings—ofender (a alguien)
day of judgment—el día del juicio
death penalty—la pena de muerte
to condemn to death—condenar a muerte
to fall from grace—caer en desgracia
I swear that I did not do it—juro que no lo hice
to swear on the Bible—jurar sobre la Biblia
to be sent to prison for __ years—ser condenado,-a a ___años de cárcel
to grieve for someone—llorar la muerte de (alguien)
resurrection of the dead—la resurrección de los muertos
it's a shame/disgrace—es una vergüenza
punishment for our sins—el castigo por nuestros pecados
a feeling of guilt—sentimiento de culpabilidad
broken-hearted—con el corazón destrozado

Scripture Passage

Here is an NIV/NVI scripture verse that may be familiar to you.[43] Increase your vocabulary by inserting the corresponding words that may be found in the vocabulary from previous lessons.

_____ joyful always, _____ continually, _____ thanks in all circumstances, for this is God's _____ for you in _____ _____. **1 Thessalonians 5:16-18**	Estén siempre alegres, oren sin cesar, den gracias a Dios en toda situación, porque esta es su voluntad para ustedes en Cristo Jesús. **1 Tesalonicenses 5:16-18**

Conversation

A disaster relief volunteer approaches a local woman in Guatemala. She appears to be wandering around the town in a daze.

VOLUNTEER: Good morning. Can I help you with something?
WOMAN: Yes, thank you. I don't have a place to stay anymore. I need your help.

VOLUNTEER: What happened to your house?
WOMAN: It was destroyed a few days ago in the hurricane, along with all my belongings. I have been living with my sister and her family temporarily, but she is struggling too. I need to find a place to stay for myself and my baby.

VOLUNTEER: I am so sorry to hear that. I work with a team that can help provide you with temporary shelter. There is also food and water there. If you would like, I can tell you where it is so that we can help you.

WOMAN: Thank you so much. This means so much to me.

VOLUNTEER: This is a tough time for you. I just want you to know that you are not alone, and that we will do all that we can to help you get through this.

VOLUNTARIO: Buenos días. ¿Puedo ayudarte en algo?
MUJER: Sí, gracias. No tengo un lugar donde quedarme. Necesito ayuda.

VOLUNTARIO: ¿Qué sucedió con tu casa?
MUJER: El huracán la destruyó hace unos días, con todas mis pertenencias. He estado viviendo con mi hermana y su familia temporeramente y a ella se le ha hecho difícil también. Necesito un lugar donde quedarme con mi bebe.

VOLUNTARIO: ¡Qué triste escuchar eso! Trabajo con un equipo que te puede ayudar a proveer un refugio temporero. También hay alimento y agua. Si deseas puedo decirte donde está el lugar para poderte ayudar.

MUJER: Muchas gracias, esto significa mucho para mí.

VOLUNTARIO: Estos son tiempos difíciles para tí. Solo quiero que sepas que no estás sola y que haremos todo lo posible para ayudarte.

agua—water	**pertenencias**—belongings
alimento—food	**proveer**—to provide
ayudar—to help	**refugio**—shelter
equipo—team	**suceder**—to happen
huracán—hurricane	**temporeramente**—temporarily
lugar—place	**tiempos difíciles**—difficult times
necesitar—to need	**triste**—sad

Chapter 5

- **Verb Combinations**
- **Old and New Testament Names**
- ***¿Quién es?*** *(Who is it?)*
- **Books of the Old and New Testament**
- **Words of Discernment**
- **Books of the Bible Word Search**
- **Past Participles**
- **Irregular Past Participles**
- **Use of Past Participles**
- **Perfect Tenses**
- **Scripture Passage**
- ***Padre Nuestro,*** *The Lord's Prayer (NVI/NIV)*
- ***Padre Nuestro,*** *The Lord's Prayer (Reina Valera/KJV)*
- **Select Bible Parables and Miracles**
- **Parables and Miracles**
- **Spanish Conversation**
- **Scripture Passage**
- **Psalm 23**
- **Words of Discernment**
- **Present Participles**
- **Irregular Present Participles**
- **Progressive Tenses**
- **Additional Uses of Present Participles**
- **Spanish Conversation**
- **Ecclesiastes 3:1-8**
- **Words of Discernment**
- **Selected Mystery Scriptures**
- **Workbook Review Exercises**
- **Translation Exercises**
- **English-Spanish Expressions**
- **Heavenly Minded Crossword**

Verb Combinations

There are some verbs that can be used in combination with other words as building blocks to help create commands. A few of these combinations are listed here.

favor de + infinitive *(command)*[1]
Favor de sentarse. *Sit down.*
Favor de lavarse las manos. *Wash your hands.*
Favor de venir aquí. *Come here.*
Favor de leer el versículo. *Read the verse.*
Favor de hablar despacio. *Speak slowly.*

Ejercicio A

Translate the following commands into Spanish, using the above verb combination format.

1. Go to the airport.
2. Interpret this verse.
3. Learn your lesson.
4. Wait here.
5. Support your community.
6. Close the door.
7. Carry my suitcase.
8. Bring me towels.
9. Obey your parents.
10. Return tomorrow.
11. Don't turn here.
12. Use the map.

Old and New Testament Names[2]

In Spanish, the Old and New Testament names are called *los nombres del testamento antiguo y nuevo.*

Aaron—Aarón
Abel—Abel
Abraham—Abraham
Adam—Adán
angel—el ángel
Antichrist—Anticristo
Ark of the Covenant—la arca del pacto
ascension—la ascensión
atonement—la expiación
Babylonians—los babilonios
Barnabas—Bernabé
Barrabas—Barrabás
Benjamin—Benjamín
Bethlehem—Belén
Cain—Caín
Canaan—Canaán
Christ—Cristo
circumcision—la circuncisión
Daniel—Daniel
David—David
Delilah—Dalila
Eden—Edén
Egypt—Egipto
Egyptians—los egipcios
Eli—Elí
Elijah—Elías
Elisha—Eliseo
Enoch—Enoc

Esau—Esaú
Esther—Ester
Eve—Eva
Ezekiel—Ezequiel
Galilee—Galilea
Garden of Eden—el huerto/ jardín del Edén
gentiles—los gentiles
Gethsemane—Getsemaní
Gideon—Gedeón
Goliath—Goliat
Gomorrah—Gomorra
Hades—Hades
Hagar—Agar
Herod—Herodes
high priest—el sumo sacerdote
Holy Trinity—la santísima trinidad
Isaac—Isaac
Isaiah—Isaías
Ishmael—Ismael
Israel—Israel
Israelite—los israelitas
Jacob—Jacob
Jehovah—Jehová
Jeremiah—Jeremías
Jerico—Jericó
Jerusalem—Jerusalén
Jesus—Jesús

Jews—los judíos
Job—Job
John—Juan
John the Baptist—Juan el bautista
Jonah—Jonás
Jonathan—Jonatán
Jordan—Jordán
Joseph—José
Joshua—Josué
Judah—Judá
Judas—Judas
Lamb of God—el Cordero de Dios
Law of Moses—la ley de Moisés
Lazarus—Lázaro
Lebanon—Líbano
Lord's Supper—la Santa Cena
Lot—Lot
Mark—Marcos
Martha—Marta
Mary—María
Mary Magdalene—María
    Magdalena
Moses—Moisés
Mount Olive—monte de los olivos
Naomi—Noemí
Nazareth—Nazaret
Nebuchadnezzar—
    Nabucodonosor
Nicodemus—Nicodemo
Noah—Noé
Passover—la Pascua
Paul—Pablo
Pentecost—Pentecostés
Peter—Pedro

Pharaoh—El Faraón
Pharisee—Fariseo
Philip—Felipe
Philistine—Filisteo
Pontius Pilate—Poncio Pilato
Potiphar—Potifar
prophet—el profeta
Rachel—Raquel
Rebecca—Rebeca
Red Sea—Mar Rojo
Resurrection—la resurrección
Reuben—Rubén
Ruth—Ruth
Samaritan—Samaritano
Samson—Sansón
Samuel—Samuel
Sarah—Sara
Satan—Satán/Satanás
Saul—Saúl/Saulo
Scripture—la escritura
Seth—Set
Sodom—Sodoma
Solomon—Salomón
Son of Man—el Hijo de hombre
synagogue—la sinagoga
temple—el templo
Timothy—Timoteo
wisemen—los magos
Zacchaeus—Zaqueo
Zion—Sion

¿Quien es? *(Who is It?)*

Match the description on the left with its corresponding name on the right.

1. El ángel caído de Dios	a. Juan el Bautista
2. Los padres terrenales de Jesús	b. David
3. Moisés los sacó de Egipto	c. Satán
4. Jesús fue bautizado por este hombre	d. Adán y Eva
5. El rey famoso de Israel	e. Jonás
6. Este profeta fue tragado por un pez enorme	f. Jesús
7. Ellos pecaron en el huerto del Edén	g. María y José
8. Murió por nuestros pecados clavado en una cruz	h. los israelitas
9. El rey de los Babilonios	i. Goliat
10. David mató a este gigante	j. Nabucodonosor

Books of the Old and New Testament

In Spanish, the books of the Old and New Testament are called *Libros del Antiguo y Nuevo Testamento.*

TABLE 5.1—Books of the Old Testament[3]

Génesis—Genesis	**Isaías**—Isaiah
Éxodo—Exodus	**Jeremías**—Jeremiah
Levítico—Leviticus	**Lamentaciones**—Lamentations
Números—Numbers	**Ezequiel**—Ezekiel
Deuteronomio—Deuteronomy	**Daniel**—Daniel
Josué—Joshua	**Oseas**—Hosea
Jueces—Judges	**Joel**—Joel
Rut—Ruth	**Amós**—Amos
Samuel—Samuel	**Abdías**—Obadiah
Reyes—Kings	**Jonás**—Jonah
Crónicas—Chronicles	**Miqueas**—Micah
Esdras—Ezra	**Nahúm**—Nahum
Nehemías—Nehemiah	**Habacuc**—Habakkuk
Ester—Esther	**Sofonías**—Zephaniah
Job—Job	**Hageo**—Haggai
Salmos—Psalms	**Zacarías**—Zechariah
Proverbios—Proverbs	**Malaquías**—Malachi
Eclesiastés—Ecclesiastes	
Cantares—Song of Solomon	

TABLE 5.2—Books of the New Testament[4]

Mateo—Matthew	**Tesalonicenses**—Thessalonians
Marcos—Mark	**Timoteo**—Timothy
Lucas—Luke	**Tito**—Titus
Juan—John	**Filemón**—Philemon
Hechos—Acts	**Hebreos**—Hebrews
Romanos—Romans	**Santiago**—James
Corintios—Corinthians	**Pedro**—Peter
Gálatas—Galatians	**Judas**—Jude
Efesios—Ephesians	**Apocalipsis**—Revelation
Filipenses—Philippians	
Colosenses—Colossians	

Words of Discernment

Three of the four words in each group are related. Find the word that does not belong and note what the remaining words have in common.

____ 1. A. la salvación   B. la cruz   C. la crucifixión   D. el culto

_____

____ 2. A. Sofonías   B. Santiago   C. Crónicas   D. Reyes

_____

____ 3. A. Lucas   B. Juan   C. Pedro   D. Moisés

_____

____ 4. A. Isaías   B. Jeremías   C. Ezequiel   D. Apocalipsis

_____

Books of the Bible Word Search

There are 38 of the Old and New Testament books hidden in the puzzle below, as shown in the example. How many of these can you find?

~~A~~	~~P~~	~~O~~	~~C~~	~~A~~	~~L~~	~~I~~	~~P~~	~~S~~	~~I~~	~~S~~	E	P	I	S
J	O	B	S	O	I	S	E	F	E	I	Z	R	E	O
D	A	N	I	E	L	O	T	Í	S	S	E	O	Z	M
L	Z	A	É	A	J	O	E	L	T	E	Q	V	A	L
É	A	R	E	X	M	M	S	O	E	N	U	E	C	A
A	C	M	S	C	O	A	A	E	R	É	I	R	O	S
O	A	T	E	Ó	R	D	L	R	N	G	E	B	R	A
I	R	I	S	N	M	Ó	O	A	C	S	L	I	I	C
M	Í	T	N	Ú	T	A	N	G	Q	O	E	O	N	A
O	A	O	E	M	U	A	I	I	A	U	S	S	T	N
N	S	C	P	E	R	O	C	S	C	I	Í	N	I	T
O	O	I	I	R	S	P	E	I	A	A	T	A	O	A
R	H	T	L	O	A	E	N	T	O	Í	S	N	S	R
E	C	Í	I	S	E	D	S	A	O	N	A	Z	A	E
T	E	V	F	N	U	R	E	C	H	M	E	S	N	S
U	H	E	M	U	Q	O	S	W	C	Ú	I	S	A	P
E	C	L	E	S	I	A	S	T	É	S	M	T	U	Í
D	J	E	R	E	M	Í	A	S	E	C	E	U	J	Ó

Amós	Ester	Juan	Proverbios
~~Apocalipsis~~	Éxodo	Jueces	Rut
Cantares	Ezequiel	Lamentaciones	Salmos
Colosenses	Filipenses	Levítico	Santiago
Corintios	Génesis	Malaquías	Tesalonicenses
Crónicas	Hechos	Marcos	Timoteo
Daniel	Isaías	Miqueas	Tito
Deuteronomio	Jeremías	Nahúm	Zacarías
Eclesiastés	Job	Números	
Efesios	Joel	Pedro	

Past Participles

The majority of past participles are regular. They are formed by removing the ending of the infinitive verb and adding the following endings, depending upon whether the verb is an **-ar**, **-er** or **-ir** verb. Use the following guidelines to help you.

- **-ar** verbs → add **-ado** to the stem form

hablar	→	habl**ado**	*spoken*
salvar	→	salv**ado**	*saved*
invitar	→	invit**ado**	*invited*
usar	→	us**ado**	*used*

- **-er** verbs → add **-ido** to the stem form

esconder	→	escond**ido**	*hidden*
comer	→	com**ido**	*eaten*
saber	→	sab**ido**	*known*

- **-ir** verbs → add **-ido** to the stem form

vivir	→	viv**ido**	*lived*
sufrir	→	sufr**ido**	*suffered*
salir	→	sal**ido**	*left*

Note: When the stem ends in **-a**, **-e**, or **-o**, a written accent is often placed over the **í** of **ido**.[5]

caer	→	ca**í**do	*fallen*
creer	→	cre**í**do	*believed*
leer	→	le**í**do	*read*

Irregular Past Participles

A small group of verbs have irregular past participles and do not follow the regular rules. A few of them are listed here.

abrir	**abierto**	*opened*	ir	**ido**	*gone*
cubrir	**cubierto**	*covered*	morir	**muerto**	*died*
decir	**dicho**	*said*	poner	**puesto**	*put*
devolver	**devuelto**	*given back*	romper	**roto**	*broken*
escribir	**escrito**	*written*	ver	**visto**	*seen*
hacer	**hecho**	*done, made*	volver	**vuelto**	*returned*

Uses of Past Participles

There are multiple uses for past participles. One of them is to describe a noun or nouns. In this case, the past participle is used as an adjective. Past participles, when used as an adjective, must agree in both gender and number with the noun being described.[6]

un aeropuerto cerrado	*a closed airport*
el Señor crucificado	*the crucified Lord*
los edificios destruidos	*the destroyed buildings*
los ángeles caídos	*the fallen angels*
una maleta abierta	*an open suitcase*
un corazón destrozado	*a broken heart*

Ejercicio B

Translate the following phrases into Spanish, as shown below.

1. the written invitations   *las invitaciones escritas*

2. the gifts given back

3. a closed bible

4. the prepared food

5. the baptized children

Past participles are also used to form sentences in the passive voice, where the subject receives the action of the verb. In English, the passive voice is expressed using some form of the verb *to be* along with the past participle. In Spanish, the verb **ser** is used, along with the past participle. When the past participle is used with **ser** in the passive sentence, the endings agree in both gender and number with the noun they modify. If the performer of the action is mentioned in the sentence, the preposition **por** *(by)* may be used.[7]

El aeropuerto fue cerrado por los oficiales. *The airport was closed by the officials.*

El Señor fue crucificado. *The Lord was crucified.*

Los edificios serán destruidos por el huracán. *The buildings will be destroyed by the hurricane.*

La maleta fue abierta por mi madre. *The suitcase was opened by my mother.*

Su corazón era destrozado por su esposa. *His heart was broken by his wife.*

Ejercicio C

Translate the following sentences into Spanish, as shown below.

1. The invitations will be written by María. *Las invitaciones serán escritas por María.*

2. Yesterday, the gifts were given back by my sister.

3. The window was opened by the thief.

4. The food was prepared by my mother.

5. Our children will be baptized by our pastor.

The Perfect Tenses

The different tenses of **haber** can be used with past participles to create what is referred to as the perfect tenses. The verb **haber** is used as the helping verb and can be conjugated in various tenses and persons like any other verb. When the past participle is used with the helping verb, it is considered as part of the verb structure and therefore does not agree with anything in gender or number. When the past participle is used in this regard, it always ends in the letter **-o**.[8]

The perfect tense can be identified in English by some form of the verb *to have* before the past participle (*I have studied, they had studied, we had studied, etc.*).

TABLE 5.3—Examples of the Use of the Perfect Tenses[9]

	Present Perfect *I have used, known, left, etc.*		**Pluperfect** *I had used, known, left, etc.*		**Past Perfect*** *I had used, known, left, etc.*	
yo	he		había		hube	
tú	has		habías		hubiste	
él/ella	ha	usado	había	usado	hubo	usado
usted	ha	sabido	había	sabido	hubo	sabido
nosotros, -as	hemos	salido	habíamos	salido	hubimos	salido
ellos/ellas	han		habían		hubieron	
ustedes	han		habían		hubieron	

	Future Perfect *I shall (will) have used, known, left, etc.*		**Conditional Perfect** *I should (would) have used, known, left, etc.*	
yo	habré		habría	
tú	habrás		habrías	
él/ella	habrá	usado	habría	usado
usted	habrá	sabido	habría	sabido
nosotros, -as	habremos	salido	habríamos	salido
ellos/ellas	habrán		habrían	
ustedes	habrán		habrían	

See the following examples that use the perfect tenses:

He usado la toalla. *I have used the towel.*
¿Habías oído las buenas noticias? *Had you heard the good news?*
Los misioneros habrán salido. *The missionaries will have left.*
No los he visto. *I have not seen them.*
Yo había usado el mapa cuando salía. *I had used the map when I left.*
Ella lo habría sabido. *She should have known it.*

*Note: the past perfect tense is only used after conjunctions such as **apenas, cuando, en cuanto** or **después que**.[10]

Ejercicio D

Fill in the blanks with the correct perfect tense, as shown below.

1. Ayer yo *(had opened)* <u>hube abierto</u> la ventana.
2. Tú *(have seen)* _____ el programa.
3. Miguel y yo *(have lived)* _____aquí en Chile.
4. Los pastores *(have spoken)* _____.
5. El huracán *(will have destroyed)* _____ las ciudades.

Scripture Passage

Underline the past participles in the scripture[11] below.

El Padre mismo los ama porque me han amado y han creído que yo he venido de parte de Dios. **Juan 16:27**	The Father himself loves you because you have loved me and have believed that I came from God. **John 16:27**

Padre Nuestro (NVI/NIV)[12]
The Lord's Prayer—Matthew 6:9-13

Spanish	English
Padre nuestro que estás en el cielo,	Our Father in heaven,
santificado sea tu nombre.	hallowed be your name,
Venga tu reino,	your kingdom come,
hágase tu voluntad	your will be done,
en la tierra como en el cielo.	on earth as it is in heaven.
Danos hoy nuestro pan cotidiano.	Give us today our daily bread.
Perdónanos nuestras deudas, como también nosotros hemos perdonado a nuestros deudores.	And forgive us our debts, as we also have forgiven our debtors.
Y no nos dejes caer en tentación, sino líbranos del maligno.	And lead us not into temptation, but deliver us from the evil one.

Padre Nuestro (Reina Valera/KJV)[13]
The Lord's Prayer—Matthew 6:9-13

Spanish	English
Padre nuestro que estás en los cielos,	Our Father which art in heaven,
santificado sea tu nombre.	Hallowed be thy name.
Venga tu reino.	Thy kingdom come,
Hágase tu voluntad,	Thy will be done
como en el cielo,	in earth, as it is
así también en la tierra.	in heaven.
El pan nuestro de cada día, dánoslo hoy.	Give us this day our daily bread.
Y perdónanos nuestras deudas, como también nosotros perdonamos a nuestros deudores.	And forgive us our debts, as we forgive our debtors.
Y no nos metas en tentación, mas líbranos del mal; porque tuyo es el reino, y el poder, y la gloria, por todos los siglos. Amén.	And lead us not into temptation, but deliver us from evil: For thine is the kingdom, and the power, and the glory, for ever. Amen.

Ejercicio E

Circle the correct words to complete the Spanish NVI version of the Lord's Prayer. You may check your answers on the previous pages.

Padre nuestro que estás en el (cielo / iglesia / camino **),**

santificado sea tu (Biblia / hombre / nombre **),**

venga tu (gloria / Dios / reino **),**

hágase tu (servicio / voluntad / alma **)**

en la (cruz/ tierra / paz **) como en el cielo.**

Danos hoy nuestro (pan / Mesías / ira **) cotidiano.**

Perdónanos nuestras (adicciónes / deudas / misas **),**

como (ninguno / nadie / también **) nosotros hemos**

perdonado a nuestros (deudores / lujurías / infierno**).**

Y no nos dejes caer en (tentación / idolatría / Anticristo **),**

sino líbranos del (espíritu / maligno / blasfemia **).**

Select Bible Parables and Miracles

When reading the parables listed below, familiarity with the English version may aid in your understanding of the Spanish version. In your devotion time, pick a parable to read in a bilingual Bible and compare both versions. Not all parables are listed here.

TABLE 5.4—Well-known Bible Parables and Miracles[14]

English Version	Spanish Version
1. Water Turned into Wine (John 2:1)	1. El Agua Cambiada en Vino (Juan 2:1)
2. Jesus Calms the Storm (Matt 8:23)	2. Jesús Calma la Tormenta (Mateo 8:23)
3. Feeding of 5,000 (Matt 14:15)	3. La Alimentación de los Cinco Mil (Mateo 14:15)
4. Walking on the Sea (Matt 14:22)	4. El Andar sobre el Mar (Mateo 14:22)
5. A Miraculous Catch of Fish (Luke 5:4)	5. La Pesca Milagrosa (Lucas 5:4)
6. The Sower and the Soils (Matt 13:3)	6. El Sembrador y los Terrenos (Mateo 13:3)
7. The Mustard Seed (Matt 13:31)	7. La Semilla de Mostaza (Mateo 13:31)
8. The Leaven (Matt 13:33)	8. La Levadura (Mateo 13:33)
9. The Great Banquet (Luke 14:16)	9. La Gran Cena (Lucas 14:16)
10. The Prodigal Son (Luke 15:11)	10. El Hijo Pródigo (Lucas 15:11)
11. The Good Samaritan (Luke 10:25)	11. El Buen Samaritano (Lucas 10:25)
12. The Wedding Feast (Matt 22:1)	12. La Fiesta de Bodas (Mateo 22:1)

Parables and Miracles

In the exercise below, match the following versions of English parables and miracles in the left column with their corresponding Spanish versions[15] from the right column, as shown in the example.

F	1	The wedding feast	a	El agua cambiada en vino
	2	The great banquet	b	El buen Samaritano
	3	The sower and the soils	c	El sembrador y los terrenos
	4	Walking on the sea	d	El hijo pródigo
	5	The good Samaritan	e	La gran cena
	6	The feeding of 5,000	f	La fiesta de bodas
	7	The prodigal son	g	La levadura
	8	Water turned into wine	h	La semilla de mostaza
	9	The leaven	i	La alimentación de los cinco mil
	10	The mustard seed	j	El andar sobre el mar

Conversation

Ricardo is visiting his coworker Miguel at his home.

RICARDO: Good morning, Miguel. How has this week been for you since your accident?

MIGUEL: My recovery has been slow and I am doing well physically. However, the accident really shook me up because I could have died from it. Now I am beginning to wonder if I will go to heaven one day when I die. I am not sure if I am saved. I feel comfortable asking you about it because I know that you are a Christian and your spiritual life seems to be in order. How can I know for sure about mine?

RICARDO: Miguel, it would be my great privilege to discuss salvation with you. First of all, do you know who Jesus Christ is?

MIGUEL: Isn't He the Son of God?

RICARDO: Yes, He is, but Jesus also did something very special for us. He is the giver of life, and He loves all who are ready to accept Him as their personal Savior. God sent Him to earth in order that Jesus might die in place of us for our sins. As the Bible says in John 3:16: "For God so loved this world that He gave His one and only Son, that whoever believes in Him shall not perish but have eternal life" (NIV). God gives us this invitation through Jesus Christ.

MIGUEL: What should I do to accept this invitation?

RICARDO: Repeat this prayer with me, and sincerely believe this in your heart.

> *Dear God, I recognize that I am a sinner, and in this moment I repent of my sins, believing faithfully that Jesus, your only Son, died for me, nailed on a cross, in order that by means of His blood, my sins have been forgiven. It is for this that I recognize Jesus as my Lord and Savior.*
>
> *Having repented of my sins, I have the full conviction that by the blood of Jesus, I now have a part in the kingdom of heaven. We thank You, God Most High, for this precious gift of salvation. Amen.*

MIGUEL: Yes, you've convinced me. I will do it.

⋉ ⋉ ⋉

RICARDO: Buenos días, Miguel. ¿Cómo ha sido esta semana para ti desde tu accidente?

MIGUEL: Mi recuperación ha sido lenta y me siento bien físicamente. Sin embargo, el accidente me trastornó porque me pude haber muerto. Ahora estoy comenzando a pensar si iré al cielo cuando muera. No estoy seguro si estoy salvo. Me siento cómodo preguntándote sobre esto porque sé que eres cristiano y tu vida espiritual parece estar en orden. ¿Cómo puedo estar seguro sobre la mía?

RICARDO: Miguel, para me sería un privilegio discutir la salvación contigo. Primeramente ¿sabes quién es Jesucristo?

MIGUEL: ¿Es el hijo de Dios?

RICARDO: Sí, lo es, pero Jesús hizo algo muy especial para nosotros. Él es el dador de la vida, y ama a todo aquellos que están dispuestos a aceptarlo como su Salvador principal. Dios lo envió a la tierra para que Jesús muriera en lugar de nosotros por nuestros pecados. Como dice la biblia en Juan 3:16 >>Porque tanto amó Dios al mundo, que dio a su Hijo unigénito, para que todo el que cree en él no se pierda, sino que tenga vida eterna (NVI). Dios nos dio esta invitación a través de Jesucristo.

MIGUEL: ¿Qué debo hacer para aceptar esta invitación?

RICARDO: Repite esta oración conmigo y créelo sinceramente en tu corazón:

Amado Dios, reconozco que soy pecador y en este momento me arrepiento de mis pecados, creyendo fielmente que Jesús, Tu único Hijo, murió por mí, clavado en una cruz, para que por medio de Su sangre, mis pecados fueran perdonados. Es por esto, que reconozco a Jesucristo, como mi Señor y Salvador. Habiéndome arrepentido de mis pecados, tengo la plena convicción de que por la sangre de Jesús, ahora tengo parte en el reino de los cielos. Gracias, Dios Altísimo, por haberme privilegiado con el precioso regalo de la Salvación. Amén.

MIGUEL: Sí, me ha convencido. Lo haré.

a través de—through

arrepentirse—to repent

clavado—nailed

comenzar—to begin

cómodo,-a—comfortable

convencer—to convince

corazón—heart

dador—giver

discutir—to discuss

dispuesto—ready

en lugar de—instead of

estar salvo,-a—to be saved

fielmente—faithfully

físicamente—physically

haber muerto—to have died

lento,-a—slowly

orden—order

pecados—sins

perdonado—forgiven

plena—full

por medio de—by means of

primeramente—first

privilegio—a privilege

recuperación—recovery

repetir—to repeat

Salvador—Savior

sangre—blood

sin embargo—however

tierra—earth

trastornar—to upset, disturb

unigénito—only begotten

Scripture Passage

Underline the past participles in the NVI/NIV scriptures[16] below.

Y una voz del cielo decía: "Éste es mi Hijo amado; estoy muy complacido con él." **Mateo 3:17**	And a voice from heaven said, "This is my Son, whom I love; with him I am well pleased." **Matthew 3:17**

Psalm 23

Many people are familiar with this "Shepherd's Psalm." May you find great comfort in reading it in both the Spanish as well as the English version. Both the NVI and NIV versions[17] are listed here.

1 El Señor es mi pastor, nada me falta;	1 The Lord is my shepherd, I shall not be in want.
2 en verdes pastos me hace descansar. Junto a tranquilas aguas me conduce;	2 He makes me lie down in green pastures, he leads me beside quiet waters,
3 me infunde nuevas fuerzas. Me guía por sendas de justicia por amor a su nombre.	3 he restores my soul. He guides me in paths of righteousness for his name's sake.
4 Aun si voy por valles tenebrosos, no temo peligro alguno porque tú estás a mi lado; tu vara de pastor me reconforta.	4 Even though I walk through the valley of the shadow of death, I will fear no evil, for you are with me; your rod and your staff, they comfort me.
5 Dispones ante mí un banquete en presencia de mis enemigos. Has ungido con perfume mi cabeza; has llenado mi copa a rebosar.	5 You prepare a table before me in the presence of my enemies. You anoint my head with oil; my cup overflows.
6 La bondad y el amor me seguirán todos los días de mi vida; y en la casa del Señor habitaré para siempre.	6 Surely goodness and love will follow me all the days of my life, and I will dwell in the house of the Lord forever.

Words of Discernment

Three of the four words in each group are related. Find the word that does not belong and note what the remaining words have in common.

_____ 1.   A. Adán   B. David   C. Herodes   D. Salomón

_____

_____ 2.   A. el ayuno   B. el viernes santo   C. la pascua   D. la navidad

_____

Present Participles

There are verb forms in English sentences that have **-ing** endings, such as *speaking, eating, working*, etc. The corresponding form of this in Spanish ends in **-ndo.** With **-ar** verbs, the present participle is normally formed by adding **-ando** to the stem of the verb. For **-er** and **-ir** verbs, it is normally formed by adding **-iendo** to the stem of the verb.[18]

TABLE 5.5—Forming Present Particples in Regular Verbs

Infinitive	Stem Form + Ending	Present Participle	English Equivalent
orar	or + **ando**	orando	*praying*
beber	beb + **iendo**	bebiendo	*drinking*
vivir	viv + **iendo**	viviendo	*living*

Ejercicio F

Change the following infinitive verbs into the present participle form as shown.

1.	alabar	*alabando*	6.	recibir	
2.	comer		7.	estudiar	
3.	comprar		8.	salir	
4.	aprender		9.	hablar	
5.	preparar		10.	sufrir	

Irregular Present Participles

Many verbs are also irregular in the present participle form. A few of them are listed here.

TABLE 5.6—Common Irregular Present Participles[19]

bendecir	*to bless*	**bendiciendo**	*blessing*
caer	*to fall*	**cayendo**	*falling*
construir	*to build*	**construyendo**	*building*
creer	*to believe*	**creyendo**	*believing*
decir	*to say*	**diciendo**	*saying*
destruir	*to destroy*	**destruyendo**	*destroying*
dormir	*to sleep*	**durmiendo**	*sleeping*
huir	*to flee*	**huyendo**	*fleeing*
ir	*to go*	**yendo**	*going*
leer	*to read*	**leyendo**	*reading*
mentir	*to lie*	**mintiendo**	*lying*
morir	*to die*	**muriendo**	*dying*
oír	*to hear*	**oyendo**	*hearing*
pedir	*to ask*	**pidiendo**	*asking*
poder	*to be able*	**pudiendo**	*being able*
reír	*to laugh*	**riendo**	*laughing*
repetir	*to repeat*	**repitiendo**	*repeating*
seguir	*to follow*	**siguiendo**	*following*
servir	*to serve*	**sirviendo**	*serving*
traer	*to bring*	**trayendo**	*bringing*
venir	*to come*	**viniendo**	*coming*

Progressive Tenses

In English, the progressive tenses are formed by using the verb *to be* with the present participle of the main verb that you are using, to form sentences such as *"I am speaking," "I was speaking," "I will be speaking,"* etc. The progressive tenses in Spanish are formed by using the verb **estar** plus the present participle.[20]

This tense is used to indicate an ongoing action as it unfolds in the present or past moment.[21]

El pastor está predicando en la capilla.
The pastor is preaching in the chapel.

Estaba estudiando cuando ellos entraron.
I was studying when they entered.

Mi padre está viviendo ahora en San Juan.
My father is living now in San Juan.

María y yo estabamos hablando cuando occurío.
Maria and I were talking when it occurred.

Ejercicio G

Conjugate the present tense of the verb **estar**, and use the present participle form, as shown below.

1. (ellos) hablar	*ellos están hablando*
2. (tú) pensar	
3. (Marco y yo) escuchar	
4. (el misionero) viajar	
5. (el niño) llorar	
6. (yo) servir	
7. (nosotros) comprar	
8. (Pedro) traer	
9. (el ladrón) huir	
10. (mis amigos) leer	
11. (los creyentes) alabar	
12. (los voluntarios) construir	

Additional Uses of Present Participles

The present participle may also be used to relate the manner by which an action is carried out. It may be used with a clause introduced by *since, when,* or *as,* or with the form *by _____ + -ing.*[22]

Yendo en coche, llegamos tarde a Chile.
When going by car, we arrive late in Chile.

Pagando con tarjeta de crédito es mejor.
By paying with a credit card, it is better.

Leyendo la biblia, los estudiantes aprenden mucho.
By reading the bible, the students learn much.

Note, however, that the infinitive form, not the **-ndo** form, is used after a preposition in Spanish,[23] or when the verb is used as a noun. In English, we call these verbs gerunds.[24]

La madre descansó antes de ir a la iglesia.
The mother rested before going to the church.

El misionero habló después de comer.
The missionary spoke after eating.

Al empezar el servicio, el coro cantó.
Upon beginning the service, the choir sang.

Estoy cansada de trabajar.
I am tired of working.

Leer es bueno.
Reading is good.

Orar es poderoso.
Praying is powerful.

Conversation

A missionary from Texas introduces himself to a pastor in Mexico and asks him about the needs of his church and what he can do to help the local community.

MISSIONARY: Good morning, Pastor. My name is Joe Smith, and I am the mission leader from Grace Church in Amarillo, Texas.

PASTOR: Good morning, and welcome. It is a pleasure to have you here in our church.

MISSIONARY: Thank you. I would like to know more details about the needs of your church and how our team may be able to help you. I mentioned to you earlier that our group of seven volunteers will be in this area for two weeks.

PASTOR: Great. As you may have already noticed, our community has many needs. The most urgent need that we discussed previously is for the construction of an orphanage. We need the materials and finances to make this possible, along with your expertise in construction work.

MISSIONARY: Our church has collected an offering for you. In addition, several in our group have had past construction experience, and I know that they would be delighted to help. When can our team start?

PASTOR: Wonderful! Let's start on Monday morning. Thank you.

MISIONERO: Buenos días, Pastor. Mi nombre es José Smith, y soy el líder de la misión de la Iglesia Grace en Amarillo, Texas.

PASTOR: Buenos días y bienvenido. Es un placer tenerlo aquí en nuestra iglesia.

MISIONERO: Gracias. Me gustaría conocer más detalles acerca de las necesidades de su iglesia y como nuestro equipo de trabajo puede ayudarle. Como he mencionado a usted antes que nuestro grupo de siete voluntarios estarán en esta zona durante dos semanas.

PASTOR: Grandioso. Como te habrás dado cuenta, nuestra comunidad tiene muchas necesidades. La necesidad más urgente que discutimos anteriormente es para la construcción de un orfanato. Necesitamos los materiales y ayuda económica para hacer esto posible, junto con su experiencia en trabajos de construcción.

MISIONERO: Nuestra iglesia ha recolectado una ofrenda para usted. Además, varios en nuestro grupo han tenido experiencia en construcción y sé que estarían encantados de ayudarle. ¿Cuándo puede empezar nuestro equipo?

PASTOR: ¡Maravilloso! Vamos a empezar el lunes por la mañana. Gracias.

acerca—about
anteriormente—previously
ayudar—to help
bienvenido,-a—welcome
discutir—to discuss
durante—during
empezar—to begin
encantado,-a—delighted

equipo—team
junto—together
líder—leader
ofrenda—offering
orfanato—orphanage
placer—pleasure
recolectado—collected
voluntario—volunteer

Ecclesiastes 3:1-8

There are many Spanish infinitive **-ar**, **-er** and **-ir** verbs in the following scripture passage[25], and they mean "to _____." Underline each one of them and write the meaning above it, as shown below.

1 Todo tiene su momento oportuno; hay un tiempo para todo lo que se hace bajo el cielo:	**1** There is a time for everything, and a season for every activity under heaven:
2 un tiempo para <u>nacer</u>, *(to be born)* y un tiempo para morir; un tiempo para plantar, y un tiempo para cosechar;	**2** a time to be born and a time to die, a time to plant and a time to uproot,
3 un tiempo para matar, y un tiempo para sanar; un tiempo para destruir, y un tiempo para construir;	**3** a time to kill and a time to heal, a time to tear down and a time to build,
4 un tiempo para llorar, y un tiempo para reír; un tiempo para estar de luto, y un tiempo para saltar de gusto;	**4** a time to weep and a time to laugh, a time to mourn and a time to dance,
5 un tiempo para esparcir piedras, y un tiempo para recogerlas; un tiempo para abrazarse, y un tiempo para despedirse;	**5** a time to scatter stones and a time to gather them, a time to embrace and a time to refrain,

6 un tiempo para intentar,
   y un tiempo para desistir;
   un tiempo para guardar,
   y un tiempo para desechar;
	6 a time to search
	   and a time to give up,
	   a time to keep
	   and a time to throw away,

7 un tiempo para rasgar,
   y un tiempo para coser;
   un tiempo para callar,
   y un tiempo para hablar;
	7 a time to tear
	   and a time to mend,
	   a time to be silent
	   and a time to speak,

8 un tiempo para amar,
   y un tiempo para odiar;
   un tiempo para la guerra,
   y un tiempo para la paz.
	8 a time to love
	   and a time to hate,
	   a time for war
	   and a time for peace.

Words of Discernment

Three of the four words in each group are related. Find the word that does not belong and note what the remaining words have in common.

_____ 1. A. la mentira   B. la idolatría   C. la envidia   D. el novio

_____

_____ 2. A. la invitación   B. el diablo   C. los espíritus malos   D. Satanás

_____

_____ 3. A. la prostitución   B. la violación   C. el adulterio   D. la paz

_____

Selected Mystery Scriptures

Here are multiple scripture passages[26] that may be familiar to you. Increase your word vocabulary by inserting the corresponding words (Spanish or English) that may have been previously included in your lessons. Answers may be found in a bilingual NVI/NIV Bible version.

3 La <u>gracia</u>, la <u>misericordia</u> y la <u>paz</u> de Dios el Padre y de <u>Jesucristo</u>, el Hijo del Padre, estarán con nosotros en <u>verdad</u> y en <u>amor</u>.
2 Juan 3

3 _____, _____ and _____ from God the Father and from _____ _____, the Father's Son, will be with us in _____ and _____.
2 John 3

13 Ahora, pues, permanecen estas tres virtudes: la <u>fe</u>, la <u>esperanza</u> y el <u>amor</u>. Pero la más excelente de ellas es el <u>amor</u>.
1 Corintios 13:13

13 And now these three remain: _____, _____ and _____. But the greatest of these is _____.
1 Corinthians 13:13

2 a mi querido hijo Timoteo: Que _____ el Padre y _____ _____ nuestro _____ te concedan gracia, misericordia y paz.
2 Timoteo 1:2

2 To Timothy, my dear son: Grace, mercy and peace from <u>God</u> the Father and <u>Christ Jesus</u> our <u>Lord</u>.
2 Timothy 1:2

5 nuestro <u>evangelio</u> les llegó no solo con palabras sino también con <u>poder</u>, es decir, con el <u>Espíritu Santo</u> y con profunda convicción.
1 Tesalonicenses 1:5

5 our _____ came to you not simply with words, but also with _____, with the _____ _____ and with deep conviction.
1 Thessalonians 1:5

16 Porque tanto amó <u>Dios</u> al mundo, que dio a su <u>Hijo</u> <u>unigénito</u>, para que todo el que cree en él no se pierda, sino que tenga <u>vida</u> <u>eterna</u>. **17** Dios no envió a su <u>Hijo</u> al <u>mundo</u> para <u>condenar</u> al <u>mundo</u>, sino para <u>salvar</u>lo por medio de él. **18** El que <u>cree</u> en él no es <u>condenado</u>, pero el que no <u>cree</u> ya está <u>condenado</u> por no haber creído en el nombre del Hijo <u>unigénito</u> de Dios.

Juan 3: 16-18

16 For _____ so loved the world that he gave his one and _____ _____, that whoever believes in him shall not perish but have _____ _____. **17** For God did not send his _____ into the _____ to _____ the _____, but to _____ the world through him. **18** Whoever _____ in him is not _____, but whoever does not _____ stands _____ already because he has not believed in the name of God's _____ _____ _____ Son.

John 3:16-18

16 <u>Estén</u> siempre alegres, **17** <u>oren</u> sin cesar, **18** <u>den</u> gracias a Dios en toda situación, porque esta es Su <u>voluntad</u> para ustedes en Cristo Jesús.

1 Tesalonicenses 5:16-18

16 _____ joyful always; **17** _____ continually; **18** _____ thanks in all circumstances, for this is God's _____ for you in Christ Jesus.

1 Thessalonians 5:16-18

7 Pidan, y se les <u>dará</u>; <u>busquen</u>, y <u>encontrarán</u>; <u>llamen</u>, y se les <u>abrirá</u>. **8** Porque todo el que <u>pide</u>, <u>recibe</u>; el que <u>busca</u>, <u>encuentra</u>; y al que <u>llama</u>, se le <u>abre</u>.
Mateo 7:7-8

7 _____ and it will be _____ to you; _____ and you will _____; _____ and the door will be _____ to you. **8** For everyone who _____ _____; he who _____ _____; and to him who _____, the door will be _____.
Matthew 7:7-8

10 <u>Quédense</u> quietos, <u>reconozcan</u> que yo soy Dios.
Salmos 46:10

10 _____ still, and _____ that I am God.
Psalms 46:10

5 Confía en el _____ de todo _____, y no en tu propia inteligencia. **6** Reconócelo en todos tus _____, y él allanará tus _____.
Proverbios 3:5-6

5 Trust in the <u>Lord</u> with all your <u>heart</u> and lean not on your own understanding; **6** in all your <u>ways</u> acknowledge him, and he will make your <u>paths</u> straight.
Proverbs 3:5-6

105 Tu <u>palabra</u> es una lámpara a mis pies; es una <u>luz</u> en mi sendero.
Salmos 119:105

105 Your _____ is a lamp to my feet; and a _____ for my path.
Psalm 119:105

21 No todo el que me dice: "_____, _____", entrará en el _____ de los _____,

21 Not everyone who says to me, '<u>Lord</u>, <u>Lord</u>,' will enter the <u>kingdom</u> of <u>heaven</u>, but only he

sino sólo el que hace la _____ de mi _____ que está en el _____. **22** Muchos me dirán en aquel día: "_____, _____, ¿no profetizamos en tu _____, y en tu _____ expulsamos _____ e hicimos muchos _____?" **23** Entonces les diré claramente: "Jamás los conocí. ¡Aléjense de mí, _____ de _____!"

Mateo 7:21-23

who does the <u>will</u> of my <u>Father</u> who is in <u>heaven</u>. **22** Many will say to me on that day, '<u>Lord</u>, <u>Lord</u>, did we not prophesy in your <u>name</u>, and in your <u>name</u> drive out <u>demons</u> and perform many <u>miracles</u>?' **23** Then I will tell them plainly, 'I never knew you. Away from me, you <u>evildoers</u>!'

Matthew 7:21-23

12 Una vez más Jesús se dirigió a la gente, y les dijo: —Yo <u>soy</u> la <u>luz</u> del <u>mundo</u>. El que me sigue no andará en <u>tinieblas</u>, sino que tendrá la <u>luz</u> de la <u>vida</u>.

Juan 8:12

12 When Jesus spoke again to the people, he said, "I _____ the _____ of the _____. Whoever follows me will never walk in _____, but will have the _____ of _____."

John 8:12

19 Así que mi _____ les proveerá de _____ lo que necesiten, conforme a las gloriosas _____ que tiene en _____ _____.

Filipenses 4:19

19 And my <u>God</u> will meet <u>all</u> your needs according to his glorious <u>riches</u> in <u>Christ</u> <u>Jesus</u>.

Philippians 4:19

28 «Vengan a mí todos ustedes que están cansados y agobiados, y yo les daré descanso. **29** Carguen con mi yugo y aprendan de mí, pues yo soy apacible y humilde de corazón, y encontrarán descanso para su alma. **30** Porque mi yugo es suave y mi carga es liviana.»
Mateo 11:28-30

6 Estoy convencido de esto: el que comenzó tan _____ _____ en ustedes la irá perfeccionando hasta el _____ de _____ _____.
Filipenses 1:6

25 En aquel tiempo Jesús dijo: «Te alabo, Padre, Señor del cielo y de la tierra, porque habiendo escondido estas cosas de los sabios e instruidos, se las has revelado a los que son como niños. **26** Sí, Padre, porque esa fue tu buena voluntad.»
Mateo 11:25-26

28 "_____ to me, all you who are weary and burdened, and I will _____ you rest. **29** Take my yoke upon you and _____ from me, for I _____ gentle and humble in _____, and you will find rest for your souls. **30** For my yoke _____ easy and my burden is light."
Matthew 11:28-30

6 being confident of this, that he who began a good work in you will carry it on to completion until the day of Christ Jesus.
Philippians 1:6

25 At that time _____ said, "I _____ you, Father, _____ of _____ and _____, because you have hidden these _____ from the _____ and learned, and revealed them to little _____. **26** Yes, _____, for this was your _____ pleasure."
Matthew 11:25-26

15 No _____ al _____ ni nada de lo que hay en él. Si alguien _____ al _____, no tiene el _____ del Padre.
1 Juan 2:15

5 Manténganse <u>libres</u> del <u>amor</u> al <u>dinero</u>, y conténtense con lo que <u>tienen</u>, porque Dios ha dicho: "Nunca te <u>dejaré</u>; jamás te <u>abandonaré</u>." **6** Así que podemos decir con toda <u>confianza</u>: "El <u>Señor</u> es quien me ayuda; no <u>temeré</u>. ¿Qué me puede <u>hacer</u> un simple mortal?"
Hebreos 13:5-6

36 ¿ De qué sirve ganar el _____ _____ si se pierde la vida?
Marcos 8:36

12 Ciertamente, la <u>palabra</u> de Dios es <u>viva</u> y poderosa, y más cortante que cualquier espada de dos filos. Penetra hasta lo más profundo del <u>alma</u> y del <u>espíritu</u>, hasta la médula de los huesos, y <u>juzga</u> los pensamientos y

15 Do not <u>love</u> the <u>world</u> or anything in the world. If anyone <u>loves</u> the <u>world</u>, the <u>love</u> of the Father is not in him.
1 John 2:15

5 Keep your lives _____ from the _____ of _____ and be content with what you _____, because God has said, "Never will I _____ you; never will I _____ you." **6** So we say with _____, "The _____ is my helper; I will not be _____. What can man _____ to me?"
Hebrews 13:5-6

36 What good is it for a man to gain the <u>whole</u> <u>world</u>, yet forfeit his soul?
Mark 8:36

12 For the _____ of God is _____ and active. Sharper than any double-edged sword, it penetrates even to dividing _____ and _____, joints and marrow; it _____

las intenciones del <u>corazón</u>.
Hebreos 4:12

the thoughts and attitudes of the
_____.
Hebrews 4:12

23 Hagan lo que hagan, _____ de buena gana, como para el _____, y no como para nadie en este mundo.
Colosenses 3:23

23 Whatever you do, <u>work</u> at it with all your heart, as working for the <u>Lord</u>, not for men.
Colossians 3:23

11 Porque yo sé muy bien los planes que <u>tengo</u> para ustedes— afirma el <u>Señor</u>—planes de bienestar y no de calamidad, a fin de darles un <u>futuro</u> y una <u>esperanza</u>.
Jeremías 29:11

11 "For I know the plans I _____ for you," declares the _____, "plans to prosper you and not to harm you, plans to give you _____ and a _____."
Jeremiah 29:11

17 —¿_____ _____ me preguntas sobre lo que es _____? —respondió Jesús—. Solamente hay _____ que es _____. Si quieres entrar en la _____, _____ los _____.
Mateo 19: 17

17 "<u>Why</u> do you ask me about what is <u>good</u>?" Jesus replied. "There is only <u>One</u> who is <u>good</u>. If you want to enter <u>life</u>, <u>obey</u> the <u>commandments</u>."
Matthew 19:17

27 Luego le dijo a <u>Tomás</u>: —<u>Pon</u> tu dedo aquí y <u>mira</u> mis manos. Acerca tu <u>mano</u> y métela en mi

27 Then he said to _____, "_____ your finger here; _____ my hands. Reach out

costado. Y no seas incrédulo, sino hombre de fe. **28** —<u>Señor</u> mío y <u>Dios</u> mío! —exclamó Tomás. **29**— <u>Porque</u> me has visto, has creído —le dijo Jesús; <u>dichosos</u> los que no han visto y sin embargo <u>creen</u>.
Juan 20:27-29

your _____ and put it into my side. Stop doubting and believe." **28** Thomas said to him, "My _____ and my _____!" **29** Then Jesus told him, "_____ you have seen me, you have believed; _____ are those who have not seen and yet have _____."
John 20:27-29

27 Mis ovejas oyen mi _____; yo las _____ y ellas me siguen.
Juan 10:27

27 My sheep listen to my <u>voice</u>; I <u>know</u> them, and they follow me.
John 10:27

9 <u>Sin</u> <u>embargo</u>, como está escrito: «<u>Ningún</u> ojo ha visto, <u>ningún</u> oído ha escuchado, <u>ninguna</u> mente humana ha concebido lo que <u>Dios</u> ha preparado para quienes lo <u>aman</u>.»
1 Corintios 2:9

9 _____, as it is written: "_____ eye has seen, _____ ear has heard, _____ mind has conceived what _____ has prepared for those who _____ him."
1 Corinthians 2:9

12 El prudente ve el _____ y lo evita; el inexperto sigue adelante y _____ las consecuencias.
Proverbios 27: 12

12 The prudent see <u>danger</u> and take refuge, but the simple keep going and <u>suffer</u> for it.
Proverbs 27:12

1 Ahora bien, <u>hermanos</u>, ustedes no <u>necesitan</u> que se les escriba acerca de tiempos y fechas, **2** porque ya saben que el <u>día</u> <u>del</u> <u>Señor</u> llegará como <u>ladrón</u> en la <u>noche</u>. **3** Cuando estén diciendo, «<u>Paz</u> y <u>seguridad</u>", vendrá de improviso sobre ellos la <u>destrucción</u>, como le llegan a la mujer encinta los <u>dolores</u> de parto. De ninguna manera podrán <u>escapar</u>. **4** Ustedes, en cambio, <u>hermanos</u>, no están en la <u>oscuridad</u> para que ese día los sorprenda como un <u>ladrón</u>. **5** Todos ustedes son <u>hijos</u> de la <u>luz</u> y del <u>día</u>. No somos de la <u>noche</u> ni de la <u>oscuridad</u>.

1 Tesalonicenses 5:1-5

1 Now, _____, about times and dates we do not _____ to write to you, **2** for you know very well that the _____ ___ _____ _____ will come like a _____ in the_____. **3** While people are saying, "_____ and _____," _____ will come on them suddenly, as labor _____ on a pregnant woman, and they will not _____. **4** But you, _____, are not in _____ so that this day should surprise you like a _____. **5** You are all _____ of the_____ and sons of the _____. We do not belong to the _____ or to the _____.

1 Thessalonians 5:1-5

25 Entonces _____ le dijo: — Yo soy la _____ y la _____. El que _____ en mí _____, aunque muera; **26** y todo el que _____ y _____ en mí no morirá jamás.

Juan 11:25-26

25 <u>Jesus</u> said to her: "I am the <u>resurrection</u> and the <u>life</u>. He who <u>believes</u> in me will <u>live</u>, even though he dies; **26** and whoever <u>lives</u> and <u>believes</u> in me will never die.

John 11:25-26

1 Luego el <u>Espíritu</u> llevó a <u>Jesús</u> al desierto para que el <u>diablo</u> lo sometiera a tentación. **2** Después de ayunar <u>cuarenta días</u> y <u>cuarenta noches</u>, tuvo hambre. **3** El <u>tentador</u> se le acercó y le propuso: —Si eres el <u>Hijo</u> de <u>Dios</u>, ordena a estas piedras que se conviertan en pan. **4** <u>Jesús</u> le respondió: —Escrito está: "No solo de pan vive el hombre, sino de toda <u>palabra</u> que sale de la boca de <u>Dios</u>".
Mateo 4:1-4

1 Then _____ was led by the _____ into the desert to be tempted by the _____. **2** After fasting _____ _____ and _____ _____, he was hungry. **3** The _____ came to him and said, "If you are the _____ of _____, tell these stones to become bread." **4** _____ answered, "It is written: 'Man does not live on bread alone, but on every _____ that comes from the mouth of _____.'
Matthew 4:1-4

29 Por tanto, si tu ojo derecho te hace _____, sácatelo y tíralo. Más te vale _____ una sola parte de tu cuerpo, y no que todo él sea arrojado al _____. **30** Y si tu mano derecha te hace _____, córtatela y arrójala. Más te vale _____ una sola parte de tu cuerpo, y no que todo él vaya al _____.
Mateo 5:29-30

29 If your right eye causes you to <u>sin</u>, gouge it out and throw it away. It is better for you to <u>lose</u> one part of your body than for your whole body to be thrown into <u>hell</u>. **30** And if your right hand causes you to <u>sin</u>, cut it off and throw it away. It is better for you to <u>lose</u> one part of your body, than for your whole body to go into <u>hell</u>.
Matthew 5:29-30

13 Todo lo <u>puedo</u> en <u>Cristo</u> que me fortalece.
Filipenses 4:13

13 I _____ do everything through _____ who gives me strength.
Philippians 4:13

9 —¡Hosanna al _____ de David!
—¡_____ el que viene
en el _____ ___ _____!
—¡_____ en las alturas!
Mateo 21:9

9 "Hosanna to the <u>Son</u> of David!"
"<u>Blessed</u> is he who comes in the
<u>name of the <u>Lord</u>!" "<u>Hosanna</u> in
the highest!"
Matthew 21:9

44 "Dijo el <u>Señor</u> a mi <u>Señor</u>: 'Siéntate
a mi derecha, hasta que ponga a tus
<u>enemigos</u> debajo de tus pies.'"
Mateo 22:44

44 "The _____ said to my _____:
'Sit at my right hand until I put your
_____ under your feet.'"
Matthew 22:44

3 Doy _____ a mi ____ cada
_____ que me acuerdo de ____.
Filipenses 1:3

3 I <u>thank</u> my <u>God</u> every <u>time</u> I
remember <u>you</u>.
Philippians 1:3

16 «Éste es el <u>pacto</u> que haré con
ellos <u>después</u> de aquel tiempo—
dice el <u>Señor</u>—: Pondré mis <u>leyes</u>
en su <u>corazón</u>, y las <u>escribiré</u> en
su mente.»
Hebreos 10:16

16 "This is the _____ I will
make with them _____ that
time, says the _____. I will put
my _____ in their _____, and
I will _____ them on their minds."
Hebrews 10:16

6 Yo soy el camino, la _____
y la _____. —le
contestó Jesús—. Nadie llega al
_____ sino por mí.
Juan 14: 6

6 Jesus answered: "I am the way
and the <u>truth</u> and the <u>life</u>. No
one comes to the <u>Father</u> except
through me."
John 14:6

7 Así que sométanse a <u>Dios</u>. Resistan al <u>diablo</u>, y él huirá de ustedes. **8** Acérquense a <u>Dios</u>, y él se acercará a <u>ustedes</u>.
Santiago 4:7-8

7 Submit yourselves, then, to _____. Resist the _____, and he will flee from you. **8** Come near to _____, and he will come near to _____.
James 4:7-8

31—Si se mantienen fieles a mis _____, serán realmente mis _____, **32** y conocerán la _____, y la _____ los hará libres.
Juan 8:31-32

31 "If you hold to my <u>teaching</u>, you are really my <u>disciples</u>. **32** Then you will know the <u>truth</u>, and the <u>truth</u> will set you free."
John 8:31-32

8 «Yo soy el <u>Alfa</u> y la <u>Omega</u> —dice el <u>Señor Dios</u>—, el que <u>es</u> y que <u>era</u> y que ha de <u>venir</u>, el <u>Todopoderoso</u>.»
Apocalipsis 1:8

8 "I am the _____ and the ____," says the _____ _____, "who ___, and who ____, and who is to _____, the _____."
Revelation 1:8

7 Pues _____ no nos ha dado un _____ de timidez, sino de _____, de _____ y de dominio propio.
2 Timoteo 1:7

7 For <u>God</u> did not give us a <u>spirit</u> of timidity but a spirit of <u>power</u>, of <u>love</u> and of self-dicipline.
2 Timothy 1:7

1 No te <u>jactes</u> del día de <u>mañana</u>, porque no sabes lo que el <u>día</u> traerá.
Proverbios 27:1

1 Do not _____ about _____, for you do not know what a _____ may bring forth.
Proverbs 27:1

4 «¿ Qué es el _____, para que en él pienses? ¿ Qué es el ser humano, para _____ lo tomes en cuenta?»
Salmos 8:4

4 What is <u>man</u> that you are mindful of him, the son of man <u>that</u> you care for him?
Psalms 8:4

1 La <u>respuesta</u> amable calma el <u>enojo</u>, pero la agresiva echa leña al fuego.
Proverbios 15:1

1 A gentle _____ turns away _____, but a harsh word stirs up anger.
Proverbs 15:1

Workbook Review Exercises

Fill in the blanks with the correct form of the word given in parentheses.

1. (creador,-a)   Dios es mi _____.
2. (prometer)   Dios nos _____ la salvación.
3. (redimir)   Jesús _____ a muchas personas por la cruz.
4. (heredar)   Nosotros _____ la vida eterna.
5. (proveer)   Dios _____ por nuestras necesidades.
6. (bendecido,-a) El creyente está _____.
7. (perdonar)   Ellos nos _____.
8. (deber, ir)   Nosotros _____ _____ a la iglesia ahora.
9. (someterse)   La mujer se _____ a su esposo.
10. (invitar)   Yo te _____ a mi fiesta.
11. (enseñar)   Nuestro pastor _____ los estudios bíblicos.
12. (ayunar)   El equipo de oración _____ la semana pasada.
13. (diezmar)   Yo _____ mi ofrenda.
14. (necesitar)   Los sin techo _____ mucho.
15. (destrozado,-a) Él está _____ porque _____ su dinero
    (apostar)   la semana pasada.
16. (engañar)   Satán _____ a los pecadores.

17. (blasfemar) Ellos _____ mucho.
18. (adulterar) Los paganos _____ mucho.
19. (sufrir) El año pasado, María _____la pérdida de su casa en el desastre.
20. (enseñar) Esta semana que viene, Pablo _____ el evangelio de Jesucristo.

Translation Exercises

Change the following sentences into Spanish.

1. Jesus loves me.

2. Glory to God in heaven.

3. My redeemer lives.

4. Jesus did signs and wonders.

5. I gave my life to Jesus Christ.

6. I believe in miracles.

7. We persevere in our Christian faith.

8. Our hope is in Christ.

9. We forgive with God's grace.

10. He trusts in the wisdom of the Holy Spirit.

11. Evangelism is a gift of the Spirit.

12. Today we fast.

13. The fellowship group starts Wednesday.

14. Where is the funeral service?

15. We serve communion the first Sunday of each month.

16. Our church attendance grows.

17. We have choir practice on Tuesday.

18. Would you like to be baptized?

19. I grieve my father's death.

20. The unbelievers will suffer the Tribulation.

21. Satan accuses believers.

22. She is a victim of rape.

23. He suffers from addiction and alcoholism.

24. Gambling is her weakness.

25. We visit the Florida Prison on Tuesdays.

English-Spanish Expressions[27]

Careful!	*¡Cuidado!*
Don't worry.	*No se preocupe.*
Do you understand?	*¿Entiende usted?*
Excuse me.	*Perdon./Disculpe./Con permiso.*
God bless you.	*Que Dios le bendiga.*
Go with God.	*Vaya con Dios.*
Happy birthday!	*¡Feliz cumpleaños!*
How are you?	*¿Cómo está?*
How do you say it?	*¿Cómo se dice?*
How do you spell it?	*¿Cómo se deletrea?*
How do you write it?	*¿Cómo se escribe?*
How much does it cost?	*¿Cuánto cuesta?*
How old are you?	*¿Cuántos años tiene?*
Hurry up!	*¡Apúrese!*
I am sorry.	*Lo siento.*
I don't know.	*No sé.*
May I help you?	*¿Puedo ayudarle?*
More slowly.	*Más despacio.*
Nice to meet you.	*Mucho gusto.*
Please.	*Por favor.*
See you tomorrow.	*Nos vemos./Hasta mañana.*
Take me to...	*Lléveme a...*
Thank you.	*Gracias.*
Welcome.	*Bienvenido,-a*
What does it mean?	*¿Qué significa?*
What happened?	*¿Qué pasó?*
What is wrong?	*¿Qué pasó?*
What is your name?	*¿Cuál es su nombre?/¿Cómo se llama?*
What time is it?	*¿Qué hora es?*
Where are you from?	*¿De dónde es?*
You are welcome.	*¡De nada!*

CROSS WORD PUZZLE

Test your knowledge of Spanish words pertaining to God, heaven and salvation by filling in the blanks on the following page.

ACROSS	DOWN
2. salvation	1. she reads
5. rapture	3. so
10. the Holy Spirit *(3 words)*	4. crucifixion
14. *Señor* (abbrev.)	6. a + el
15. some (masc.)	7. to pray
17. spirit	8. Jesus Christ
18. child (masc.)	9. eternity
19. rich	11. holiness
20. heaven	12. I love
21. place	13. all powerful
23. power, to be able to	14. sovereign
25. holiness	16. to save
26. adornment	22. to pray
28. God	24. to promise
29. less	27. God is _____ *presente*
30. one	31. of
32. of	33. alone, by one's self
35. to bless	34. honor
39. Almighty	36. her
43. the (article, neut.)	37. negative
44. reflexive pronoun	38. like
45. anger	40. he says
47. merciful	41. I pray
48. affection	42. for
	44. to be
	46. my

HEAVENLY-MINDED CROSSWORD

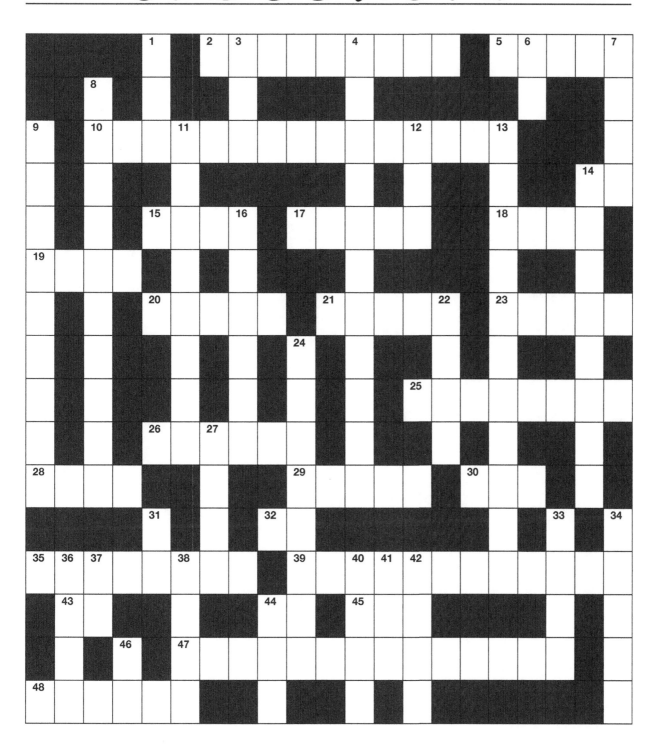

Appendix

- **Direct and Indirect Object Pronouns**
- **Cardinal Numbers**
- **Ordinal Numbers**
- **Verb Conjugation**
- **Verb Conjugation Examples**
- **Pronouns at a Glance**
- **Verb Tenses at a Glance**
- **Common Spanish Suffixes**
- **Irregular Verbs and Their Tenses**
- **Create Your Own Verb Practice Sheets**
- ***Oración* (Prayer)**
- **English Infinitive Verb Forms**
- **Spanish Infinitive Verb Forms**
- **Vocabulary (English to Spanish)**
- **Vocabulary (Spanish to English)**
- **Answers**
- **References**
- **Bibliography**
- **Index**
- **Page Index of Scripture Verses**
- **God's Pathway to Salvation**

Appendix

There is a variety of information here that can be used as supplemental reference material. You may find quick reference charts here, as well as other data to help you formulate sentences.

TABLE 6.1—Direct and Indirect Object Pronouns[1,2]

	Direct	Indirect
yo	me *(me)*	me *(to/for me)*
tú	te *(you, fam.)*	te *(to/for you, fam.)*
él	lo *(him, it)*	le *(to/for him)*
ella	la *(her, it)*	le *(to/for her)*
usted	lo *(you, formal masc.)* la *(you, formal fem.)*	le *(to/for you, form.)*
nosotros	nos *(us, masc./fem.)*	nos *(to/for us)*
ellos	los *(them, masc.)*	les *(to/for them)*
ellas	las *(them, fem.)*	les *(to/for them)*
ustedes	los *(you, formal masc.)* las *(you, formal fem.)*	les *(to/for you, formal pl.)*

TABLE 6.2—Cardinal Numbers[3]

0	cero	zero
1	uno	one
2	dos	two
3	tres	three
4	cuatro	four
5	cinco	five
6	seis	six
7	siete	seven
8	ocho	eight
9	nueve	nine
10	diez	ten
11	once	eleven
12	doce	twelve
13	trece	thirteen
14	catorce	fourteen
14	quince	fifteen
16	dieciséis	sixteen
17	diecisiete	seventeen
18	dieciocho	eighteen
19	diecinueve	nineteen
20	veinte	twenty
21	veintiuno	twenty-one
22	veintidós	twenty-two
30	treinta	thirty
31	treinta y uno	thirty-one
40	cuarenta	forty
50	cincuenta	fifty
60	sesenta	sixty

  Visit us at www.SpanishForChristianService.com

70	setenta	seventy
80	ochenta	eighty
90	noventa	ninety
100	cien(to)	one hundred
101	ciento uno	one hundred one
110	ciento diez	one hundred ten
200	doscientos	two hundred
300	trescientos	three hundred
400	cuatrocientos	four hundred
500	quinientos	fix hundred
600	seiscientos	six hundred
700	setecientos	seven hundred
800	ochocientos	eight hundred
900	novecientos	nine hundred
1000	mil	one thousand
1.000.000	un millón	one million
2.000.000	dos millones	two million

TABLE 6.3—Ordinal Numbers[4]

1	primero,-a	first
2	segundo,-a	second
3	tercero,-a	third
4	cuarto,-a	fourth
5	quinto,-a	fifth
6	sexto,-a	sixth
7	séptimo,-a	seventh
8	octavo,-a	eighth
9	noveno,-a	ninth
10	décimo,-a	tenth

Verb Conjugation[5]

TABLE 6.4—Present Tense of Regular *-ar, -er* and *-ir* Verbs

	-ar	-er	-ir
yo	-o	-o	-o
tú	-as	-es	-es
él/ella	-a	-e	-e
usted	-a	-e	-e
nosotros, -as	-amos	-emos	-imos
ellos/ellas	-an	-en	-en
ustedes	-an	-en	-en

TABLE 6.5—Imperfect Tense of Regular *-ar, -er* and *-ir* Verbs

	-ar	-er	-ir
yo	-aba	-ía	-ía
tú	-abas	-ías	-ías
él/ella	-aba	-ía	-ía
usted	-aba	-ía	-ía
nosotros, -as	-ábamos	-íamos	-íamos
ellos/ellas	-aban	-ían	-ían
ustedes	-aban	-ían	-ían

TABLE 6.6—Past Tense of Regular *-ar, -er* and *-ir* Verbs

	-ar	-er	-ir
yo	-é	-í	-í
tú	-aste	-iste	-iste
él/ella	-ó	-ió	-ió
usted	-ó	-ió	-ió
nosotros, -as	-amos	-imos	-imos
ellos/ellas	-aron	-ieron	-ieron
ustedes	-aron	-ieron	-ieron

TABLE 6.7—Future Tense of Regular *-ar, -er* and *-ir* Verbs

	-ar	-er	-ir
yo	-é	-é	-é
tú	-ás	-ás	-ás
él/ella	-á	-á	-á
usted	-á	-á	-á
nosotros, -as	-emos	-emos	-emos
ellos/ellas	-án	-án	-án
ustedes	-án	-án	-án

TABLE 6.8—Conditional Tense of Regular *-ar, -er* and *-ir* Verbs

	-ar	-er	-ir
yo	-ía	-ía	-ía
tú	-ías	-ías	-ías
él/ella	-ía	-ía	-ía
usted	-ía	-ía	-ía
nosotros, -as	-íamos	-íamos	-íamos
ellos/ellas	-ían	-ían	-ían
ustedes	-ían	-ían	-ían

TABLE 6.9—Subjunctive Mood of Regular *-ar, -er* and *-ir* Verbs

	-ar	-er	-ir
yo	-e	-a	-a
tú	-es	-as	-as
él/ella	-e	-a	-a
usted	-e	-a	-a
nosotros, -as	-emos	-amos	-amos
ellos/ellas	-en	-an	-an
ustedes	-en	-an	-an

TABLE 6.10—Command Mood of Regular *-ar, -er* and *-ir* Verbs

	-ar	**-er**	**-ir**
yo	—	—	—
tú	-a no —es	-e no —as	-e no —as
él/ella	-e	-a	-a
usted	-e	-a	-a
nosotros, -as	-emos	-amos	-amos
ellos/ellas	-en	-an	-an
ustedes	-en	-an	-an

Verb Conjugation Examples

TABLE 6.11—Examples of Present Tense Regular *-ar, -er* and *-ir* Verbs

	-ar	**-er**	**-ir**
yo	amo	bebo	comparto
tú	amas	bebes	compartes
él/ella	ama	bebe	comparte
usted	ama	bebe	comparte
nosotros, -as	amamos	bebemos	compartimos
ellos/ellas	aman	beben	comparten
ustedes	aman	beben	comparten

TABLE 6.12—Examples of Imperfect Tense Regular *-ar, -er* and *-ir* Verbs

	-ar	**-er**	**-ir**
yo	amaba	bebía	compartía
tú	amabas	bebías	compartías
él/ella	amaba	bebía	compartía
usted	amaba	bebía	compartía
nosotros, -as	amábamos	bebíamos	compartíamos
ellos/ellas	amaban	bebían	compartían
ustedes	amaban	bebían	compartían

TABLE 6.13—Examples of Past Tense Regular *-ar, -er* and *-ir* Verbs

	amar	beber	compartir
yo	am**é**	beb**í**	compart**í**
tú	am**aste**	beb**iste**	compart**iste**
él/ella	am**ó**	beb**ió**	compart**ió**
usted	am**ó**	beb**ió**	compart**ió**
nosotros, -as	am**amos**	beb**imos**	compart**imos**
ellos/ellas	am**aron**	beb**ieron**	compart**ieron**
ustedes	am**aron**	beb**ieron**	compart**ieron**

TABLE 6.14—Examples of Future Tense of Regular *-ar, -er* and *-ir* Verbs

	amar	beber	compartir
yo	amar**é**	beber**é**	compartir**é**
tú	amar**ás**	beber**ás**	compartir**ás**
él/ella	amar**á**	beber**á**	compartir**á**
usted	amar**á**	beber**á**	compartir**á**
nosotros, -as	amar**emos**	beber**emos**	compartir**emos**
ellos/ellas	amar**án**	beber**án**	compartir**án**
ustedes	amar**án**	beber**án**	compartir**án**

TABLE 6.15—Examples of Conditional Tense Regular *-ar, -er* and *-ir* Verbs

	amar	beber	compartir
yo	amar**ía**	beber**ía**	compartir**ía**
tú	amar**ías**	beber**ías**	compartir**ías**
él/ella	amar**ía**	beber**ía**	compartir**ía**
usted	amar**ía**	beber**ía**	compartir**ía**
nosotros, -as	amar**íamos**	beber**íamos**	compartir**íamos**
ellos/ellas	amar**ían**	beber**ían**	compartir**ían**
ustedes	amar**ían**	beber**ían**	compartir**ían**

TABLE 6.16—Examples of Subjunctive Mood Regular *-ar*, *-er* and *-ir*

	amar	**beber**	**compartir**
yo	am**e**	beb**a**	compart**a**
tú	am**es**	beb**as**	compart**as**
él/ella	am**e**	beb**a**	compart**a**
usted	am**e**	beb**a**	compart**a**
nosotros, -as	am**emos**	beb**amos**	compart**amos**
ellos/ellas	am**en**	beb**an**	compart**an**
ustedes	am**en**	beb**an**	compart**an**

TABLE 6.17—Examples of Command Mood Regular *-ar*, *-er* and *-ir* Verbs

	amar	**beber**	**compartir**
yo	—	—	—
tú	am**a**; no am**es**	beb**e**; no beb**as**	compart**e**; no compart**as**
él/ella	am**e**	beb**a**	compart**a**
usted	am**e**	beb**a**	compart**a**
nosotros, -as	am**emos**	beb**amos**	compart**amos**
ellos/ellas	am**en**	beb**an**	compart**an**
ustedes	am**en**	beb**an**	compart**an**

TABLE 6.18—Examples of Progressive and Past Participles

	amar	**beber**	**compartir**
Progressive (estar +) (to be + -ing)	am-**ando** (loving)	beb-**iendo** (drinking)	compart-**iendo** (sharing)

Pronouns

TABLE 6.19—Subject, Demonstrative, Relative and Interrogative Pronouns[6]

SUBJECT		DEMONSTRATIVE			RELATIVE		INTERROGATIVE	
I	yo	this	éste	ésta	who	quien quienes	Who?	¿Quién? ¿Quiénes?
you	tú	these	éstos	éstas	whom	que quien		
he	él	that	ése aquél	ésa aquélla	which	que cual	Which?	¿Cuál?
she	ella	those	ésos aquéllos	ésas aquéllas	what	que	What?	¿Qué?
you *(form.)*	usted				that	que	Whom?	¿A quién?
we	nosotros				whose	quien quienes	Whose?	¿De quién? ¿De quiénes? ¿A quién?
they	ellos, ellas, ustedes							

TABLE 6.20—Indefinite, Possessive and Reflexive Pronouns[7]

INDEFINITE			POSSESSIVE			REFLEXIVE	
any	algún alguno alguna	algunos algunos algunas	mine	el mío la mía	los míos las mìas	myself	me
some	uno una	unos unas	yours	el tuyo la tuya	los tuyos las tuyas	yourself	te
every	todo toda	todos todas	his, hers	el suyo la suya	los suyos las suyas	himself, herself, itself, one's self	se
each	cada		ours	el nuestro la nuestra	los nuestros las nuestras	ourselves	nos
few	algunos algunas		theirs	el suyo la suya	los suyos las suyas	themselves	se

Verb Tenses at a Glance[8,9]
(Using "Amar—to love" as an Example)

Present Tense—Spanish has no equivalent for the English *am* (is, are) or *do* (does) in the present tense. Use this tense to describe something that is happening at the present time. (The single verb *amo* means *I am loving, I do love, or I love.*)

Imperfect Tense—Use this tense to describe events that *used to* happen or *repeated or habitual events in the past.* The translation of this tense in English depends upon the context. (e.g., *yo amaba* means *I used to love, I was loving.*)

Past Tense—Use to express *an action that was completed* at a definite time in the past. (e.g., *yo amé* means *I did love, I loved.*)

Future Tense—Use this tense to describe actions in the future that use *shall* and *will* in English. (e.g., *yo amaré* means *I shall love* or *I will love.*)

Conditional Tense—This tense expresses an idea that is *dependent on a condition* which is either expressed or understood. Use this tense to express the English equivalent of *would* or *should*. (e.g., *yo amaría* means *I would love* or *I should love.*)

Subjunctive Mood—Use this tense when you want to express *possibility* or *uncertainty*. Many times it is translated as *may*...It is used to express doubt or when a contrary-to-fact supposition is made. (e.g., *yo ame* means *I may love.*)

Command Mood—Use this tense to give instruction or to tell someone to do something. (Ex: ¡*amen ustedes!* means *you love!*)

Reflexive —A reflexive verb is one whose subject and object are the same. The *subject acts upon itself*. A reflexive verb is indicated by the pronoun **se** attached to the infinitive verb. (e.g., *Amarse* means *to love one's self. Ella se ama* means *she loves herself.*)

Common Spanish Suffixes[10]

This table may be used as a tool to assist in increasing your knowledge of vocabulary words. With an awareness of these Spanish suffixes, words can be created by adding them to the endings of words.

TABLE 6.21—Frequently Used Spanish Suffixes

SUFFIX	MEANING	ENG.EQUIV.	FOUND IN	EXAMPLES
-able	*able to, capable of*	-able	adjectives	adorable culpable
-ano, -ana	*like, relating to, native of*	-an	nouns, adjectives	soberano cristiano pagano
-anza	*quality, state of being, condition, process*	-ance	nouns	la venganza la confianza
-ción	*result of action, state of being*	-tion	nouns	la humilación la salvación la invitación la adopción la adoración
-dad, -edad	*state of being, forms abstract noun*	-ness, -hood	nouns	la bondad la santidad la enfermedad la debilidad
-dor, -dora	*one who denotes profession*	-er, -or	nouns	creador,-a buscador,-a adorador,-a pecador,-a
-encia	*act, state of being, result of action*	-ence, -ency	nouns	la herencia la paciencia la asistencia
-ente	*like, doing, related to*	-ing, -ent	adjectives	omnipotente omnipresente diferente siguiente

-ico, -ica	like, relating to	-ic	adjectives	angélico, bíblico, Católico, evangélico, satánico
-idad	state of being, quality	-ity	nouns	la eternidad la necesidad la unidad la humilidad
-ificar	to make (like)	-ify	verbs	crucificar santificar glorificar justificar purificar
-ismo	system, act, characteristic, loyalty to	-ism	nouns	cristianismo compañerismo el alcoholismo
-ito, -ita	diminutive	(none)	nouns	el pobrecito
-ito, -ita	like, relating to, one who	-ite	adjectives, nouns	(el) israelita el ingénito
-mente	forms adverbs	-ly	adverbs	fielmente lealmente
-miento	act, state of being, result of action	-ment	nouns	el sacramento el mandamiento el sentimiento
-oso, -osa	full of, having	-ous, -ful, -y	adjectives	cariñoso,-a misericordioso
-sión	state of being, result of action	-sion	nouns	la visión la conversión
-tad, -stad	state of being, forms abstract nouns	-ty	nouns	la lealtad la majestad la libertad

Visit us at www.SpanishForChristianService.com

Irregular Verbs and Their Tenses[11]

TABLE 6.22—*conocer*

CONOCER (to know)	Present	Imperfect	Past
yo	conozco	conocía	conocí
tú	conoces	conocías	conociste
él/ella	conoce	conocía	conoció
usted	conoce	conocía	conoció
nosotros, -as	conocemos	conocíamos	conocimos
ellos/ellas	conocen	conocían	conocieron
ustedes	conocen	conocían	conocieron

	Future	Conditional	Subjunctive
yo	conoceré	conocería	conozca
tú	conocerás	conocerías	conozcas
él/ella	conocerá	conocería	conozca
usted	conocerá	conocería	conozca
nosotros, -as	conoceremos	conoceríamos	conozcamos
ellos/ellas	conocerán	conocerían	conozcan
ustedes	conocerán	conocerían	conozcan

	Command
yo	—
tú	conoce; no conozcas
él/ella	conozca
usted	conozca
nosotros, -as	conozcamos
ellos/ellas	conozcan
ustedes	conozcan

TABLE 6.23—*creer*

CREER (to believe)	Present	Imperfect	Past
yo	creo	creía	creí
tú	crees	creías	creíste
él/ella	cree	creía	creyó
usted	cree	creía	creyó
nosotros, -as	creemos	creíamos	creímos
ellos/ellas	creen	creían	creyeron
ustedes	creen	creían	creyeron

	Future	Conditional	Subjunctive
yo	creeré	creería	crea
tú	creerás	creerías	creas
él/ella	creerá	creería	crea
usted	creerá	creería	crea
nosotros, -as	creeremos	creeríamos	creamos
ellos/ellas	creerán	creerían	crean
ustedes	creerán	creerían	crean

	Command
yo	—
tú	cree; no creas
él/ella	crea
usted	crea
nosotros, -as	creamos
ellos/ellas	crean
ustedes	crean

TABLE 6.24—*dar*

DAR (to give)	Present	Imperfect	Past
yo	doy	daba	di
tú	das	dabas	diste
él/ella	da	daba	dio
usted	da	daba	dio
nosotros, -as	damos	dábamos	dimos
ellos/ellas	dan	daban	dieron
ustedes	dan	daban	dieron

	Future	Conditional	Subjunctive
yo	daré	daría	dé
tú	darás	darías	des
él/ella	dará	daría	dé
usted	dará	daría	dé
nosotros, -as	daremos	daríamos	demos
ellos/ellas	darán	darían	den
ustedes	darán	darían	den

	Command
yo	—
tú	da; no des
él/ella	dé
usted	dé
nosotros, -as	demos
ellos/ellas	den
ustedes	den

TABLE 6.25—*decir*

DECIR (to say)	Present	Imperfect	Past
yo	digo	decía	dije
tú	dices	decías	dijiste
él/ella	dice	decía	dijo
usted	dice	decía	dijo
nosotros, -as	decimos	decíamos	dijimos
ellos/ellas	dicen	decían	dijeron
ustedes	dicen	decían	dijeron

	Future	Conditional	Subjunctive
yo	diré	diría	diga
tú	dirás	dirías	digas
él/ella	dirá	diría	diga
usted	dirá	diría	diga
nosotros, -as	diremos	diríamos	digamos
ellos/ellas	dirán	dirían	digan
ustedes	dirán	dirían	digan

	Command
yo	—
tú	di; no digas
él/ella	diga
usted	diga
nosotros, -as	digamos
ellos/ellas	digan
ustedes	digan

TABLE 6.26—*estar*

ESTAR (to be)	Present	Imperfect	Past
yo	estoy	estaba	estuve
tú	estás	estabas	estuviste
él/ella	está	estaba	estuvo
usted	está	estaba	estuvo
nosotros, -as	estamos	estábamos	estuvimos
ellos/ellas	están	estaban	estuvieron
ustedes	están	estaban	estuvieron

	Future	Conditional	Subjunctive
yo	estaré	estaría	esté
tú	estarás	estarías	estés
él/ella	estará	estaría	esté
usted	estará	estaría	esté
nosotros, -as	estaremos	estaríamos	estemos
ellos/ellas	estarán	estarían	estén
ustedes	estarán	estarían	estén

	Command
yo	—
tú	está; no estés
él/ella	esté
usted	esté
nosotros, -as	estemos
ellos/ellas	estén
ustedes	estén

TABLE 6.27—*haber*

HABER (to have)	Present	Imperfect	Past
yo	he	había	hube
tú	has	habías	hubiste
él/ella	ha	había	hubo
usted	ha	había	hubo
nosotros, -as	hemos	habíamos	hubimos
ellos/ellas	han	habían	hubieron
ustedes	han	habían	hubieron

	Future	Conditional	Subjunctive
yo	habré	habría	haya
tú	habrás	habrías	hayas
él/ella	habrá	habría	haya
usted	habrá	habría	haya
nosotros, -as	habremos	habríamos	hayamos
ellos/ellas	habrán	habrían	hayan
ustedes	habrán	habrían	hayan

	Command
yo	—
tú	he; no hayas
él/ella	haya
usted	haya
nosotros, -as	hayamos
ellos/ellas	hayan
ustedes	hayan

Visit us at www.SpanishForChristianService.com

TABLE 6.28—*hacer*

HACER (to make, to do)	Present	Imperfect	Past
yo	hago	hacía	hice
tú	haces	hacías	hiciste
él/ella	hace	hacía	hizo
usted	hace	hacía	hizo
nosotros, -as	hacemos	hacíamos	hicimos
ellos/ellas	hacen	hacían	hicieron
ustedes	hacen	hacían	hicieron

	Future	Conditional	Subjunctive
yo	haré	haría	haga
tú	harás	harías	hagas
él/ella	hará	haría	haga
usted	hará	haría	haga
nosotros, -as	haremos	haríamos	hagamos
ellos/ellas	harán	harían	hagan
ustedes	harán	harían	hagan

	Command
yo	—
tú	haz; no hagas
él/ella	haga
usted	haga
nosotros, -as	hagamos
ellos/ellas	hagan
ustedes	hagan

TABLE 6.29—*ir*

IR *(to go)*	Present	Imperfect	Past
yo	voy	iba	fui
tú	vas	ibas	fuiste
él/ella	va	iba	fue
usted	va	iba	fue
nosotros, -as	vamos	íbamos	fuimos
ellos/ellas	van	iban	fueron
ustedes	van	iban	fueron

	Future	Conditional	Subjunctive
yo	iré	iría	vaya
tú	irás	irías	vayas
él/ella	irá	iría	vaya
usted	irá	iría	vaya
nosotros, -as	iremos	iríamos	vayamos
ellos/ellas	irán	irían	vayan
ustedes	irán	irían	vayan

	Command
yo	—
tú	ve; no vayas
él/ella	vaya
usted	vaya
nosotros, -as	vamos (no vayamos)
ellos/ellas	vayan
ustedes	vayan

TABLE 6.30—*poder*

PODER (to be able, can)	Present	Imperfect	Past
yo	puedo	podía	pude
tú	puedes	podías	pudiste
él/ella	puede	podía	pudo
usted	puede	podía	pudo
nosotros, -as	podemos	podíamos	pudimos
ellos/ellas	pueden	podían	pudieron
ustedes	pueden	podían	pudieron

	Future	Conditional	Subjunctive
yo	podré	podría	pueda
tú	podrás	podrías	puedas
él/ella	podrá	podría	pueda
usted	podrá	podría	pueda
nosotros, -as	podremos	podríamos	podamos
ellos/ellas	podrán	podrían	puedan
ustedes	podrán	podrían	puedan

	Command
yo	—
tú	puede; no puedas
él/ella	pueda
usted	pueda
nosotros, -as	podamos
ellos/ellas	puedan
ustedes	puedan

TABLE 6.31—*poner*

PONER *(to put, place)*	Present	Imperfect	Past
yo	pongo	ponía	puse
tú	pones	ponías	pusiste
él/ella	pone	ponía	puso
usted	pone	ponía	puso
nosotros, -as	ponemos	poníamos	pusimos
ellos/ellas	ponen	ponían	pusieron
ustedes	ponen	ponían	pusieron

	Future	Conditional	Subjunctive
yo	pondré	pondría	ponga
tú	pondrás	pondrías	pongas
él/ella	pondrá	pondría	ponga
usted	pondrá	pondría	ponga
nosotros, -as	pondremos	pondríamos	pongamos
ellos/ellas	pondrán	pondrían	pongan
ustedes	pondrán	pondrían	pongan

	Command
yo	—
tú	pon; no pongas
él/ella	ponga
usted	ponga
nosotros, -as	pongamos
ellos/ellas	pongan
ustedes	pongan

Visit us at www.SpanishForChristianService.com

TABLE 6.32—*querer*

QUERER (to want, wish)	Present	Imperfect	Past
yo	quiero	quería	quise
tú	quieres	querías	quisiste
él/ella	quiere	quería	quiso
usted	quiere	quería	quiso
nosotros, -as	queremos	queríamos	quisimos
ellos/ellas	quieren	querían	quisieron
ustedes	quieren	querían	quisieron

	Future	Conditional	Subjunctive
yo	querré	querría	quiera
tú	querrás	querrías	quieras
él/ella	querrá	querría	quiera
usted	querrá	querría	quiera
nosotros, -as	querremos	querríamos	queramos
ellos/ellas	querrán	querrían	quieran
ustedes	querrán	querrían	quieran

	Command
yo	—
tú	quiere; no quieras
él/ella	quiera
usted	quiera
nosotros, -as	queramos
ellos/ellas	quieran
ustedes	quieran

TABLE 6.33—*saber*

SABER (to know)	Present	Imperfect	Past
yo	sé	sabía	supe
tú	sabes	sabías	supiste
él/ella	sabe	sabía	supo
usted	sabe	sabía	supo
nosotros, -as	sabemos	sabíamos	supimos
ellos/ellas	saben	sabían	supieron
ustedes	saben	sabían	supieron

	Future	Conditional	Subjunctive
yo	sabré	sabría	sepa
tú	sabrás	sabrías	sepas
él/ella	sabrá	sabría	sepa
usted	sabrá	sabría	sepa
nosotros, -as	sabremos	sabríamos	sepamos
ellos/ellas	sabrán	sabrían	sepan
ustedes	sabrán	sabrían	sepan

	Command
yo	—
tú	sabe; no sepas
él/ella	sepa
usted	sepa
nosotros, -as	sepamos
ellos/ellas	sepan
ustedes	sepan

TABLE 6.34—*salir*

SALIR (to go out, leave)	Present	Imperfect	Past
yo	salgo	salía	salí
tú	sales	salías	saliste
él/ella	sale	salía	salió
usted	sale	salía	salió
nosotros, -as	salimos	salíamos	salimos
ellos/ellas	salen	salían	salieron
ustedes	salen	salían	salieron

	Future	Conditional	Subjunctive
yo	saldré	saldría	salga
tú	saldrás	saldrías	salgas
él/ella	saldrá	saldría	salga
usted	saldrá	saldría	salga
nosotros, -as	saldremos	saldríamos	salgamos
ellos/ellas	saldrán	saldrían	salgan
ustedes	saldrán	saldrían	salgan

	Command
yo	—
tú	sal; no salgas
él/ella	salga
usted	salga
nosotros, -as	salgamos
ellos/ellas	salgan
ustedes	salgan

TABLE 6.35—*ser*

SER (to be)	Present	Imperfect	Past
yo	soy	era	fui
tú	eres	eras	fuiste
él/ella	es	era	fue
usted	es	era	fue
nosotros, -as	somos	éramos	fuimos
ellos/ellas	son	eran	fueron
ustedes	son	eran	fueron

	Future	Conditional	Subjunctive
yo	seré	sería	sea
tú	serás	serías	seas
él/ella	será	sería	sea
usted	será	sería	sea
nosotros, -as	seremos	seríamos	seamos
ellos/ellas	serán	serían	sean
ustedes	serán	serían	sean

	Command
yo	—
tú	sé; no seas
él/ella	sea
usted	sea
nosotros, -as	seamos
ellos/ellas	sean
ustedes	sean

TABLE 6.36—*tener*

TENER (to have)	Present	Imperfect	Past
yo	tengo	tenía	tuve
tú	tienes	tenías	tuviste
él/ella	tiene	tenía	tuvo
usted	tiene	tenía	tuvo
nosotros, -as	tenemos	teníamos	tuvimos
ellos/ellas	tienen	tenían	tuvieron
ustedes	tienen	tenían	tuvieron

	Future	Conditional	Subjunctive
yo	tendré	tendría	tenga
tú	tendrás	tendrías	tengas
él/ella	tendrá	tendría	tenga
usted	tendrá	tendría	tenga
nosotros, -as	tendremos	tendríamos	tengamos
ellos/ellas	tendrán	tendrían	tengan
ustedes	tendrán	tendrían	tengan

	Command
yo	—
tú	ten; no tengas
él/ella	tenga
usted	tenga
nosotros, -as	tengamos
ellos/ellas	tengan
ustedes	tengan

TABLE 6.37—*venir*

VENIR *(to come)*	Present	Imperfect	Past
yo	vengo	venía	vine
tú	vienes	venías	viniste
él/ella	viene	venía	vino
usted	viene	venía	vino
nosotros, -as	venimos	veníamos	vinimos
ellos/ellas	vienen	venían	vinieron
ustedes	vienen	venían	vinieron

	Future	Conditional	Subjunctive
yo	vendré	vendría	venga
tú	vendrás	vendrías	vengas
él/ella	vendrá	vendría	venga
usted	vendrá	vendría	venga
nosotros, -as	vendremos	vendríamos	vengamos
ellos/ellas	vendrán	vendrían	vengan
ustedes	vendrán	vendrían	vengan

	Command
yo	—
tú	ven; no vengas
él/ella	venga
usted	venga
nosotros, -as	vengamos
ellos/ellas	vengan
ustedes	vengan

Visit us at www.SpanishForChristianService.com

TABLE 6.38—*ver*

VER *(to see)*	Present	Imperfect	Past
yo	veo	veía	vi
tú	ves	veías	viste
él/ella	ve	veía	vio
usted	ve	veía	vio
nosotros, -as	vemos	veíamos	vimos
ellos/ellas	ven	veían	vieron
ustedes	ven	veían	vieron

	Future	Conditional	Subjunctive
yo	veré	vería	vea
tú	verás	verías	veas
él/ella	verá	vería	vea
usted	verá	vería	vea
nosotros, -as	veremos	veíamos	veamos
ellos/ellas	verán	verían	vean
ustedes	verán	verían	vean

	Command
yo	—
tú	ve; no veas
él/ella	vea
usted	vea
nosotros, -as	veamos
ellos/ellas	vean
ustedes	vean

Create Your Own
Verb Tense Practice Sheets

TABLE 6.39

yo			
tú			
él/ella			
usted			
nosotros, -as			
ellos/ellas			
ustedes			

yo			
tú			
él/ella			
usted			
nosotros, -as			
ellos/ellas			
ustedes			

yo			
tú			
él/ella			
usted			
nosotros, -as			
ellos/ellas			
ustedes			

Verb Tense Practice Sheets

yo			
tú			
él/ella			
usted			
nosotros, -as			
ellos/ellas			
ustedes			

yo			
tú			
él/ella			
usted			
nosotros, -as			
ellos/ellas			
ustedes			

yo			
tú			
él/ella			
usted			
nosotros, -as			
ellos/ellas			
ustedes			

Verb Tense Practice Sheets

yo			
tú			
él/ella			
usted			
nosotros, -as			
ellos/ellas			
ustedes			

yo			
tú			
él/ella			
usted			
nosotros, -as			
ellos/ellas			
ustedes			

yo			
tú			
él/ella			
usted			
nosotros, -as			
ellos/ellas			
ustedes			

Verb Tense Practice Sheets

yo			
tú			
él/ella			
usted			
nosotros, -as			
ellos/ellas			
ustedes			

yo			
tú			
él/ella			
usted			
nosotros, -as			
ellos/ellas			
ustedes			

yo			
tú			
él/ella			
usted			
nosotros, -as			
ellos/ellas			
ustedes			

Verb Tense Practice Sheets

yo			
tú			
él/ella			
usted			
nosotros, -as			
ellos/ellas			
ustedes			

yo			
tú			
él/ella			
usted			
nosotros, -as			
ellos/ellas			
ustedes			

yo			
tú			
él/ella			
usted			
nosotros, -as			
ellos/ellas			
ustedes			

Visit us at www.SpanishForChristianService.com

Verb Tense Practice Sheets

yo			
tú			
él/ella			
usted			
nosotros, -as			
ellos/ellas			
ustedes			

yo			
tú			
él/ella			
usted			
nosotros, -as			
ellos/ellas			
ustedes			

yo			
tú			
él/ella			
usted			
nosotros, -as			
ellos/ellas			
ustedes			

Oración/Prayer

Here is a prayer that utilizes some of our previously learned vocabulary. The underlined words are found in some of these lists.

Padre Nuestro,	Our Father,
en el nombre de tu hijo <u>Jesús</u>,	in the name of your son Jesus,
con <u>humildad</u> yo te doy <u>gracias</u>	with humility I give you thanks
por todo lo bueno que haces	for all the goodness that you do
en mi vida:	in my life:
por darme la <u>vida</u> y la salud	for giving me life, health,
y la oportunidad de <u>adorar</u> y	and the chance to adore and
<u>glorificar</u> Tu <u>Santo</u> Nombre.	glorify your Holy Name.
Te pido que tus <u>promesas</u>	I ask you that your promises
sucedan en mi vida diaria,	may occur in my daily life,
y que tu <u>misericordia</u> y tu <u>gracia</u>	and that your mercy and grace
me acompañen siempre,	may accompany me always,

para seguir <u>fielmente</u> tus caminos, guiado por tu <u>amor</u> y tu <u>bondad</u>, por medio del <u>Espíritu</u> <u>Santo</u>.	to follow faithfully your paths, guided by your love and goodness, by means of the Holy Spirit.
<u>Dios</u> <u>soberano</u> y <u>eterno</u>, te pido una <u>bendición</u> para todos quienes me rodean, especialmente para mi <u>iglesia</u>, mi familia y para mi vida.	Sovereign and eternal God, I ask you for a blessing for all those who surround me, especially for my church, my family, and for my life.
Todo esto te lo presento, en el nombre de tu hijo, nuestro <u>Señor</u> y <u>Salvador</u> Jesús. Amen	All this I present to you, in the name of your son, our Lord and Savior Jesus. Amen

English Infinitive Verb Forms

(English To Spanish)

abort—abortar

abstain—abstenerse, evitar

abuse—abusar, maltratar

accept—aceptar

accompany—acompañar

accuse—acusar

adopt—adoptar, ahijar

adore—adorar, venerar *(more often used in the Catholic faith)*

adulterate—adulterar

afflict—afligir, apenar

agree—acordar

anger—enojar

anoint—ungir

answer—contestar

appreciate—agradecer, apreciar

approve—aprobar

arrive—llegar

ask—pedir

atone—expiar

attend—asistir a

avoid—evitar

awaken—despertarse

baptize—bautizar

bathe oneself—bañarse

be—ser, estar

be able—poder

be born—nacer

(be) jealous—envidiar

beg—mendigar, pedir limosna

begin—comenzar, empezar

believe—creer

belong—pertenecer

blame—culpar

blaspheme—blasfemar

bless—bendecir

boast—jactarse

break—romper, quebrantar

bribe—sobornar

bring—traer

build—construir, edificar

burn—quemar

bury—enterrar, sepultar

buy—comprar

call—llamar

call collect—llamar a cobro revertido

call together—convocar

care *(to be concerned)*—preocuparse

care for *(someone)*—cuidar a

carry—llevar

cease—cesar

chaperone—acompañar

charge *(of)*—encargarse

chat—charlar

cheat—engañar

check—examinar, revisar

cleanse—purgar

close—cerrar

collect—recolectar

come—venir

come back—volver

comfort—confortar

command—mandar

commit—cometer

commit adultery—adulterar

commit suicide—suicidarse

complain—quejarse

condemn—condenar

confess—confesar

congratulate—felicitar, congratular

conquer—vencer

console—consolar, confortar

construct—construir
converse—conversar
convert—convertir
corrupt—corromper
cost—costar
cover—cubrir
covet—codiciar
create—crear
crucify—crucificar
cry—llorar
cure—curar
curse—maldecir
deceive—engañar
decide—decidir
dedicate—consagrar a
deliver from—librar
demand—exigir
deny—negar
desire—desear, anhelar
desist—desistir
destroy—destruir, destrozar
die—morir, fallecer
dine—cenar
direct—dirigir
discourage—desanimar
discuss—discutir
disobey—desobedecer
distance—alejar, distanciar
disturb—trastornar
divorce—divorciar
do—hacer
donate—hacer una donación, donar
doubt—dudar
drink—beber, tomar
drive—conducir, manejar
dwell—habitar
eat—comer
eat breakfast—desayunar
educate—educar
elect—elegir

email—enviar un mensaje electrónico
embitter—amargar
embrace—abrazarse
encourage—animar, motivar
end—terminar
enjoy—gozar
enslave—esclavizar
enter—entrar
entrust—confiar en
envy—envidiar, codiciar
escape—escapar
escort—escortar, acompañar
eulogize—elogiar
evangelize—evangelizar
examine—probar, examinar
exceed—sobrar
exchange *(money)*—cambiar dinero
exile—exiliar
explain—explicar
fail—fracasar
fall—caer
fast—ayunar
fax—mandar por fax
fear—temer por, tener miedo
feed—alimentar
feel—sentir
fill—llenar
find—encontrar
finish—terminar
fix—arreglar *(repair)*, fijar (*a position*)
flee—huir
fly—volar
follow—seguir
fool—engañar
forgive—perdonar
free—librar
fulfill—cumplir
gain—ganar

gamble—apostar
gather—recoger
give—dar
give back—devolver
give testimony—dar testimonio
give the blessing—dar la bendición
glorify—glorificar, alabar
go—ir
go to bed—acostarse
gossip—chismear
grant—conceder
grieve—lamentar
grow—crecer
guide—guiar
harvest—cosechar
hate—odiar
have—tener
have an abortion—abortar
heal—sanar
hear—oír
help—ayudar
hide—esconder
honor—honrar
hope—esperar
host—hospedar
hug—abrazarse
hunger—tener hambre
hurt—doler
influence—influir
inherit—heredar
instill—infundir
insult—insultar
intercede—interceder con
interpret—interpretar
intoxicate/ become intoxicated—emborrachar
invite—invitar
judge—juzgar
justify—justificar
keep—guardar

kidnap—secuestar
kill—matar
kneel—arrodillarse
knock (on the door)—llamar a la puerta
know—conocer, saber
lack—faltar
laugh—reír
lead—conducir
learn—aprender
leave—salir
level—allanar, nivelar
lie—mentir
like—gustar
listen—escuchar
live—vivir
lodge (a guest)—hospedar
look at—mirar
lose—perder
love (each other)—amarse
love (someone)—amar
lust—lujuriar
make—hacer
make the sign of the cross—persignarse
marry—casarse con
meet—encontrar, reunir, quedar
mend—coser
mistreat—maltratar
motivate—motivar
mourn—lamentar, llorar por
move—mover
murder—asesinar, matar
nail—clavar
name (to be named)—llamarse
near—acercarse
need—necesitar
neglect—descuidar
obey—obedecer
observe—observar

occur—ocurrir, suceder
open—abrir
organize—organizar
overcome—vencer
overflow—rebosar
owe—deber
pardon—perdonar
pay—pagar
permit—permitir
persecute—perseguir
persevere—perseverar
persist—persistir
phone—llamar por teléfono, telefonear
place—poner
plant—plantar
play—jugar
pledge—comprometer
praise—alabar, elogiar
pray—orar, rezar *(mostly used in the Catholic faith)*
preach—predicar
prepare—preparar, disponer
present—presentar
promise—prometer
pronounce—pronunciar
prophesy—profetizar
prostitute—prostituirse
protect—proteger
provide—proveer
punish—castigar
put—poner
raise *(from the dead)*—resucitar
rape—violar
read—leer
receive—recibir
redeem—redimir, salvarse
refuse—rechazar
rejoice—regocijar
relate—relacionar

remain—permanecer, quedar
remember—recordar, acordar
remove—sacar
repeat—repetir
repent—arrepentirse de
require—necesitar, exigir, requerir
respect—respetar, honrar
rest—descansar
restore—restaurar
return—regresar, volver
rob—robar
ruin—arruinar
run—correr
run up debt—endeudarse
sacrifice—sacrificar
sanctify—santificar
save *(a life, a soul)*—salvarse
say—decir
say goodbye—despedirse
scatter—esparcir
seal—sellar
search—intentar
see—ver
seek—buscar
select—elegir
send—enviar, mandar
serve—servir
shame—avergonzar
share—compartir
shave—afeitarse
shelter—refugiar
shop—ir de compras
show—enseñar
silence—callar
sin—pecar
sit—sentarse
slander—maldecir
sleep—dormir
smile—sonreír
smoke—fumar

sow—sembrar
speak—hablar
sponsor—patrocinar
squander—derrochar
starve—privar de comida, pasar hambre
steal—robar
strengthen—fortalecer
study—estudiar
submit—someter a, rendirse
sue—demandar
suffer—sufrir, padecer
supply—proveer, suplir
support—apoyar
surrender—rendirse, someter a
surround—rodear
survive—sobrevivir
swallow—tragar
swear—jurar
take—tomar, llevar
take out—sacar
talk—hablar, conversar con, charlar
teach—enseñar
tear—rasgar
telephone—telefonear, llamar por teléfono
tell—decir, contar
tempt—tentar
test—probar, examinar
testify—testificar, declarar
thank—agradecer a
think—pensar
thirst—tener sed
threaten—amenazar
throw away—desechar
tithe—diezmar
tolerate—aguantar
travel—viajar
trust—confiar en
turn—dar la vuelta

understand—comprender, entender
unite—unirse, juntarse
upset—trastornar
use—usar
visit—visitar
volunteer—ofrecerse como voluntario
wait—esperar
walk—caminar
want—querer
warn—avisar
wash—lavar
watch—observar
wed—casarse con
welcome—darle la bienvenida a
work—trabajar
work miracles—hacer milagros
work wonders—hacer maravillas
worship—adorar, venerar *(more often used in the Catholic faith)*
write—escribir
yearn—anhelar

Spanish Infinitive Verb Forms
(Spanish To English)

abortar—to have an abortion, to abort

abrazarse—to embrace, hug

abrir—open

abstenerse—to abstain, avoid

abusar de—to abuse *(i.e., drugs, or to take unfair advantage of)*

aceptar—accept

acercar—to bring near/close

acompañar—to chaperone

acordar—to agree, to decide, to remember

acostarse—to go to bed

acusar—to accuse

adoptar—to adopt *(an approach, a child)*

adorar—to adore, to worship

adulterar—to commit adultery

afeitarse—to shave

afligir—to afflict

afligirse—to grieve

agradecer a—to thank, appreciate

aguantar—to tolerate, hold

ahijar—to adopt *(a child)*

alabar—to praise, to glorify

alejar—to distance

alimentar—to feed

allanar—to level, smooth

amar—to love

amargar—to embitter

amarse—to love each other

amenazar—to threaten

anhelar—to yearn, desire

animar—to encourage

apenar—to afflict, aggrieve

apostar—to gamble, bet

apoyar—to support

aprender—to learn

aprobar—to approve

arreglar—to fix *(repair)*

arrepentirse de—to repent

arrodillarse—to kneel

arruinar—to ruin, destroy

asesinar—to assassinate, murder

asistir a—to attend

avergonzar—to shame, embarrass

avisar—to warn

ayudar—to help

ayunar—to fast

bañarse—to bathe *(oneself)*

bautizar—to baptize

beber—to drink

bendecir—to bless

blasfemar—to blaspheme

buscar—to seek, to search

caer—to fall

callar—to silence

cambiar *(dinero)*—to exchange *(money)*

caminar—to walk

cargar—to charge *(a price)*

casarse con—to wed, to marry

castigar—to punish

cenar—to dine

cerrar—to close

cesar—to cease

charlar—to chat, to talk

chismear—gossip

clavar—to nail

cobrar—to charge *(a price)*

codiciar—to envy, covet

comenzar—to begin

comer—to eat
cometer—to commit, carry out
compartir—to share
comprar—to buy
comprender—to understand
comprometer—to submit, pledge
conceder—to grant, to agree to
condenar—to condemn
conducir—to lead, to drive
confesar—to confess
confiar en—to trust, to confide in
confortar—to comfort
congratular—to congratulate
conocer—to know *(someone)*
consagrar a—to dedicate to
consolar—to comfort
construir—to construct, to build
contar—to tell
contestar—to answer
conversar con—to talk with
convertir—to convert
convocar—to call together, summon
correr—to run
corromper—to corrupt
cosechar—to harvest
coser—to mend, sow
costar—to cost
crear—to create
crecer—to grow
creer—to believe
crucificar—to crucify
cubrir—to cover
cuidar—to care for *(someone)*
culpar—to blame
cumplir—to fulfill, to complete
curar—to cure
dar—to give
dar la bendición—to give the blessing
dar la vuelta—to turn

dar pena—to sorrow
dar testimonio—to testify, to give testimony
darle la bienvenida a—to welcome
deber—to owe, ought to
decir—to say
declarar—to testify
dejar—to leave alone, to let stand
demandar—to sue
derrochar—to squander, to waste
desanimar—to discourage
desayunar—to eat breakfast
descansar—to rest
descuidar—to neglect
desear—to desire, want
desechar—to throw away
desistir—to desist
desobedecer—to disobey
despedirse—to say goodbye
despertarse—to awaken
destrozar—to destroy
destruir—to destroy
devolver—to give back
diezmar—to tithe
dirigir—to direct
discutir—to discuss
disponer—to prepare
distanciar—to distance
divorciar—to divorce
doler—to hurt
donar—to donate
dormir—to sleep
dudar—to doubt
edificar—to build, edify
educar—to educate, bring up
elegir—to select, elect
elogiar—to eulogize, praise
emborrachar—to intoxicate, become intoxicated
empezar—to begin

Visit us at www.SpanishForChristianService.com

encargarse—to be in charge of, take care of

encontrar—to find, meet

endeudarse—to run up debts

engañar—to deceive, cheat, fool

enojar—to anger

enseñar—to teach, show

entender—to understand

enterrar—to bury

entrar—to enter

enviar un mensaje electrónico—to email

envidiar—to envy

escapar—to escape

esclavizar—to enslave

esconder—to hide

escribir—to write

escuchar—to listen

esparcir—to scatter

esperar—to hope, to wait

estar—to be

estar de vacaciones—to vacation

estudiar—to study

evangelizar—to evangelize

evitar—to avoid

examinar—to test, examine, check

exigir—to demand, require

exiliar—to exile

expiar—to atone

explicar—to explain

fallecer—to die

faltar—to lack

felicitar—to congratulate

fijar—to fix *(a position)*

fortalecer—to strengthen

fracasar—to fail,break, disappoint

fumar—to smoke

ganar—to gain

glorificar—to glorify

gozar—to enjoy

guardar—to keep

guiar—to guide

habitar—to dwell

hablar—to speak

hacer—to make, to do

hacer maravillas—to work wonders

hacer milagros—to work miracles

hacer una donación—to donate

heredar—to inherit

honrar—to honor

hospedar—to lodge, to receive as a guest

huir—to flee

influir—to influence

infundir—to instill

insultar—to insult

intentar—to search, try

interceder con—to intercede with

interpretar—to interpret

invitar—to invite

ir—to go

ir de compras—to go shopping

jactarse—to boast

jugar—to play

juntarse—to unite, get together, meet

jurar—to swear

justificar—justify

juzgar—to judge

lamentar—to grieve

lavar—to wash

leer—to read

librar—to free, deliver from

llamar a cobro revertido—to call collect

llamar a la puerta—to call, knock

llamar por teléfono—to phone

llamarse—to be named

llegar—to arrive

llenar—to fill

llevar—to carry, to take

llorar—to cry
llorar por—to grieve
lujuriar—to lust
maldecir—to curse, slander
maltratar—to mistreat
mandar—to command, send
mandar por fax—to fax
manejar—to drive
matar—to kill, to murder
mendigar—to beg
mentir—to lie
meter—to insert, to put in
morir—to die
motivar—to motivate, encourage
mover—to move
nacer—to be born
necesitar—to need, require
negar—to deny
nivelar—to level (something, with people)
obedecer—to obey
observar—to observe
ocurrir—to occur
odiar—to hate
ofrecerse como voluntario—to volunteer
oír—to hear
orar—to pray
organizar—to organize
padecer—to suffer
pagar—to pay
pasar hambre—to starve
patrocinar—to sponsor
pecar—to sin
pedir—to ask
pedir limosna—to beg
pensar—to think
perder—to lose
perdonar—to forgive
permanecer—to remain

permitir—to permit
perseguir—to persecute, to chase
perseverar—to persevere
persistir—to persist
pertenecer—to belong
plantar—to plant
poder—to be able
poner—to place, put
predicar—to preach
preocuparse—to be concerned
preparar—to prepare
presentar—to present
privar de comida—to starve
probar—to test
profetizar—to prophesy
prohibir—to forbid
prometer—to promise
pronunciar—to pronounce
prostituirse—to prostitute
proteger—to protect
proveer—to provide
purgar—to cleanse
purificar—to purify
quebrantar—to break (an object)
quedar—to remain
quejarse—to complain
quemar—to burn
querer—to want
rasgar—to tear
rebosar—to overflow
rechazar—to resist, to refuse, to deny
recibir—to receive
recoger—to gather
recolectar—to collect, gather
recordar—to remember
redimir—to redeem
refugiarse—to take refuge, shelter
regocijar—to rejoice
regresar—to return
reír—to laugh

relacionar—to relate
rendirse—to submit, to surrender
repetir—to repeat
requerir—to require
respetar—to respect
restaurar—to restore, to recover
reunir—to meet
revisar—to check
rezar—to pray (*mostly used in the Catholic faith*)
robar—to rob, to steal
rodear—to surround
romper—to break *(an object)*
saber—to know
sacar—to remove, take out
sacrificar—to sacrifice
salir—to leave
salvarse—to save *(a life, a soul)*
sanar—to heal
santificar—to sanctify, to make holy
secuestrar—to kidnap
seguir—to follow
sellar—to seal
sembrar—to sow, plant
sentarse—to sit
sentirse—to feel
sepultar—to bury
ser—to be
servir—to serve
sobornar—to bribe
sobrar—to have too much of, to exceed
sobrevivir—to survive
someter a—to submit, surrender
sonreír—to laugh
soportar—to support
suceder—to occur, happen
sufrir—to suffer
suicidarse—to commit suicide
suplir—to supply

telefonear—to telephone
temer por—to fear for
tener—to have
tener hambre—to hunger
tener miedo—to fear
tener sed—to thirst
tentar—to tempt
terminar—to end
testificar—to testify
tomar—to take, drink
trabajar—to work
traer—to bring
tragar—to swallow
trastornar—to upset, disturb
ungir—to anoint
unirse—to unite, get together, meet
usar—to use
vencer—to conquer, defeat, overcome
venerar—*(more often used in the Catholic faith)* to worship, adore, revere
venir—to come
ver—to see
viajar—to travel
violar—to rape
virar—to change direction
visitar—to visit
volar—to fly
volver—to return, come back

Vocabulary/Vocabulario
(English To Spanish)

Aaron—Aarón
Abel—Abel
abomination (n.)—la abominación
abort (v.)—abortar
abortion (n.)—el aborto
Abraham—Abraham
abstain (v.)—abstenerse, evitar
abstinence (n.)—la abstinencia
abuse (n.)—el abuso
abuse *(someone)* (v.)—maltratar
abuse *(drugs)* (v.)—abusar de
abyss (n.)—el abismo
accept (v.)—aceptar
accident (n.)—el accidente
accompany (v.)—acompañar
according to—según
accusation (n.)—la acusación
accuse (v.)—acusar
Acts—Hechos
Adam—Adán
addict (n.)—el/la adicto,-a
addiction (n.)—la adicción
addictive—que crea dependencia
adopt (v.)—adoptar, ahijar
adoption (n.)—la adopción
adorable—adorable
adoration (n.)—la adoración
adore (v.)—adorar
adorer (n.)—el/la adorador,-ra
adult (n.)—el/la adulto,-a
adulterate (v.)—adulterar
adultery (n.)—el adulterio
Advent (n.)—el Advenimiento
Adventist—adventista
adversity (n.)—la adversidad
afflict (v.)—afligir, apenar

affliction (n.)—la aflicción
after—después
afternoon (n.)—la tarde
age (n.)—la edad
agree (v.)—acordar
airplane (n.)—el avión
airport (n.)—el aeropuerto
alcoholic (n.)—el/la alcohólico,-a
alcoholism (n.)—el alcoholismo
all—todo,-a
alleluia—aleluya
allergic—ser alérgico,-a
allergy (n.)—la alergia
almighty—todopoderoso
also—también
altar (n.)—el altar
altercation (n.)—el altercado, la disputa
although—aunque
always—siempre
amen—amén
Amos—Amós
angel(s) (n.)—el ángel, los ángeles
angelic—angélico,-a
anger (n.)—la ira, el enojo
anger (v.)—enojar
anoint (v.)—ungir
anointed—ungido,-a
answer (n.)—la respuesta
answer (v.)—contestar
Antichrist (n.)—el Anticristo
Apocalypse (n.)—el apocalipsis
apostle (n.)—el apóstol
Apostle's Creed (n.)—el credo apostólico
appointment (n.)—la cita

appreciate (v.)—agradecer, apreciar
approve (v.)—aprobar
April—abril
Ark of the Covenant—la arca del pacto
arrival (n.)—la llegada
arrive (v.)—llegar
ascension (n.)—la ascensión
ask (v.)—pedir
at—a, en
atheist (n.)—el/la ateo,-a
atone (v.)—expiar
atonement (n.)—la expiación
attend (v.)—asistir a
attendance (n.)—la asistencia
August—agosto
aunt (n.)—la tía
avoid (v.)—evitar
awaken (v.)—despertarse
Babylonians—los Babilonios
back (n.)—la espalda
bad—mal/ malo,-a
bank (n.)—el banco
banquet (n.)—el banquete
baptism (n.)—el bautizo
Baptist (n.)—el/ la bautista
baptize (v.)—bautizar
Barnabas—Bernabé
Barrabas—Barrabás
bathe *(oneself)*(v.)—bañarse
be (v.)—ser, estar
be able to (v.)—poder
because—porque
before—antes de
beg (v.)—mendigar, pedir limosna
beggar (n.)—el/la mendigo,-a
begin (v.)—comenzar, empezar
behavior (n.)—la conducta
belief (n.)—la creencia
believe (v.)—creer

believer (n.)—el/la creyente
belong (v.)—pertenecer
belongings (n.)—las pertenencias
beloved—querido,-a
Benjamin—Benjamín
besides—además
Bethlehem—Belén
Bible (n.)—la Biblia
Bible studies (n.)—los estudios bíblicos
biblical—bíblico
bill (n.)—la cuenta
birth (v.)—dar a luz
bishop (n.)—el obispo
bitterness (n.)—la amargura
blame (n.)—la culpa
blame (v.)—culpar
blaspheme (v.)—blasfemar
blasphemous words—las palabras blasfemas
blasphemy (n.)—la blasfemia
bless (v.)—bendecir
blessed—*(a thing)* bendito,-a , *(a person)* bendecido,-a; dichoso,-a
blessing (n.)—la bendición
blood (n.)—la sangre
blue—azul
boast (v.)—jactarse
boasting (n.)—la jactancia
boat (n.)—el bote
body (n.)—el cuerpo
book (n.)—el libro
both—ambos,-as
boy (n.)—el chico, el muchacho
boyfriend (n.)—el novio *(fiancé)*
bread (n.)—el pan
break *(an object)* (v.)—romper, quebrantar
bribe (n.)—el soborno

bribe (v.)—sobornar
bride (n.)—la novia
bridegroom (n.)—el novio
bridesmaid (n.)—la madrina de boda
bring (v.)—traer
broken (*home*)—una familia dividida; (*person*) destrozado,-a, deshecho;*(object)* roto,-a, quebrado,-a
brother (n.)—el hermano
brute (n.)—la fiera
Buddist—budista
build (v.)—construir, edificar
building (n.)—el edificio
building fund—el fondo para la construcción
bulletin (n.)—el boletín
burden (n.)—la carga
burn (n.)—la quemadura
burn (v.)—quemar
bury (v.)—enterrar, sepultar
bus (n.)—el autobús
but—pero, sino
buy (v.)—comprar
Cain—Caín
call (v.)—llamar
call collect (v.)—llamar a cobro revertido
call together (v.)—convocar
Canaan—Canaán
car (n.)—el coche, el carro
card (n.)—la tarjeta
care (n.)—el cuidado
care *(to be concerned) (v.)*—preocuparse
care for*(someone)* (v.)—cuidar a
careful—cuidado
carry (v.)—llevar
cash (n.)—el efectivo, el dinero
cash (v.)—cobrar

Catholic—católico,-a
cease (v.)—cesar
cellphone (n.)—el teléfono celular
century (n.)—el siglo
challenge (n.)—el desafío
chance (n.)—la oportunidad
chapel (n.)—la capilla
chaperone (v.)—acompañar
chaplain (n.)—el capellán
chapter (n.)—el capítulo
character (n.)—el carácter
charge *(a price)* (v.)—cobrar, cargar
charge of (v.)—encargarse
charisma (n.)—el carisma
charity (n.)—la caridad
chat (v.)—charlar
cheat (v.)—engañar
cheating (n.)—el engaño
check *(money)* (n.)—el cheque
check (v.)—examinar, revisar
chest (n.)—el pecho
child (n.)—el niño, la niña
choice (n.)—el recurso
choir (n.)—el coro
chorus (n.)—el coro
chosen—elegido
Christ—Cristo
Christian—cristiano,-a
Christianity (n.)—el cristianismo
Christmas (n.)—la Navidad
Christmas Eve—la nochebuena
Chronicles—Crónicas
church (n.)—la iglesia
church bulletin—el boletín de la iglesia
circumcision (n.)—la circuncisión
city (n.)—la ciudad
class (n.)—la clase
clean—limpio,-a
cleanse (v.)—purgar

clinic (n.)—la clínica
close—cerca
close (v.)—cerrar
clothes (n.)—la ropa
cocaine (n.)—la cocaína
cold (n.)—el frío
collect (v.)—recolectar
Colossians—Colosenses
come (v.)—venir
come back (v.)—volver
comfort (n.)—el confort, el consuelo
comfort (v.)—confortar
comfortable—cómodo,-a
coming of Christ—el advenimiento
command (v.)—mandar
commandments (n.)—los mandamientos
commit (v.)—cometer
commit adultery (v.)—adulterar
commit suicide (v.)—suicidarse
commitment (n.)—la obligación
communion (n.)—la comunión
community (n.)—la comunidad, el vecindario
complain (v.)—quejarse
complaint (n.)—la queja
computer (n.)—el computador
concern (n.)—la preocupación
condemn (v.)—condenar
condemned—condenado,-a
conduct (n.)—la conducta
confess (v.)—confesar
confession (n.)—la confesión
confidence (n.)—la confianza
confirmation (n.)—la confirmación
conflict (n.)—el conflicto
congratulate (v.)—felicitar, congratular
congratulations (n.)—las felicitaciones

congregation (n.)—la congregación
conquer (v.)—vencer
conscience (n.)—la conciencia
console (v.)—consolar, confortar
construct (v.)—construir
converse (v.)—conversar
conversion (n.)—la conversión
convert (n.)—el/la converso,-a
convert (v.)—convertir
conviction (n.)—la convicción
Corinthians—Corintios
corrupt (v.)—corromper
corrupt—corrupto,-a, corrompido,-a
corruption (n.)—la corrupción
cost (n.)—el precio
cost (v.)—costar
couple (n.)—la pareja
courage (n.)—la virtud
cousin (n.)—el/la primo,-a
covenant (n.)—el pacto
cover (v.)—cubrir
covet (v.)—codiciar
covetous—codicioso,-a
cramp (n.)—el calambre
create (v.)—crear
creation (n.)—la creación
creator (n.)—el creador, la creadora
credit card (n.)—la tarjeta de crédito
crime (n.)—el crimen, el delito
cross (n.)—la cruz
crucified—crucificado,-a
crucifix (n.)—el crucifijo
crucifixion (n.)—la crucifixión
crucify (v.)—crucificar
cruel person (n.)—la fiera
cry (v.)—llorar
cult (n.)—la secta
cure (v.)—curar
curse (n.)—la maldición
curse (v.)—maldecir

custom (n.)—la costumbre
Customs *(office)* (n.)—la aduana
daily—cotidiano, diario,-a
danger (n.)—el peligro
Daniel—Daniel
daring—audaz
darkness (n.)—las tinieblas, la oscuridad
date *(time)* (n.)—la fecha
daughter (n.)—la hija
David—David
day (n.)—el día
deacon (n.)—el diácono
dead—muerto,-a
Dead Sea—el mar Muerto
death (n.)—la muerte, el fallecimiento
debt (n.)—la deuda
debtor (n.)—el deudor/la deudora
deceased—difunto,-a; fallecido,-a
deceive (v.)—engañar
December—diciembre
deception (n.)—el engaño
decide (v.)—acordar
declare (v.)—declarar
dedicate (v.)—consagrar a
deeds (n.)—las obras, las acciones
Delilah—Dalila
deliver from (v.)—librar
demand (v.)—exigir
denomination (n.)—la denominación
deny (v.)—negar, rechazar
departure (n.)—la salida
desert (n.)—el desierto
desire (n.)—el deseo
desire (v.)—anhelar, desear
desist (v.)—desistir
destroy (v.)—destruir, destrozar, arruinar
destruction (n.)—la destrucción

Deuteronomy—Deuteronomio
devil (n.)—el diablo
devotion (n.)—la devoción
devout—devoto,-a, piadoso,-a
die (v.)—morir, fallecer
different—diferente
difficult—difícil
difficulty (n.)—la dificultad
dine (v.)—cenar
direct (v.)—dirigir
direction (n.)—la dirección
dirty—sucio,-a
disagreement (n.)—el desacuerdo
disaster (n.)—el desastre
disciple (n.)—el/la discípulo,-a
discipline (n.)—la disciplina
discourage (v.)—desanimar
discuss (v.)—discutir
disease (n.)—la enfermedad
disobedience (n.)—la desobediencia
disobey (v.)—desobedecer
disorder (n.)—el trastorno
distance (v.)—alejar, distanciar
divine—divino
divorce (v.)—divorciar
dizzy—tener mareos
do (v.)—hacer
doctrine (n.)—la doctrina
document (n.)—el documento
donate (v.)—hacer una donación, donar
donation (n.)—la donación
door (n.)—la puerta
doubt (n.)—la duda
doubt (v.)—dudar
dream (n.)—el sueño
drink (n.)—la bebida
drink (v.)—beber, tomar
drive (v.)—conducir, manejar
drought (n.)—la sequía

drug abuse (n.)—la drogadicción
drug addict —el/la drogadicto,-a
during—durante
dwell (v.)—habitar
early—temprano
earth (n.)—la tierra
earthquake (n.)—el terremoto
east (n.)—el este
Easter (n.)—la Pascua
eat (v.)—comer
eat breakfast (v.)—desayunar
Ecclesiastes—Eclesiastés
Eden—Edén
educate (v.)—educar
Egypt—Egipto
Egyptians—Egipcios
eight—ocho
elder (n.)—el/la anciano,-a
elect (n.)—el elegido
elect (v.)—elegir
eleven—once
Eli—Elí
Elijah—Elías
Elisha—Eliseo
email (n.)—el correo electrónico
email (v.)—enviar un mensaje
    electrónico
embitter (v.)—amargar
embrace (v.)—abrazarse
emergency (n.)—la emergencia
emotion (n.)—la emoción
emotionally moving—
    conmovedor,-a
encourage (v.)—animar
encouragement (n.)—el ánimo,
end (n.)—el fin
end (v.)—terminar
enemy (n.)—el/la enemigo,-a
engaged—prometido,-a;
    comprometido,-a

engagement (n.)—el compromiso
English *(language)* (n.)—el inglés
enjoy (v.)—gozar
Enoch—Enoc
enslave (v.)—esclavizar
enter (v.)—entrar
entrance (n.)—la entrada
entrust (v.)—confiar en
envy (n.)—la envidia
envy (v.)—envidiar, codiciar
Ephesians—Efesios
Episcopal—episcopal
Esau—Esaú
escape (v.)—escapar, huir
escort (n.)—el/la acompañante
escort (v.)—escortar, acompañar
Esther—Ester
eternal—eterno,-a
eternal life (n.)—la vida eterna
eternity (n.)—la eternidad
Eucharist (n.)—la Eucaristía
eulogize (v.)—elogiar
eulogy (n.)—el elogio
evangelic—evangélico,-a
evangelism (n.)—el evangelismo
evangelize (v.)—evangelizar
Eve—Eva
even—hasta, todavía, aún
evening (n.)—la noche
evil—malo,-a
evil (n.)—la maldad, el mal
evil spirits—los espíritus malos
exact--exacto
exam (n.)—el examen
examine (v.)—probar, examinar
excellent—excelente
except—sino
exchange *(money)* (v.)—cambiar
    dinero
exile (n.)—el exilio

exile (v.)—exiliar
exit (n.)—la salida
Exodus—Éxodo
exorcist (n.)—el/la exorcista
explain (v.)—explicar
eye (n.)—el ojo
Ezekiel—Ezequiel
Ezra—Esdras
face (n.)—el rostro, la cara
fail (v.)—fracasar
failure (n.)—el fracaso
faith (n.)—la fe
faithful—fiel, leal
faithfully—fielmente, lealmente
faithfulness (n.)—la fidelidad, la
    lealtad
fall (n.)—el otoño
fall (v.)—caer
false—falso
false prophet—el/la profeta falso,-a
false witnesses—los testígos falsos
family (n.)—la familia
family counselors—los consejeros
    familiares
famine (n.)—el hambre
far—lejos
fast (n.)—el ayuno
fast (v.)—ayunar
fast and prayer—ayuno y oración
father (n.)—el padre
father-in-law (n.)—el suegro
fax (v.)—mandar por fax
fear (n.)—el miedo
fear for (v.)—temer por, tener miedo
February—febrero
feed (v.)—alimentar
feeling (n.)—el sentimiento
fellowship (n.)—el compañerismo
fever (n.)—la fiebre
fiancé (n.)—el novio

fiancée (n.)—la novia
fifteen—quince
fifty—cincuenta
fill (v.)—llenar
financing (n.)—el financiamiento
find (v.)—encontrar
finish (n.)—el fin
finish (v.)—terminar
first—primero
fish (n.)—el pez
five—cinco
fix (v.)—arreglar *(repair)*, fijar
    (position)
flee (v.)—huir
flood (n.)—la inundación, el diluvio
    (biblical)
flu (n.)—el gripe
fly (v.)—volar
focus (n.)—el enfoque
follow (v.)—seguir
follower (n.)—el seguidor, la
    seguidora
following—siguiente
food (n.)—la comida, el alimento
fool (n.)—el/la tonto,-a; el/la
    necio,-a
fool (v.)—engañar
foot (n.)—el pie
for—para, por
forbid (v.)—prohibir
forgive (v.)—perdonar
forgiveness (n.)—el perdón
forty—cuarenta
four—cuatro
fourteen—catorce
free (v.)—librar
free—gratis
freedom (n.)—la libertad
Friday—el viernes
friend (n.)—el/la amigo,-a

friendship (n.)—la amistad
from—desde, de
Fruit of the Spirit—el fruto del Espíritu
fulfill (v.)—cumplir
fulfillment (n.)—el cumplimiento
full—pleno,-a
fund (n.)—el fondo
fundraising (n.)—el levantar fondos
funds available—fondos disponibles
funeral (n.)—el funeral, fúnebre
funeral home (n.)—la funeraria
funeral service—el servicio funerario
future (n.)—el futuro
gain (v.)—ganar
Galatians—Gálatas
Galilee—Galilea
gamble (v.)—apostar
gambling (n.)—el juego con apuestas
gambling debt—la deuda de juego
garbage (n.)—la basura
garden (n.)—el huerto *(vegetable)* el jardín *(flower)*
Garden of Eden—el huerto/jardín del Edén
gas station (n.)—el gasolinera
gather (v.)—recoger
generally—generalmente
Genesis—Génesis
gentiles—los gentiles
gentleness (n.)—la ternura
Gethsemane—Getsemaní
giant (n.)—el gigante
Gideon—Gedeón
gift (n.)—el regalo, el don
gift of tongues—el don de las lenguas
gifted—talentoso,-a
gifts of the Spirit—los dones espirituales

girl (n.)—la niña, la muchacha
girlfriend (n.)—la amiga
give (v.)—dar
give testimony (v.)—dar testimonio
give the blessing (v.)—dar la bendición
giver (n.)—el dador, la dadora
gloomy—tenebroso,-a
glorify (v.)—glorificar, alabar
glory (n.)—la gloria
go (v.)—ir
God—Dios
godchild (n.)—el/la ahijado,-a
godfather (n.)—el padrino
godmother (n.)—la madrina
gold (n.)—el oro
Goliath—Goliat
Gomorrah—Gomorra
good—buen; bueno,-a; buenos,-as
Good Friday—el Viernes Santo
goodness (n.)—la bondad
gospel (n.)—el evangelio
gossip (n.)—el chisme
gossip (v.)—chismear
go to bed (v.)—acostarse
grace (n.)—la gracia
granddaughter (n.)—la nieta
grandfather (n.)—el abuelo
grandmother (n.)—la abuela
grandson (n.)—el nieto
grant (v.)—conceder
grave (n.)—la sepultura
greed (n.)—la codicia
greedy—codicioso,-a
greetings (n.)—los saludos
grief (n.)—la pena, el dolor
grieve (v.)—lamentar
groom (n.)—el novio
grow (v.)—crecer
growth (n.)—el crecimiento

guest (n.)—el/la huésped,-a
guide (v.)—guiar
guilt (n.)—la culpa
guilty—culpable
Habakkuk—Habacuc
Hades—Hades
Hagar—Agar
Haggai—Hageo
hand (n.)—la mano
happy—feliz
harvest (v.)—cosechar
haste (n.)—la prisa
hate (v.)—odiar
have (v.)—tener
he—él
head (n.)—la cabeza
heal (v.)—sanar
health (n.)—la salud
hear (v.)—oír
heart (n.)—el corazón
heat (n.)—el calor
heaven (n.)—el cielo
Heavenly Father—el Padre celestial
Hebrews—Hebreos
Hell (n.)—el infierno
help (n.)—la ayuda, el socorro
help (v.)—ayudar
helper (n.)—el/la ayudante
here—aquí
heresy (n.)—la herejía
Herod—Herodes
hide (v.)—esconder
high priest—el sumo sacerdote
Hindu—hindú
holiday (n.)—el día de feriado
holiness (n.)—la santidad
holy—santo,-a; sagrado,-a
Holy Land—la Tierra Santa
Holy Spirit—El Espíritu Santo
Holy Trinity—la Santísima Trinidad

holy water—el agua bendita
Holy Week—la Semana Santa
home (n.)—la casa, el hogar
homeless—los sin techo, los sin hogar, los sin vivienda
homeless shelter—la casa de refugio
homosexual (n.)—el/la homosexual
homosexuality (n.)—la homosexualidad
honeymoon (n.)—la luna de miel
honor (n.)—el honor, la honra
honor (v.)—honrar
hope (n.)—la esperanza
hope (v.)—esperar
Hosea—Oseas
hospital (n.)—el hospital
host (n.)—el/la huésped,-a
hotel (n.)—el hotel
hour (n.)—la hora
house (n.)—la casa, la vivienda
however—sin embargo
human nature—la naturaleza humana
humanitarian—humanitaria
humble—humilde
humiliation (n.)—la humillación
humility (n.)—la humildad
hundred—ciento, cien
hunger (n.)—el hambre
hunger (v.)—tener hambre
hungry—hambriento,-a
hurricane (n.)—el huracán
hurt (v.)—doler
husband (n.)—el esposo, el marido
hymn (n.)—el himno
hymn book—el himnario
hypocrisy (n.)—la hipocresía
hypocrite (n.)—el/la hipócrita
I—yo
idol (n.)—el ídolo

idolatry (n.)—la idolatría
illegal—ilegal
illegal resident—indocumentado, a
illness (n.)—la enfermedad
immigrant (n.)—el/la inmigrante
immigrant community—la comunidad de inmigrantes
immortal—inmortal
important—importante
in—en
influence (n.)—la influencia
influence (v.)—influir
inherit (v.)—heredar
inheritance (n.)—la herencia
innocent—inocente
instead—en lugar de
instill (v.)—infundir
insult (v.)—insultar
integrity (n.)—la integridad
intercede (v.)—interceder con
intercession (n.)—la intercesión
intercessor (n.)—el/la intercesor,-a
interpret (v.)—interpretar
interpretation (n.)—la interpretación
interpreter (n.)—el/la intérprete
intoxicate/ become intoxicated (v.)—emborrachar
invitation (n.)—la invitación
invite (v.)—invitar
Isaac—Isaac
Isaiah—Isaías
Ishmael—Ismael
Israel—Israel
Israelite—Israelita
Jacob—Jacob
James—Santiago
January—enero
jealousy (n.)—los celos
Jehovah—Jehová

Jehovah's Witness—el testigo de Jehová
Jeremiah—Jeremías
Jericho—Jericó
Jerusalem—Jerusalén
Jesus—Jesús
Jesus Christ—Jesucristo
Jews—los judíos
Job—Job
Joel—Joel
John—Juan
John the Baptist—Juan el Bautista
Jonah—Jonás
Jonathan—Jonatán
Jordan—Jordán
Joseph—José
Joshua—Josué
joy (n.)—la alegría, el gozo
joyful—alegre
joyfully—alegremente
Judah—Judá
Judas—Judas
Jude—Judas
judge (v.)—juzgar
Judges—Jueces
judgment (n.)—la sentencia, el juicio
Judgment Day—el día del juicio final
July—julio
June—junio
juvenile—juvenil
keep (v.)—guardar
kidnap (v.)—secuestrar
kill (v.)—matar
killer (n.)—asesino,-a
kind—amable
kindness (n.)—la bondad, la amabilidad
king (n.)—el rey
kingdom (n.)—el reino
Kings—Reyes

kneel (v.)—arrodillarse

knock *(on the door)* (v.)—llamar a la puerta

know (v.)—conocer, saber

knowledge (n.)—el conocimiento

lack (n.)—la falta

lack (v.)—faltar

Lamb of God—el cordero de Dios

Lamentations—Lamentaciones

lamp (n.)—la lámpara

language (n.)—el idioma

last night—anoche

late—-tarde

later—luego, más tarde

laugh (v.)—reír

Law of Moses—la ley de Moisés

layman (n.)—el/la seglar

Lazarus—Lázaro

lazy—perezoso,-a

lead (v.)—conducir

leader (n.)—el líder

leadership team—el equipo de líderes

learn (v.)—aprender

leave *(a place)* (v.)—salir

leaven (n.)—la levadura

Lebanon—Líbano

left—a la izquierda

Lent (n.)—la Cuaresma

less—menos

lesson (n.)—la lección

letter (n.)—la carta

level (n.)—el nivel

level (v.)—allanar, nivelar

Leviticus—Levítico

lie (n.)—la mentira

lie (v.)—mentir

life (n.)—la vida

light (n.)—la luz

light—liviano,-a, ligero,-a

like—como

like (v.)—gustar

listen (v.)—escuchar

live (v.)—vivir

lodge (v.)—hospedar *(a guest)*

look at (v.)—mirar

Lord—el Señor

Lord Jesus—el Señor Jesús

Lord's prayer—el Padrenuestro

Lord's Supper—la santa cena

lose (v.)—perder

loss (n.)—la pérdida

lost—perdido,-a

Lot—Lot

lottery (n.)—la lotería

love (n.)—el amor

love *(each other)* (v.)—amarse

love *(someone)* (v.)—amar

loving—amoroso,-a

loyal—leal, fiel

loyally—lealmente

loyalty (n.)—la lealtad

luck (n.)—la suerte

Luke—Lucas

lust (n.)—la lujuria

lust (v.)—lujuriar

Lutheran—luterano,-a

luxury (n.)—el lujo

magic (n.)—la magia

mail (n.)—el correo

majesty (n.)—la majestad

make (v.)—hacer

make the sign of the cross (v.)—persignarse

Malachi—Malaquías

man (n.)—el hombre

many—mucho,-a *(sing.)*; muchos,-as *(pl.)*

map (n.)—el mapa

March—marzo

Visit us at www.SpanishForChristianService.com

marijuana (n.)—la marihuana
Mark—Marcos
marriage (n.)—el casamiento
marriage license—la licencia de
   matrimonio
married *(person)*—casado,-a
marry (v.)—casarse con
Martha—Marta
Mary—María
Mary Magdalene—María Magdalena
mass (n.)—la misa
materialism (n.)—el materialismo
materials (n.)—los materiales
matrimony (n.)—el matrimonio
Matthew—Mateo
May—mayo
medication (n.)—el medicamento
meek—manso,-a
meekness (n.)—la mansedumbre
meet (v.)—encontrar, reunir, quedar
member *(of the church)*(n.)—el/la
   miembro,-a *(de la iglesia)*
mend (v.)—coser
Mennonite—menonita
merciful—misericordioso,-a
mercy (n.)—la misericordia
Messiah (n.)—el Mesías
Messianic—mesiánico,-a
Methodist (n.)—el/ la metodista
Micah—Miqueas
midnight (n.)—la medianoche
mind (n.)—el mente
minister (n.)—el/la pastor,-a
ministry (n.)—el ministerio
miracle (n.)—el milagro, el prodigio
mirror (n.)—el espejo
misfortune (n.)—la desdicha, la
   desgracia
mission (n.)—la misión
missionary (n.)—el/la misionero,-a

mister (n.)—el señor
mistreat (v.)—maltratar
Monday—el lunes
money (n.)—el dinero
monk (n.)—el monje
month (n.)—el mes
more—más
morning (n.)—la mañana
Moses—Moisés
Most High—Altísimo,-a
mother (n.)—la madre
mother-in-law (n.)—la suegra
motivate (v.)—motivar
motor-taxi (n.)—el mototaxi
Mount Olive—monte de los olivos
mourn (v.)—lamentar
mouth (n.)—la boca
move (v.)—mover
movie (n.)—el cine, la película
much—mucho,-a
mud (n.)—el lodo
murder (n.)—el asesinato, el
   homicidio
murder (v.)—asesinar, matar
music (n.)—la música
mystery (n.)—el misterio
Nahum—Nahúm
nail (n.)—el clavo
nail (v.)—clavar
nailed—clavado
name (n.)—el nombre
Naomi—Noemí
nauseous—tener náusea
Nazareth—Nazaret
near (v.)—acercarse
near—cerca *(a place)*, acerca *(a time)*
Nebuchadnezzar—Nabucodonosor
necessary—necesario
need (n.)—la necesidad
need (v.)—necesitar

neglect (n.)—la negligencia, el descuido

neglect (v.)—descuidar

Nehemiah—Nehemías

neighbor (n.)—prójimo,-a; vecino,-a

nephew (n.)—el sobrino

never—nunca

new—nuevo,-a

news (n.)—las noticias

next—próximo,-a

nice—amable

Nicodemus—Nicodemo

niece (n.)—la sobrina

night (n.)—la noche

nine—nueve

Noah—Noé

Noah's ark—la arca de Noé

no one—nadie, ningún, ninguno,-a

noon (n.)—el mediodía

north (n.)—el norte

nothing—nada

November—noviembre

now—ahora

Numbers—Números

nun (n.)—la monja

nursery (n.)—el cuarto de los niños

oath (n.)—el juramento

Obadiah—Abdías

obedience (n.)—la obedencia

obey (v.)—obedecer

observe (v.)—observar

obstacle (n.)—el obstáculo

occur (v.)—ocurrir, suceder

October—octubre

offense (n.)—la ofensa

offering (n.)—la ofrenda

old—viejo,-a

older—mayor

omnipotent—omnipotente, todopoderoso,-a

omnipresent—omnipresente

omniscient—omnisciente

on—en, sobre

one—un; uno,-a

only—solamente

only begotten—unigénito,-a

open (v.)—abrir

opportunity (n.)—la oportunidad

option (n.)—el recurso

order (n.)—el/la orden

organize (v.)—organizar

orientation (n.)—la orientación

orphan (n.)—el/la huérfano,-a

orphanage (n.)—el orfanato

Orthodox—ortodoxo

overcome (v.)—vencer

overflow (v.)—rebosar

owe (v.)—deber

own—propio

pagan (n.)—el/la pagano,-a

pain (n.)—el dolor

Palm Sunday—Domingo de Ramos

paper (n.)—el papel

parable (n.)—la parábola

pardon (n.)—el perdón

pardon (v.)—perdonar

parents (n.)—los padres

parole (n.)—la libertad condicional, la probatoria

party (n.)—la fiesta

Passover (n.)—la Pascua de los judíos

passport (n.)—el pasaporte

past—pasado,-a

pastor (n.)—el/la pastor,-a

pasture (n.)—el pasto

path (n.)—la senda, el camino, el sendero

patience (n.)—la paciencia

Paul—Pablo

pay (v.)—pagar
peace (n.)—la paz
peaceful—tranquilo, -a
pen (n.)—la pluma, el bolígrafo
penance (n.)—la penitencia
Pentateuch (n.)—el pentateuco
Pentecost (n.)— el Pentecostés
Pentecostal—de pentecostés
people (n.)—la gente
permit (v.)—permitir
persecute (v.)—perseguir
persecution (n.)—la persecución
perseverance (n.)—la perseverancia
persevere (v.)—perseverar
persist (v.)—persistir
persistence (n.)—la persistencia
perverse—perverso,-a
Peter—Pedro
pew (n.)—el banco
pharaoh (n.)—el faraón
Pharisee—fariseo
pharmacy (n.)—la farmacia
Philemon—Filemón
Philip—Felipe
Philippians—Filipenses
Philistine—filisteo
phone (n.)—el teléfono
phone (v.)—llamar por teléfono
phone card (n.)—la tarjeta de
    telefónica
physically—físicamente
pious—piadoso,-a
place (n.)—el sitio, el lugar
place (v.)—poner
plan (n.)—el plan
plant (v.)—plantar
planter (n.)—el/la sembrador,-a
play (v.)—jugar
pleasure (n.)—el gusto
police (n.)—la policía

political asylum—el asilo político
Pontius Pilate—Poncio Pilato
poor (n.)—el pobre
pope (n.)—el papa
pornography (n.)—la pornografía
Portuguese *(language)* (n.)—el
    portugués
post office (n.)—el correo
Potiphar—Potifar
poverty (n.)—la pobreza
power (n.)—el poder
praise (n.)—la alabanza
praise (v.)—alabar, elogiar
praising God—alabando a Dios
pray (v.)—orar, rezar (*Catholic*)
prayer (n.)—la oración
prayer team—el equipo de oración
preach (v.)—predicar
preacher (n.)—el/la predicador, -a
pregnancy (n.)—el embarazo
pregnant—encinta
prepare (v.)—preparar, disponer
Presbyterian—presbiteriano,-a
present (v.)—presentar
pride (n.)—el orgullo
priest (n.) *(Catholic)*—el sacerdote
priestess (n.)—la sacerdotisa
primarily—primeramente
prison (n.)—la cárcel, la prisión
prison officer—el/la carcelero,-a
prisoner (n.)—el/la preso,-a
privilege (n.)—el privilegio
problem (n.)—el problema
proceeds (n.)—las ganancias, los
    beneficios
prodigal (n.)—el/la pródigo,-a
program (n.)—el programa
promise (n.)—la promesa
promise (v.)—prometer
pronounce (v.)—pronunciar

prophecy (n.)—la profecía
prophesy (v.)—-profetizar
prophet (n.)—el profeta
prostitute (n.)—la prostituta
prostitute (v.)—prostituirse
prostitution (n.)—la prostitución
protect (v.)—proteger
protection (n.)—la protección
Protestant—protestante
Proverbs—Proverbios
provide (v.)—proveer
provision (n.)—la provisión
Psalms—Salmos
punish (v.)—castigar
pure—puro, -a
purgatory (n.)—el purgatorio
purity (n.)—la pureza
purpose (n.)—el propósito
put (v.)—poner
Quaker—cuáquero,-a
question (n.)—la pregunta
rabbi (n.)—el rabí
Rachel—Raquel
rain (n.)—la lluvia
raise *(from the dead)* (v.)—
    resucitar
rape (n.)—la violación
rape (v.)—violar
rapid—rápido,-a
rapidly—rápidamente
rapist (n.)—el/la violador,-a
rapture (n.) *(of the church)*—el rapto
    (de la iglesia)
read (v.)—leer
reason (n.)—la razón
Rebecca—Rebeca
rebelliousness (n.)—la rebeldía
receive (v.)—recibir
recovery (n.)—la recuperación
Red Cross—la cruz roja

redeem (v.)—redimir, salvar
Redeemer (n.)—el Redentor
redemption (n.)—la redención
Red Sea—Mar Rojo
rejoice (v.)—regocijar
relate (v.)—relacionar
related—relacionado,-a
relationship (n.)—la relación
relative (n.)—el pariente, la parienta
relief (n.)—el alivio
religion (n.)—la religión
religious—religioso,-a
remain (v.)—permanecer, quedar
remember (v.)—recordar, acordar
remove (v.)—sacar
repeat (v.)—repetir
repent (v.)—arrepentirse de
repentance (n.)—el arrepentimiento
require (v.)—necesitar, exigir,
    requerir
resist (v.)—rechazar
respect (n.) —el respeto
respect (v.)—respetar, honrar
rest (n.)—el descanso
rest (v.)—descansar
restaurant (n.)—el restaurante
restoration (n.)—la restauración
restore (v.)—restaurar
restroom (n.)—el cuarto de baño
resurrection (n.)—la resurrección
retreat (n.)—el retiro
return (v.)—regresar, volver
Reuben—Rubén
revelation (n.)—la revelación
Revelation—Apocalipsis
reverence (n.)—la reverencia
reverend—reverendo,-a
reward (n.)—la recompensa
rich—rico,-a
riches (n.)—las riquezas

Visit us at www.SpanishForChristianService.com

right *(legal term)*—derecho
right *(side)*—derecha
right and wrong—el bien y el mal
righteousness (n.)—la rectitud
road (n.)—el camino
rob (v.)—robar
robber (n.)—el ladrón, la ladrona
rod (n.)—la vara
role (n.)—el papel
Romans—Romanos
rosary (n.)—el rosario
roundtrip—de ida y vuelta
ruin (v.)—arruinar
run (v.)—correr
run up debts (v.)—endeudarse
Ruth—Rut
Sabbath (n.)—el sábado
sacrament (n.)—el sacramento
sacred—sagrado,-a
sacrifice (n.)—el sacrificio
sacrifice (v.)—sacrificar
sacrilege (n.)—el sacrilegio
sad—triste
sadness (n.)—la tristeza
safe—salvo,-a
saint (n.)—el/la santo,-a
salvation (n.)—la salvación
samaritan (n.)—el/la samaritano,-a
Samson—Sansón
Samuel—Samuel
sanctification (n.)—la santificación
sanctify (v.)—santificar
sanctuary (n.)—el santuario
Sarah—Sara
Satan (n.)—Satán, Satanás
Satanic—satánico,-a
Saturday—el sábado
Saul—Saúl *(king),* Saulo *(Paul)*
save *(a soul, a life)* (v.)—salvar
Savior (n.)—el Salvador

say (v.)—decir
say goodbye (v.)—despedirse
scatter (v.)—esparcir
schedule of services—el horario de servicios
scholarship (n.)—la beca
school (n.)—la escuela
scripture (n.)—la escritura
sea (n.)—el mar
seal (v.)—sellar
search (v.)—buscar, intentar
secretary (n.)—el/la secretario,-a
security (n.)—la seguridad
see (v.)—ver
seed (n.)—la semilla
seek (v.)—buscar
seeker (n.)—el/la buscador,-a
self-control—dominio propio
selfish—egoísta
send (v.)—enviar, mandar
September—septiembre
servant (n.)—el sirviente, la sirvienta
serve (v.)—servir
service (n.)—el servicio
Seth—Set
seven—siete
shame (n.)—la vergüenza
shame (v.)—avergonzar
share (n.)—la parte, la porción
share (v.)—compartir
shave (v.)—afeitarse
she—ella
shelter (n.)—el refugio
shelter (v.)—refugiar
shepherd (n.)—el pastor
shop (n.)—la tienda
shop (v.)—ir de compras
show (v.)—enseñar
sickness (n.)—la enfermedad
side (n.)—el lado

signs & wonders—señales y maravillas
silence (v.)—callar
sin (n.)—el pecado
sin (v.)—pecar
since—pues, desde
single *(person)*—soltero,-a
sinner (n.)—el pecador, la pecadora
sister (n.)—la hermana
sit (v.)—sentarse
situation (n.)—la situación
six—seis
slander (v.)—maldecir
slave (n.)—el/la esclavo,-a
sleep (v.)—dormir
slow—lento,-a
slowly—lentamente, despacio
smile (n.)—la sonrisa
smile (v.)—sonreír
smoke (v.)—fumar
snow (n.)—la nieve
soap (n.)—el jabón
sobriety (n.)—la sobriedad
Sodom—Sodoma
Solomon—Salomón
some—unos, unas
someone—alguien
something—algo
son (n.)—el hijo
Song of Solomon—Cantares
Son of man—el hijo de hombre
soon—pronto
sorcerer (n.)—el mago, el brujo
sorceress (n.)—la bruja
sorcery (n.)—la brujería
sorrow (n.)—la tristeza
soul (n.)—el alma, el ánimo
soul-searching—el examen de conciencia
south (n.)—el sur

sovereign—soberano,-a
sovereignty (n.)—la soberanía
sow (v.)—sembrar
sower (n.)—el sembrador, la sembradora
Spanish *(language)* (n.)—el español
speak (v.)—hablar
spirit (n.)—el espíritu
spiritual—espiritual
spiritual warfare—la guerra espiritual
spirituality (n.)—la espiritualidad
sponsor (n.)—el patrocinador, la patrocinadora
sponsor (v.)—patrocinar
spouse (n.)—el/la marido,-a; el/la esposo,-a
spring (n.)—la primavera
staff *(member)* (n.)—el personal, el líder
staff *(rod)* (n.)—la vara
standard (n.)—el nivel
starvation (n.)—el hambre
starve (v.)—privar de comida, pasar hambre
statue (n.)—la estatua
steal (v.)—robar
stigma (n.)—el estigma
still *(calm)*—tranquilo,-a
still *(even)*—todavía
stomach (n.)—el estómago
stone (n.)—la piedra
store (n.)—la tienda
storm (n.)—la tempestad, la tormenta
straight *(ahead)*—derecho
strange—extraño
street (n.)—la calle
strength (n.)—la fuerza
strengthen (v.)—fortalecer

student (n.)—el/la estudiante
study (v.)—estudiar
submission (n.)—la sumisión
submit (v.)—someter a, rendirse
success (n.)—el éxito
sue (v.)—demandar
suffer (v.)—sufrir, padecer
suffering (n.)—el sufrimiento
suicide (n.)—el suicidio
suitcase (n.)—la maleta
summer (n.)—el verano
Sunday—el domingo
Sunday school (n.)—la escuela dominical
supernatural—sobrenatural
supply (n.)—la existencia, las reservas
supply (v.)—proveer, suplir
support (n.)—el apoyo
support (v.)—apoyar
surrender (v.)—rendirse, someter a
survive (v.)—sobrevivir
survivor (n.)—el/la sobreviviente
swallow (v.)—tragar
swear (v.)—jurar
swift—veloz
swiftly—velozmente
synagogue (n.)—la sinagoga
system (n.)—el sistema
tabernacle (n.)—el tabernáculo
take (v.)—tomar, llevar
talk (v.)—hablar, conversar con, charlar
taxi (n.)—el taxi
teach (v.)—enseñar
teacher (n.)—el/la maestro,-a
team (n.)—el equipo
tear (v.)—rasgar
telephone (n.)—el teléfono

telephone (v.)—telefonear
tell (v.)—decir, contar
temple (n.)—el templo
temporarily—temporeramente
tempt (v.)—tentar
temptation (n.)—la tentación
tempter (n.)—el tentador, la tentadora
ten—diez
tender—tierno,-a
terrestial—terrenal
test (v.)—probar, examinar
testify (v.)—testificar, declarar
testimony (n.)—el testimonio
thank (v.)—agradecer a
thankful—agradecido,-a
Thanksgiving (n.)—el día de Acción de Gracias
theater (n.)—el cine
then—entonces
therapist (n.)—el/la terapeuta
therapy (n.)—la terapia
there—allí
Thessalonians—Tesalonicenses
they—ellos, ellas
thief (n.)—el ladrón, la ladrona
thing (n.)—la cosa
think (v.)—pensar
thirst (n.)—la sed
thirteen—trece
thirty—treinta
thought (n.)—la idea
thousand—mil
threat (n.)—la amenaza
threaten (v.)—amenazar
three—tres
throne (n.)—el trono
throne of God—el trono de Dios
through—a través de
throw away (v.)—desechar

Thursday—el jueves
ticket (n.)—el boleto
time (n.)—el tiempo
time (n.)—la vez *(in a series)*
timidity (n.)—la timidez
Timothy—Timoteo
tired—cansado,-a
tithe (v.)—diezmar
tithing (n.)—el diezmo
Titus—Tito
to—a
today (n.)—hoy
together—junto,-a
tolerant—tolerante
tolerate (v.)—aguantar
tomb (n.)—la sepultura
tomorrow (n.)—la mañana
tonight (n.)—esta noche
towel (n.)—la toalla
tragedy (n.)—la tragedia
tragic—trágico,-a
train (n.)—el tren
tranquil—tranquilo,-a
trash (n.)—la basura
travel (v.)—viajar
traveller's check (n.)—el cheque de
   viajero
trials (n.)—las aflicciones
tribulation (n.)—la tribulación
Trinity (n.)—la Trinidad
trust (n.)—la confianza
trust (v.)—confiar en
truth (n.)—la verdad
Tuesday—el martes
turn (n.)—la vuelta
turn (v.)—dar la vuelta
twelve—doce
twenty—veinte
two—dos
unbeliever (n.)—el/la incrédulo,-a

uncle (n.)—el tío
under—debajo
understand (v.)—comprender
unfaithful—infiel
Unitarian—unitario,-a
unite (v.)—unirse, juntarse
United States—los estados unidos
unity (n.)—la unidad
until—hasta
upset (n.)—el trastorno
upset (v.)—trastornar
use (v.)—usar
usher (n.)—el ujier
vacation (v.)—estar de vacaciones
valley (n.)—el valle
vengeance (n.)—la venganza
verse (n.)—el versículo
very—muy
vice (n.)—el vicio, la mala costumbre
victim (n.)—la víctima
victorious—victorioso,-a
violence (n.)—la violencia
violent—violento
virgin (n.)—la virgen
virtue (n.)—la virtud
vision (n.)—la visión
visit (v.)—visitar
volunteer (n.)—el/la voluntario,-a
volunteer (v.)—ofrecerse como
   voluntario
vow (n.)—el voto
wait (v.)—esperar
walk (v.)—caminar
want (v.)—querer
war (n.)—la guerra
warn (v.)—avisar
warning (n.)—la advertencia, el aviso
wash (v.)—lavar
waste (v.)—derrochar
wasteful—pródigo,-a

watch (v.)—observar
water (n.)—el agua *(fem.)*
we—nosotros, nosotras
weak—débil
weakness (n.)—la debilidad
weary—cansado,-a
wed (v.)—casarse con
wedding (n.)—la boda, el casamiento
Wednesday—el miércoles
week (n.)—la semana
weekend (n.)—el fin de semana
welcome (v.)—darle la bienvenida
welcome—bienvenido,-a
welfare work—el trabajo social
well—bien
well-being (n.)—el bienestar
west (n.)—el oeste
what—que
what?—¿qué?
where?—¿dónde?
where—donde
which—cual, cuales
which?—¿cuál?, ¿cuáles?
who—quien
who?—¿quién?, ¿quiénes?
why?—¿por qué?
wicked—malo,-a
wickedness (n.)—la maldad
widow (n.)—la viuda
widower (n.)—el viudo
wife (n.)—la esposa, la mujer
will *(of God)* (n.)—la voluntad *(de Dios)*
wine (n.)—el vino
winter (n.)—el invierno
wisdom (n.)—la sabiduría
wise—sabio,-a
wisemen (n.)—los magos
wish (n.)—el deseo
wish (v.)—desear

with—con
without—sin
witness (n.)—el/la testigo
woman (n.)—la mujer
word (n.)—la palabra
Word *(of God)*—el Verbo *(de Dios)*
work (n.)—la obra, el trabajo
work (v.)—trabajar
work miracles (v.)—hacer milagros
work wonders (v.)—hacer maravillas
world (n.)—el mundo
worldliness (n.)—el mundanería
worry (n.)—la preocupación
worship (n.)—la adoración
worship (v.)—adorar, venerar *(more often used in the Catholic faith)*
worshipper (n.)—el adorador, la adoradora
write (v.)—escribir
year (n.)—el año
yearn (v.)—anhelar
yearning (n.)—el anhelo
yeast (n.)—la levadura
yesterday—ayer
yoke (n.)—el yugo
you—tú *(fam.)*; usted *(sing.form.)*; ustedes *(pl. form.)*
young—joven
youth group—el grupo de jóvenes
Zacchaeus—Zaqueo
Zechariah—Zacarías
Zephaniah—Sofonías
Zion—Sion

Vocabulario/Vocabulary

(Spanish To English)

a—to, for
Aarón—Aaron
Abdías—Obadiah
Abel—Abel
abismo (n.)—abyss
abominación (n.)—abomination
abortar (v.)—to have an abortion, abort
aborto (n.)—abortion
Abraham—Abraham
abrazarse (v.)—to embrace, hug
abril—April
abrir (v.)—to open
abstenerse (v.)—abstain
abstinencia (n.)—abstinence
abuela (n.)—grandmother
abuelo (n.)—grandfather
abusar de (v.)—to abuse *(drugs)*
abuso (n.)—abuse
accidente (n.)—accident
aceptar (v.)—to accept, approve
acerca de—about, concerning
acercar (v.)—to get or bring near
acompañante (n.)—escort
acompañar (v.)—to chaperone
acordar (v.)—to agree
acostarse (v.)—to go to bed
acusación (n.)—accusation
acusar (v.)—to accuse
Adán—Adam
además—besides
adicción (n.)—addiction
adicto,-a (n.)—addict
adopción (n.)—adoption
adoptar (v.)—to adopt *(an approach, or adopt a child)*

adorable—adorable
adoración (n.)—worship, adoration
adorador,-a (n.)—worshipper
adorar (v.)—to adore, worship
adorno (n.)—adornment
aduana (n.)—customs, customs office
adulterar (v.)—to commit adultery
adulterio (n.)—adultery
adulto,-a—adult
advenimiento (n.)—coming of Christ, Advent
adventista—Adventist
adversidad (n.)—adversity
advertencia (n.)—warning
adviento (n.)—Advent
adviso (n.)—notice, warning
aeropuerto (n.)—airport
afeitarse (v.)—to shave
aflicción (n.)—affliction, trial, grief
afligir (v.)—to afflict
afligirse (v.)—to grieve
Agar—Hagar
agosto—August
agradecer a (v.)—to thank
agradecido,-a—thankful
agua (n.)—water
aguantar (v.)—to tolerate, hold
ahijado,-a (n.)—godchild
ahijar (v.)—to adopt *(a child)*
ahora—now
al *(=a+el)*—to the
alabando a Dios—praising God
alabanza (n.)—praise
alabar (v.)—to glorify, to praise
alcohólico,-a—alcoholic
alcoholismo (n.)—alcoholism

alegre—joyful
alegremente—joyfully
alegría (n.)—joy
alejar (v.)—to distance
aleluya—alleluia
alergia (n.)—allergy
alérgico,-a—allergic
algo—something
alguien—someone
alimentar (v.)—to feed
alimento (n.)—food
alivio (n.)—relief
allá—over there
allanar (v.)—to level, to smooth
allí—there
alma (n.)—soul
altar (n.)—altar
altercado (n.)—altercation
Altísimo,-a—Most High
amabilidad (n.)—kindness
amable—nice, kind
amar (v.)—to love *(someone)*
amargar (v.)—to embitter
amargura (n.)—bitterness
amarse (v.)—to love *(each other)*
ambos,-as—both
amén—amen
amenaza (n.)—threat
amenazar (v.)—to threaten
amigo,-a (n.)—friend
amistad (n.)—friendship
amor (n.)—love
Amós—Amos
anciano,-a (n.)—elder
ángel (n.)—angel
angélico,-a—angelic
anhelar (v.)—to yearn, to desire
anhelo (n.)—yearning, desire
animar (v.)—to encourage
ánimo (n.)—soul, spirit, encouragement

anoche—last night
ansia (n.)—anxiety
antes de—before
Anticristo (n.)—Antichrist
año (n.)—year
apenar (v.)—to aggrieve, afflict
apocalipsis (n.)—Apocalypse, Revelation
apostar (v.)—to gamble
apóstol (n.)—apostle
apoyar (v.)—to support
apoyo (n.)—support, backing
aprender (v.)—to learn
aquél—that one *(masc.)*
aquélla—that one *(fem.)*
aquéllas—those ones *(fem.)*
aquéllos—those ones *(masc.)*
aquí—here
arca de Noé—Noah's ark
arca del pacto—Ark of the Covenant
arreglar (v.)—to fix
arrepentimiento (n.)—repentance
arrepentirse de (v.)—to repent of
arrodillarse (v.)—to kneel
arruinar (v.)—to ruin, to destroy
ascensión (n.)—ascension
asesinar (v.)—to kill, murder
asesinato (n.)—murder
asesino,-a (n.)—killer
asilo (n.)—asylum
asilo político—political asylum
asistencia (n.)—attendance
asistir a (v.)—attend
ateo,-a (n.)—atheist
a través de—through
audaz—daring
aún—even, still
aunque—although
autobús (n.)—bus
avergonzar (v.)—to shame, embarrass

avión (n.)—airplane
avisar (v.)—to warn
ayer—yesterday
ayuda (n.)—help, assistance
ayudante (n.)—helper
ayudar (v.)—to help
ayunar (v.)—to fast
ayuno (n.)—fast
ayuno y oración (n.)—fast and
    prayer
azul—blue
Babilonios—Babylonians
banco (n.)—pew, bench, bank
banquete (n.)—banquet
bañarse (v.)—to bathe oneself
Barrabás—Barrabas
barrio (n.)—neighborhood
basura (n.)—trash, garbage
bautista (n.)—Baptist
bautizar (v.)—to baptize
bautizo (n.)—baptism
beber (v.)—to drink
bebida (n.)—drink
beca (n.)—scholarship
Belén—Bethlehem
bendecido,-a—blessed *(a person)*
bendecir (v.)—to bless
bendición (n.)—blessing
bendito,-a—blessed *(a thing or place)*
beneficios (n.)—proceeds
Benjamín—Benjamin
Bernabé—Barnabas
bestia (n.)—brute, beast
Biblia (n.)—Bible
bíblico—biblical
bien—well
bienestar (n.)—well-being
bienvenido,-a—welcome
blasfemar (v.)—to blaspheme
blasfemia (n.)—blasphemy

boca (n.)—mouth
boda (n.)—wedding, marriage
boletín de la iglesia—church
    bulletin
boleto (n.)—ticket
bolígrafo (n.)—pen
bondad (n.)—goodness, kindness
bote (n.)—boat
bruja (n.)—sorceress, witch *(fem.)*
brujería (n.)—sorcery, witchcraft
brujo (n.)—sorcerer, magician,
    (male) witch
budista—Buddist
buen; bueno,-a; buenos,-as—good
buscador,-a (n.)—seeker
buscar (v.)—to seek, search
cabeza (n.)—head
caer (v.)—to fall
Caín—Cain
calambre (n.)—cramp
callar (v.)—to silence
calle (n.)—street
calor (n.)—heat
cambiar dinero (v.)—to exchange
    (money)
caminar (v.)—to walk
camino (n.)—road, way
Canaán—Canaan
cansado,-a—tired, weary
Cantares—Song of Solomon
capellán (n.)—chaplain
capilla (n.)—chapel
capítulo (n.)—chapter
cara (n.)—face
carácter (n.)—character
cárcel (n.)—prison
carcelero,-a (n.)—prison officer
carga (n.)—load, burden
cargar (v.)—to charge *(a price)*
caridad (n.)—charity

cariño (n.)—affection
cariñoso,-a—affectionate
carisma (n.)—charisma
carro (n.)—car
carta (n.)—letter
casa (n.)—house
casa de refugio—homeless shelter
casado,-a—married
casamiento (n.)—marriage
casarse con (v.)—to wed, marry
castigar (v.)—to punish
católico,-a—Catholic
catorce—fourteen
celos (n.)—jealousy
cenar (v.)—to dine
cerca de—near to, almost
cerrar (v.)—to close
cesar (v.)—to cease, end
charla (n.)—talk, chat
charlar (v.)—to talk, chat
cheque (n.)—check *(money)*
chico,-a (n.)—boy, girl
chisme (n.)—gossip
chismear (v.)—to gossip
cielo (n.)—heaven
cien, ciento—hundred
cinco—five
cincuenta—fifty
cine (n.)—theater
circuncisión (n.)—circumcision
cita (n.)—appointment
ciudad (n.)—city
clase (n.)—class
clavado—nailed
clavar (v.)—to nail
clavo (n.)—nail
clínica (n.)—clinic
cobrar (v.)—to charge *(a price)*
cocaína (n.)—cocaine
coche (n.)—car

codicia (n.)—greed
codiciar (v.)—to envy, covet
codicioso,-a—greedy, covetous
Colosenses—Colossians
comenzar (v.)—to begin
comer (v.)—to eat
cometer (v.)—to commit, carry out
comida (n.)—food
como—how, like
cómodo,-a—comfortable
compañerismo (n.)—fellowship
compartir (v.)—to share
comprar (v.)—to buy
comprender (v.)—to understand
compromiso (n.)—engagement
computador (n.)—computer
comunidad (n.)—community
comunidad de inmigrantes—
    immigrant community
comunión (n.)—communion
conceder (v.)—to grant, agree to
conciencia (n.)—conscience
condenado,-a—condemned
condenar (v.)—to condemn
conducir (v.)—to drive, to lead
conducta (n.)—conduct, behavior
confesar (v.)—to confess, admit
confesión (n.)—confession
confianza (n.)—trust, confidence
confiar en (v.)—trust, confide in
confirmación (n.)—confirmation
conflicto (n.)—struggle, conflict
confort (n.)—comfort
confortar (v.)—to comfort
congratular (v.)—to congratulate
congregación (n.)—congregation
conmigo—with me
conmovedor,-a—emotionally moving
conocer (v.)—to know *(someone)*
consagrar a (v.)—to dedicate to

consejeros familiares—family counselors

consigo—with him, with her, with you *(form.)*

consolar (v.)—to console, comfort

construir (v.)—to build, construct

contar (v.)—to tell

contestar (v.)—to answer

contigo—with you *(fam.)*

contraer deudas—to run up debts

conversar con (v.)—to talk with

conversión (n.)—conversion

converso,-a (n.)—convert

convertir (v.)—to convert

convicción (n.)—conviction

convocar (v.)—to call together

corazón (n.)—heart

cordero (n.) *(de Dios)*—Lamb *(of God)*

Corintios—Corinthians

coro (n.)—choir, chorus

correo (n.)—mail, post office

correo electrónico (n.)—email

correr (v.)—to run

corromper (v.)—to corrupt

corrompido,-a—corrupted

corrupción (n.)—corruption

corrupto,-a—corrupt

cosa (n.)—thing

cosechar (v.)—to harvest

coser (v.)—to mend, sew

costar (v.)—to cost

costumbre (n.)—custom, habit

cotidiano—daily

creación (n.)—creation

creador,-a (n.)—creator

crear (v.)—to create

crecer (v.)—to grow

crecimiento (n.)—growth, increase

creencia (n.)—belief, faith

creer (v.)—to believe

creyente (n.)—believer

crimen (n.)—crime

cristianismo (n.)—Christianity

cristiano,-a—Christian

Cristo—Christ

Crónicas—Chronicles

crucificado,-a—crucified

crucificar (v.)—to crucify

crucifijo (n.)—crucifix

crucifixión (n.)—crucifixion

cruz (n.)—cross

Cruz Roja—Red Cross

cual—which

cuáquero,-a—Quaker

cuarenta—forty

cuaresma (n.)—Lent

cuatro—four

cubrir (v.)—to cover

cuenta (n.)—bill

cuerpo (n.)—body

cuidado—care, careful

cuidar (v.)—to care for

culpa (n.)—guilt, blame

culpable—guilty

culpar (v.)—to blame

culto (n.)—worship

cumplimiento (n.)—fulfillment

cumplir (v.)—to fulfill, complete

curar (v.)—to cure, heal

dador,-a (n.)—giver

Dalila—Delilah

dama de honor—bridesmaid

Daniel—Daniel

dar (v.)—to give

dar la bendición (v.)—to give the blessing

darle la bienvenida a (v.)—to welcome

dar la vuelta (v.)—to turn

dar testimonio (v.)—to give testimony, testify

David—David

de—of, from

debajo—under

deber (v.)—to owe, ought to

débil—weak

debilidad (n.)—weakness

decir (v.)—to say

declarar (v.)—to testify, declare

dejar (v.)—to leave alone, let stand

del *(=de+el)*—of the

delito (n.)—crime

demandar (v.)—to demand

derecho,-a—right

desacuerdo (n.)—disagreement

desafío (n.)—challenge

desanimar (v.)—to discourage

desastre (n.)—disaster

desayunarse (v.)—to have breakfast

descansar (v.)—to rest

descanso (n.)—rest

descuidar (v.)—to neglect

descuido (n.)—neglect, negligence

desde—from, since

desdicha (n.)—misfortune

desear (v.)—to wish, desire

desechar (v.)—to throw away

deseo (n.)—wish, desire

desgracia (n.)—disgrace, misfortune

deshecho,-a—exhausted, devastated *(person)*

desierto (n.)—desert

desistir (v.)—to desist, cease

desobedecer (v.)—disobey

desobediencia (n.)—disobedience

despacio—slowly

despedirse (v.)—to say goodbye

despertarse (v.)—to awaken

después—after

destrozado,-a—broken *(person)*

destrozar (v.)—to destroy

destrucción (n.)—destruction

destruir (v.)—to destroy

deuda (n.)—debt

deuda de juego—gambling debt

deudor,-a (n.)—debtor

Deuteronomio—Deuteronomy

devolver (v.)—to give back

devoto,-a—devout

día (n.)—day

diablo (n.)—devil

diácono (n.)—deacon

día de Acción de Gracias—Thanksgiving

día de feriado—holiday

día del juicio final—Judgment Day

diario,-a—daily

dichoso,-a—blessed

diciembre—December

diez—ten

diezmar (v.)—to tithe

diezmo (n.)—tithe

diferente—different

difícil—difficult

dificultad (n.)—difficulty

difunto,-a—deceased, dead

diluvio (n.)—flood *(biblical)*

dinero (n.)—money

Dios—God

dirección (n.)—direction

dirigir (v.)—to direct

disciplina (n.)—discipline

discípulo,-a (n.)—disciple, follower

discutir (v.)—to discuss

disponer (v.)—to arrange, prepare

dispuesto—ready

disputa (n.)—dispute

distanciar (v.)—to distance

divino—divine, excellent

divorciar (v.)—to divorce
doce—twelve
doctrina (n.)—doctrine
documento (n.)—document
doler (v.)—to hurt
dolor (n.)—pain, grief
domingo—Sunday
Domingo de Ramos—Palm Sunday
dominio propio—self-control
don (n.)—gift
don de las lenguas—gift of tongues
donación (n.)—donation
donar (v.)—donate
¿dónde—where?
dones espirituales—spiritual gifts
dormir (v.)—to sleep
dos—two
drogadicción (n.)—drug addiction
drogadicto,-a—drug addict
duda (n.)—doubt
dudar (v.)—to doubt
durante—during
ebrio—intoxicated
Eclesiastés—Ecclesiastes
edad (n.)—age
Edén—Eden
edificar (v.)—to edify
edificio (n.)—building
educar (v.)—to educate, bring up
efectivo (n.)—cash
Efesios—Ephesians
Egipcios—Egyptians
Egipto—Egypt
egoísta—selfish
él—he
elegido,-a (n.)—elect, chosen
elegir (v.)—to select, elect
Eli—Elí
Elías—Elijah
Eliseo—Elisha

ella—she
ellas—they *(fem.)*
ellos—they *(masc.)*
elogiar (v.)—eulogize, praise
elogio (n.)—eulogy, praise
embarazo (n.)—pregnancy
emborrachar (v.)—to intoxicate,
   become intoxicated
emergencia (n.)—emergency
emoción (n.)—emotion
empezar (v.)—to begin
en—in, on, at
en lugar de—instead of
encargarse (v.)—to be in charge of,
   take care of
encinta—pregnant
encontrar (v.)—to find, meet
endeudarse (v.)—to run up debts
enemigo,-a (n.)—enemy
enero—January
enfermedad (n.)—sickness, disease
enfoque (n.)—focus
engañar (v.)—to deceive, cheat, fool
engaño (n.)—deception, cheating
Enoc—Enoch
enojar (v.)—to anger
enojo (n.)—anger
enseñar (v.)—to teach, show
enterrar (v.)—to bury
entonces—then
entrar (v.)—to enter
enviar (v.)—to send
enviar un mensaje electrónico
   (v.)—to email
envidia (n.)—envy
envidiar (v.)—to envy
episcopal—Episcopal
equipo (n.)—team
equipo de líderes—leadership team
equipo de oración—prayer team

ésa—that one *(fem.)*
ésas—those ones *(fem.)*
Esaú—Esau
escapar (v.)—to escape
esclavizar (v.)—to enslave
esclavo,-a (n.)—slave
esconder (v.)—to hide
escortar (v.)—to escort
escribir (v.)—to write
escritura (n.)—scripture
escuchar (v.)—to listen
escuela (n.)—school
escuela dominical—Sunday school
Esdras—Ezra
ése—that one *(masc.)*
ésos—those ones *(masc.)*
espalda (n.)—back
español *(language)* (n.)—Spanish
esparcir (v.)—to scatter
espejo (n.)—mirror
esperanza (n.)—hope
esperar (v.)—to hope, to wait
espíritu (n.)—spirit
espiritual—spiritual
espiritualidad (n.)—spirituality
Espíritu Santo—Holy Spirit
espíritus malos—evil spirits
esposo,-a (n.)—spouse
ésta—this one *(fem.)*
esta noche—tonight
estados unidos—United States
estar (v.)—to be
estar de vacaciones (v.)—to be on
    vacation
éstas—these ones *(fem.)*
estatua (n.)—statue
este (n.)—east
éste—this one *(masc.)*
Ester—Esther
estigma (n.)—stigma

éstos—these ones *(masc.)*
estudiante (n.)—student
estudiar (v.)—study
estudios bíblicos—Bible studies
eternidad (n.)—eternity
eterno,-a—eternal
Eucaristía (n.)—Eucharist
Eva—Eve
evangélico,-a—evangelic
evangelio (n.)—gospel
evangelismo (n.)—evangelism
evangelizar (v.)—to evangelize
evitar (v.)—to avoid
exacto—exact
examen (n.)—test
examen de conciencia—soul-
    searching
examinar (v.)—to examine, test
excelente—excellent
exigir (v.)—to demand
exiliar (v.)—to exile
exilio (n.)—exile
existencia (n.)—supply
éxito (n.)—success
Éxodo—Exodus
exorcista (n.)—exorcist
expiación (n.)—atonement
explicar (v.)—to explain
extraño—strange
Ezequiel—Ezekiel
fallecer (v.)—to die
fallecido,-a—deceased
fallecimiento (n.)—death
falso—false
falta (n.)—lack
faltar (v.)—to lack
familia (n.)—family
Faraón—Pharaoh
Fariseo—Pharisee
farmacia (n.)—pharmacy

fe (n.)—faith
febrero—February
fecha (n.)—date
felicitaciones (n.)—congratulations
felicitar (v.)—to congratulate
Felipe—Philip
fidelidad (n.)—faithfulness
fiebre (n.)—fever
fiel—faithful
fielmente—faithfully
fiera (n.)—beast, cruel person
fiesta (n.)—party
fijar (v.)—to fix (a position)
Filemón—Philemon
Filipenses—Philippians
Filisteo—Philistine
fin (n.)—end, finish
financiamiento (n.)—financing
físicamente—physically
fondo (n.)—fund
fondo para la construcción—
     building fund
fondos disponibles—available funds
fortalecer (v.)—to strengthen
fracasar (v.)—to break, to fail, to be
     disappointed
fracaso (n.)—disaster, failure
frío (n.)—cold
fruto del Espíritu—fruit of the Spirit
fuerza (n.)—strength
fumar (v.)—to smoke
fúnebre—funeral
funeral (n.)—funeral
funeraria (n.)—funeral home
futuro (n.)—future
Gálatas—Galatians
Galilea—Galilee
ganancias (n.)—proceeds, gains
ganar (v.)—to gain
gasolinera (n.)—gas station

Gedeón—Gideon
generalmente—generally
Génesis—Genesis
gente (n.)—people
gentiles—Gentiles
Getsemaní—Gethsemane
gigante (n.)—giant
gloria (n.)—glory
glorificar (v.)—to glorify
Goliat—Goliath
Gomorra—Gomorrah
gozar (v.)—to enjoy
gozo (n.)—joy
gracia (n.)—grace
gratis—free
gripe (n.)—flu
grupo de apoyo—support group
grupo de jóvenes—youth group
guardar (v.)—to keep
guerra (n.)—war
guerra espiritual—spiritual warfare
guiar (v.)—to guide
gustar (v.)—to like
gusto (n.)—pleasure
Habacuc—Habakkuk
habitar (v.)—to dwell
hablar (v.)—to speak
hacer (v.)—to make, to do
hacer maravillas (v.)—to work
     wonders
hacer milagros (v.)—to work
     miracles
hacer una donación (v.)—to donate
Hades—Hades
Hageo—Haggai
hambre (n.)—hunger, starvation
hambriento,-a—hungry
hasta—until
hay—there is, there are
Hebreos—Hebrews

Hechos—Acts
heredar (v.)—to inherit
herejía (n.)—heresy
herencia (n.)—inheritance
hermana (n.)—sister
hermano (n.)—brother
Herodes—Herod
hija (n.)—daughter
hijo (n.)—son
Hijo del hombre—Son of Man
himnario (n.)—hymnal
himno (n.)—hymn
hindú—Hindu
hipocresía (n.)—hipocrisy
hipócrita (n.)—hipocrite
hogar (n.)—home
hombre (n.)—man
homicidio (n.)—murder, homicide
homosexual (n.)—homosexual
homosexualidad (n.)—
    homosexuality
honor (n.)—honor
honra (n.)—dignity, self-respect
honrar (v.)—to honor, respect
hora (n.)—hour
horario de servicios—schedule of
    services
hospedar (v.)—to lodge, to receive as
    a guest
hospital (n.)—hospital
hotel (n.)—hotel
hoy—today
huérfano,-a (n.)—orphan
huerto (n.)—garden *(of vegetables)*
huerto/jardín del Edén—Garden of
    Eden
huésped,-a (n.)—guest, host
huir (v.)—to flee
humanitaria—humanitarian
humildad (n.)—humility

humilde—meek, humble
humillación (n.)—humiliation
huracán (n.)—hurricane
idea (n.)—idea, thought
idioma (n.)—language
idolatría (n.)—idolatry
ídolo (n.)—idol
iglesia (n.)—church
ilegal—illegal
importante—important
incrédulo,-a (n.)—unbeliever
indocumentado,-a—illegal resident
    (undocumented)
infermedad (n.)—illness
infiel—unfaithful
infierno (n.)—hell
influencia (n.)—influence, power
influir (v.)—to influence
infundir (v.)—to instill
ingénito—only begotten
inglés *(language)* (n.)—English
inmigrante (n.)—immigrant
inmigrante ilegal—illegal immigrant
inmortal—immortal
inocente—innocent
insultar (v.)—to insult
integridad (n.)—integrity
intentar (v.)—to try, search, attempt
interceder con (v.)—to intercede
    with
intercesión (n.)—intercession
intercesor,-a (n.)—intercessor
interpretación (n.)—interpretation
interpretar (v.)—to interpret
intérprete (n.)—interpreter
inundación (n.)—flood
invierno (n.)—winter
invitación (n.)—invitation
invitar (v.)—to invite
ir (v.)—to go

ira (n.)—anger, wrath
ir de compras (v.)—to shop
Isaac—Isaac
Isaías—Isaiah
Ismael—Ishmael
Israel—Israel
Israelita—Israelite
izquierda—left
jabón (n.)—soap
Jacob—Jacob
jactancia (n.)—boasting
jactarse (v.)—to boast
jardín (n.)—garden
Jehová—Jehovah
Jeremías—Jeremiah
Jericó—Jericho
Jerusalén—Jerusalem
Jesucristo—Jesus Christ
Jesús—Jesus
Job—Job
Joel—Joel
Jonás—Jonah
Jonatán—Jonathan
Jordán—Jordan
José—Joseph
Josué—Joshua
joven—young
Juan—John
Juan el Bautista—John the Baptist
Judá—Judah
Judas—Judas, Jude
judíos (n.)—Jews
Jueces—Judges
juego (n.)—game
juego con apuestas—gambling
jueves—Thursday
jugar (v.)—to play
julio—July
junio—June
juntarse (v.)—to unite, get together

junto,-a—together, next to
juramento (n.)—oath, curse
jurar (v.)—to swear
juvenil—juvenile
juzgar (v.)—to judge
lado (n.)—side
ladrón,-ona (n.)—robber, thief
Lamentaciones—
    Lamentations
lamentar (v.)—to grieve
lámpara (n.)—lamp, light
lavar (v.)—to wash
Lázaro—Lazarus
leal—loyal
lealmente—loyally
lealtad (n.)—loyalty
lección (n.)—lesson
leer (v.)—to read
lejos—far
lentamente—slowly
lento,-a—slow
levadura (n.)—leavening, yeast
levantar fondos—fundraising
Levítico—Leviticus
ley de Moisés—Law of Moses
Líbano—Lebanon
libertad (n.)—freedom
libertad condicional—parole
librar (v.)—to free, deliver from
libro (n.)—book
licencia de matrimonio—marriage
    license
líder (n.)—leader, staff
ligero,-a—light (*weight*)
limpio,-a—clean
llamar (v.)—to be named, to call
llamar a cobro revertido—to call
    collect
llamar a la puerta—to knock (*on the
    door*)

llamar por teléfono—to phone
llegada (n.)—arrival
llegar (v.)—to arrive
llenar (v.)—to fill
llorar (v.)—to cry
lluvia (n.)—rain
lodo (n.)—mud
los sin techo—homeless
Lot—Lot
lotería (n.)—lottery
Lucas—Luke
luego—later, afterwards
lugar (n.)—place
lujo (n.)—luxury
lujuria (n.)—lust
lujuriar (v.)—to lust
luna de miel—honeymoon
lunes—Monday
luterano,-a—Lutheran
luz (n.)—light
madre (n.)—mother
madrina (n.)—godmother
madrina de boda (n.)—maid/ matron of honor
maestro,-a (n.)—teacher
magia (n.)—magic
mago (n.)—sorcerer, magician, wise man
majestad (n.)—majesty
mal—bad, evil
Malaquías—Malachi
maldad (n.)—badness, evilness
maldecir (v.)—to curse, slander
maldición (n.)—curse
maleta (n.)—suitcase
malo,-a—bad, evil, wicked
maltratar (v.)—mistreat
mandamientos (n.)—commandments
mandar (v.)—command, order, send
mandar por fax (v.)—to fax

mano (n.)—hand
mansedumbre (n.)—meekness
manso,-a—meek, gentle
mañana (n.)—tomorrow, morning
mapa (n.)—map
mar (n.)—sea
maravillas (n.)—wonders
Marcos—Mark
mareo—dizzy
María—Mary
María Magdalena—Mary Magdalene
marido,-a (n.)—spouse
marihuana (n.)—marijuana
Mar Muerto—Dead Sea
Mar Rojo—Red Sea
Marta—Martha
martes—Tuesday
marzo—March
más—more
matar (v.)—to kill, murder
Mateo—Matthew
materiales (n.)—materials
materialismo (n.)—materialism
matrimonio (n.)—matrimony
mayo—May
mayor—older
medianoche (n.)—midnight
medicamento (n.)—medicine
mediodía (n.)—noon
mendigar (v.)—to beg
mendigo,-a (n.)—beggar
menonita—Mennonite
menor—younger
menos—less
mente (n.)—mind
mentir (v.)—to lie
mentira (n.)—lie
mes (n.)—month
mesiánico,-a—Messianic
Mesías (n.)—Messiah

meter (v.)—to insert, to put in
metodista (n.)—Methodist
miedo (n.)—fear
miércoles—Wednesday
mil—thousand
milagro (n.)—miracle
ministerio (n.)—ministry
Miqueas—Micah
mirar (v.)—look at
misa (n.)—mass
misericordia (n.)—mercy
misericordioso,-a—merciful
misión (n.)—mission
misionero,-a (n.)—missionary
misterio (n.)—mystery
Moisés—Moses
monja (n.)—nun
monje (n.)—monk
Monte de los olivos—Mount Olive
morir (v.)—to die
motivar (v.)—to motivate, encourage
mototaxi (n.)—motor-taxi
mover (v.)—to move
muchacho,-a (n.)—boy, girl
mucho,-a—much, many
muerte (n.)—death
muerto—dead
mujer (n.)—woman
mundano—worldly
mundo (n.)—world
música (n.)—music
muy—very
Nabucodonosor—Nebuchadnezzar
nada—nothing
nadie—no one
Nahúm—Nahum
naturaleza humana—human nature
náusea (n.)—nausea
Navidad (n.)—Christmas, nativity
Nazaret—Nazareth

necesario—necessary
necesidad (n.)—need
necesitar (v.)—to need
necio,-a (n.)—foolish person
negar (v.)—to deny
negligencia (n.)—neglect, negligence
Nehemías—Nehemiah
Nicodemo—Nicodemus
nieta (n.)—granddaughter
nieto (n.)—grandson
nieve (n.)—snow
ningún, ninguno,-a—no one, nobody, none
niño,-a (n.)—boy, girl
nivel (n.)—standard, level
nivelar (v.)—to level *(something, with people)*
noche (n.)—night, evening
nochebuena (n.)—Christmas Eve
Noé—Noah
Noemí—Naomi
nombre (n.)—name
nosotros,-as—we
noticias (n.)—news
novia (n.)—bride, fiancée, girlfriend
noviembre—November
novio (n.)—bridegroom, fiancé, boyfriend
nueve—nine
nuevo,-a—new
Números—Numbers
nunca—never
obedecer (v.)—to obey
obedencia (n.)—obedience
obispo (n.)—bishop
obligación (n.)—commitment, obligation
obra (n.)—deed, work
observar (v.)—to observe
obstáculo (n.)—obstacle

ocho—eight
octubre—October
ocurrir (v.)—to occur
odiar (v.)—to hate
oeste (n.)—west
ofensa (n.)—offense
ofrecerse como voluntario (v.)—to volunteer
ofrenda (n.)—offering
oír (v.)—to hear
ojo (n.)—eye
omnipotente—omnipotent, all-powerful
omnipresente—omnipresent
omnisciente—omniscient
once—eleven
oportunidad (n.)—opportunity, chance
oración (n.)—prayer
orar (v.)—to pray
orden (n.)—order
orfanato (n.)—orphanage
organizar (v.)—to organize
orgullo (n.)—pride
orientación (n.)—orientation
oro (n.)—gold
ortodoxo—Orthodox
oscuridad (n.)—darkness
Oseas—Hosea
otoño (n.)—fall, autumn
Pablo—Paul
paciencia (n.)—patience
pacto (n.)—covenant, agreement
padecer (v.)—to suffer
padre (n.)—father
Padre Divino—Heavenly Father
Padrenuestro—Our Father *(Lord's Prayer)*
padres (n.)—parents
padrino (n.)—godfather, sponsor, best man

pagano,-a (n.)—pagan
pagar (v.)—to pay
palabra (n.)—word
palabras blasfemas—blasphemous words
pan (n.)—bread
papa (n.)—pope, papa, daddy
papel (n.)—paper, role
para—for, to, in order to
parábola (n.)—parable
pareja (n.)—couple
pariente,-a (n.)—relative
parte (n.)—part, share
pasado (n.)—past
pasaporte (n.)—passport
pasar hambre (v.)—to starve
Pascua (n.)—Easter
Pascua de los judíos (n.)—Passover
pasto (n.)—pasture
pastor,-a (n.)—pastor
patrocinador,-a (n.)—sponsor
patrocinar (v.)—to sponsor, protect
paz (n.)—peace
pecado (n.)—sin, fault
pecador,-a (n.)—sinner
pecar (v.)—to sin
pecho (n.)—chest
pedir (v.)—to ask
pedir limosna (v.)—to beg
Pedro—Peter
película (n.)—movie
peligro (n.)—danger
pena (n.)—punishment, sorrow
penitencia (n.)—penance
pensar (v.)—to think
pentateuco—Pentateuch
Pentecostés—Pentecost
perder (v.)—to lose
pérdida (n.)—loss
perdido,-a—lost

perdón (n.)—forgiveness
perdonar (v.)—to forgive
perezoso,-a—lazy
permanecer (v.)—to remain
permitir (v.)—to permit
pero—but
persecución (n.)—persecution
perseguir (v.)—to persecute, to chase
perseverancia (n.)—perseverance
perseverar (v.)—to persevere
persignarse (v.)—to make the sign of
    the cross
persistencia (n.)—persistence
persistir (v.)—to persist
pertenecer (v.)—to belong
pertenencias (n.)—belongings
perverso,-a—perverse, wicked
pez (n.)—fish
piadoso,-a—devout, pious
pie (n.)—foot
piedra (n.)—stone
plan (n.)—plan, scheme
plena—full
pluma (n.)—pen, feather
pobre (n.)—the poor, indigent
pobreza (n.)—poverty
poder (n.)—power
poder (v.)—to be able
policía (n.)—police
Poncio Pilato—Pontius Pilate
poner (v.)—to put, place
por—by, by means of
por medio de—by means of
¿por qué?—why?
pornografía (n.)—pornography
porqué (n.)—reason, why
porque—because
portugués *(language)*(n.)—
    Portuguese
Potifar—Potiphar

precio (n.)—price, cost
predicador,-a (n.)—preacher
predicar (v.)—to preach
pregunta (n.)—question
preocupación (n.)—concern, worry
preocuparse (v.)—to be concerned
preparar (v.)—to prepare
presbiteriano,-a—Presbyterian
preso,-a (n.)—prisoner
primavera (n.)—spring
primeramente—primarily
primero,-a—first
primo,-a (n.)—cousin
prisa (n.)—haste
prisión (n.)—prison
privar de comida (v.)—to starve
privilegio (n.)—privilege
probar (v.)—to test
probatoria (n.)—parole
problema (n.)—problem
prodigio (n.)—miracle, wonder
pródigo,-a—wasteful, prodigal
profecía (n.)—prophecy
profeta falso,-a—false prophet
profetizar (v.)—to prophesy
programa (n.)—program
prohibir (v.)—to forbid
prójimo,-a (n.)—neighbor
promesa (n.)—promise
prometer (v.)—to promise
prometido,-a—engaged
pronto—soon
pronunciar (v.)—to pronounce
propio—own
propósito (n.)—purpose, intention
prostitución (n.)—prostitution
prostituirse (v.)—to prostitute
prostituta (n.)—prostitute
protección (n.)—protection
proteger (v.)—to protect

protestante—Protestant
proveer (v.)—to provide
Proverbios—Proverbs
provisión (n.)—provision
próximo,-a—next
puerta (n.)—door
pues—since, then, well
pureza (n.)—purity
purgar (v.)—to cleanse
purgatorio (n.)—purgatory
puro,-a—pure, virgin
que—what
¿Qué?—what?
quebrado,-a—broken
quebrar (v.)—to break
quedar (v.)—to meet, remain
queja (n.)—complaint, quarrel
quejarse (v.)—to complain
quemadura (n.)—burn
quemar (v.)—to burn
querer (v.)—to want
querido,-a—beloved
¿Quién?—who?
quien—who
quince—fifteen
rabí (n.)—rabbi
rápidamente—rapidly
rápido,-a—rapid
rapto *(de la iglesia)* (n.)—rapture *(of the church)*
Raquel—Rachel
rasgar (v.)—to tear
razón (n.)—reason
Rebeca—Rebecca
rebeldía (n.)—rebelliousness
rebosar (v.)—to overflow, run over
rechazar (v.)—to resist, to refuse, to deny
recoger (v.)—to gather
recolectar (v.)—to collect, gather
recompensa (n.)—reward

recordar (v.)—to remember
rectitud (n.)—righteousness
recuperación (n.)—recovery
recurso (n.)—choice, option
redención (n.)—redemption
Redentor (n.)—Redeemer
redimir (v.)—to redeem, buy back
refugiarse (v.)—to take refuge
refugio (n.)—shelter, refuge
regalo (n.)—gift
regocijar (v.)—to rejoice
reino (n.)—kingdom
reír (v.)—to laugh
relación (n.)—relation
relacionado,-a—related
relacionar (v.)—to relate
religión (n.)—religion
religioso,-a—religious
renacer (v.)—to be reborn
rendirse (v.)—to submit, surrender
repetir (v.)—to repeat
requerir (v.)—to require
respeto (n.)—respect, consideration
respuesta (n.)—answer, response
restauración (n.)—restoration
restaurante (n.)—restaurant
restaurar (v.)—to restore, recover
resucitar (v.)—to raise from the dead
resurrección (n.)—resurrection
retiro (n.)—retreat
reunir (v.)—to meet
revelación (n.)—revelation, apocalypse
reverencia (n.)—reverence
reverendo,-a (n.)—reverend
revisar (v.)—to check
rey (n.)—king
Reyes—Kings
rico,-a—rich
riquezas (n.)—riches

robar (v.)—to steal, rob
Romanos—Romans
romper (v.)—to break *(a thing)*
ropa (n.)—clothes
rosario (n.)—rosary
rostro (n.)—face
roto,-a—broken
Rubén—Reuben
Rut—Ruth
sábado—Saturday
saber (v.)—to know
sabiduría (n.)—wisdom
sabio,-a—wise
sacar (v.)—to take out, remove
sacerdote (n.)—priest *(Catholic)*
sacerdotisa (n.)—priestess
sacramento (n.)—sacrament
sacrificar (v.)—to sacrifice
sacrificio (n.)—sacrifice
sagrado,-a—holy, sacred
salida (n.)—exit, departure
salir (v.)—to leave *(a place)*
Salmos—Psalms
Salomón—Solomon
salud (n.)—health
salvación (n.)—salvation
Salvador (n.)—Savior
salvar (v.)—to save, redeem
salvo,-a—safe, saved
samaritano,-a (n.)—samaritan
Samuel—Samuel
sanar (v.)—to heal
sangre (n.)—blood
Sansón—Samson
santa cena—Lord's Supper
Santiago—James
santidad (n.)—holiness, godliness
santificación (n.)—sanctification
santificar (v.)—to sanctify, make holy
Santísima Trinidad—Holy Trinity

santo,-a—saint, holy
santuario (n.)—sanctuary
Sara—Sarah
Satán (n.)—Satan
Satanás (n.)—Satan
satánico,-a—satanic
Saúl/Saulo—Saul
secta (n.)—sect, cult
secuestrar (v.)—to kidnap
sed (n.)—thirst
seglar (n.)—layman
seguidor,-a (n.)—follower
seguir (v.)—to follow
según—according to
seguridad (n.)—security
seis—six
sellar (v.)—to seal
semana (n.)—week
Semana Santa—Holy Week
sembrador,-a (n.)—sower, planter
sembrar (v.)—to sow, plant
semilla (n.)—seed
senda (n.)—path
sendero (n.)—path
sentarse (v.)—to sit
sentencia (n.)—judgment
sentimiento (n.)—feeling
señales (n.)—signs, marvels
Señor (n.)—Lord
Señor Jesús—Lord Jesus
septiembre—September
sepultar (v.)—to bury
sepultura (n.)—grave, tomb
sequía (n.)—drought
ser (v.)—to be
servicio (n.)—service
servicios funerarios—funeral services
servir (v.)—to serve
Set—Seth

Visit us at www.SpanishForChristianService.com

siempre—always
siete—seven
siglo (n.)—century, ages
siguiente—following
sin—without
sin embargo—however
sin hogar—homeless
sin vivienda—homeless
sinagoga (n.)—synagogue
sino—but, except, only
Sion—Zion
sirviente,-a (n.)—servant
sistema (n.)—system
sitio (n.)—place
situación (n.)—situation
soberanía (n.)—sovereignty
soberano,-a—sovereign
soberbio,-a—haughty, arrogant
sobornar (v.)—to bribe
soborno (n.)—bribe
sobrar (v.)—to have too much of, exceed
sobre—on, on top of
sobrenatural—supernatural
sobreviviente (n.)—survivor
sobrevivir (v.)—to survive
sobriedad (n.)—sobriety
sobrina (n.)—niece
sobrino (n.)—nephew
socio,-a (n.)—*(business)* member
socorro (n.)—help
Sodoma—Sodom
Sofonías—Zephaniah
solamente—only
soltero,-a (n.)—single *(person)*, unmarried
someter a (v.)—to submit to, surrender
sonreír (v.)—to smile
sonrisa (n.)—smile

soportar (v.)—to tolerate
suceder (v.)—to occur, to happen
sucio,-a—dirty
suegra (n.)—mother-in-law
suegro (n.)—father-in-law
sueño (n.)—dream, sleep
suerte (n.)—luck
sufrimiento (n.)—suffering
sufrir (v.)—to suffer
suicidarse (v.)—to commit suicide
suicidio (n.)—suicide
sumisión (n.)—submission
sumo sacerdote—high priest
suplir (v.)—to supply
sur (n.)—south
tabernáculo (n.)—tabernacle
talentoso,-a—gifted
también—also
tanto,-a—so much
tarde (adv.)—late
tarde (n.)—afternoon
tarjeta de crédito (n.)—credit card
tarjeta telefónica (n.)—phone card
taxi (n.)—taxi
telefonear (v.)—to telephone
teléfono (n.)—telephone
teléfono celular (n.)—cellphone
temer por (v.)—to fear for
tempestad (n.)—storm
templo (n.)—temple
temporeramente—temporarily
temprano—early
tenebroso,-a—gloomy
tener (v.)—to have
tener hambre (v.)—to hunger
tener miedo (v.)—to be afraid
tener sed (v.)—to thirst
tentación (n.)—temptation
tentador (n.)—tempter
tentar (v.)—to tempt

terapeuta (n.)—therapist
terapia (n.)—therapy
terminar (v.)—to end
ternura (n.)—gentleness
terremoto (n.)—earthquake
terrenal—terrestrial
Tesalonicenses—Thessalonians
testificar (v.)—to testify
testigo,-a (n.)—witness
testigo de Jehová—Jehovah's Witness
testigos falsos—false witnesses
testimonio (n.)—testimony
tía (n.)—aunt
tiempo (n.)—time
tienda (n.)—shop
tierra (n.)—earth
Tierra Santa—Holy Land
timidez (n.)—timidity
Timoteo—Timothy
tinieblas (n.)—darkness, profound ignorance
tío (n.)—uncle
Tito—Titus
toalla (n.)—towel
todavía—even, still
todo,-a—all
todopoderoso,-a—all mighty, all powerful
tolerante—tolerant
tomar (v.)—to take, to drink
tonto,-a (n.)—fool, idiot
tormenta (n.)—storm, calamity
trabajar (v.)—to work
trabajo (n.)—work
traer (v.)—to bring
tragar (v.)—to swallow
tragedia (n.)—tragedy
trágico,-a—tragic
tranquilo,-a—peaceful

trastornar (v.)—to upset, disturb
trastorno (n.)—upset, disorder
trece—thirteen
treinta—thirty
tren (n.)—train
tres—three
tribulación (n.)—tribulation
Trinidad (n.)—Trinity
triste—sad
tristeza (n.)—sadness
trono de Dios—throne of God
tú—you *(fam.)*
ungido,-a—anointed
ungir (v.)—to anoint
unidad (n.)—unity, unit
unigénito,-a—only begotten
unirse (v.)—to unite, join
unitario,-a—Unitarian
uno,-a—one
unos,-as—some
usar (v.)—to use
usted—you *(sing., form.)*
ustedes—you *(pl., form.)*
valle (n.)—valley
vara (n.)—staff, rod
veces (n.)—times *(in a series)(pl.)*
vecindario (n.)—neighborhood
vecino,-a (n.)—neighbor
veinte—twenty
veloz—rapid
velozmente—rapidly
vencer (v.)—to overcome
venerar (v.)—to worship, revere *(more often used in the Catholic faith)*
venganza (n.)—vengeance
venir (v.)—to come
ver (v.)—to see
verano (n.)—summer
Verbo *(de Dios)*—Word *(of God)*

verdad (n.)—truth
vergüenza (n.)—shame
versículo (n.)—verse
vez (n.)—time (*in a series*) (*sing.*)
viajar (v.)—to travel
vicio (n.)—vice, bad habit
víctima (n.)—victim
victorioso,-a—victorious
vida eterna—eternal life
viejo,-a—old
viernes—Friday
Viernes Santo—Good Friday
vino (n.)—wine
violación (n.)—rape
violador,-a (n.)—rapist
violar (v.)—to rape
violencia (n.)—violence
violento—violent
virar (v.)—to change direction
virgen (n.)—virgin
virtud (n.)—virtue, courage
visión (n.)—vision
visitar (v.)—to visit
viuda (n.)—widow
viudo (n.)—widower
vivienda (n.)—house
vivir (v.)—to live
volar (v.)—to fly
voluntad *(de Dios)* (n.)—will *(of God)*
voluntario,-a (n.)—volunteer
volver (v.)—to return, come back
vosotros,-as—you *(plu., fam.)*
voto (n.)—vow
vuelta (n.)—turn
yo—I
yugo (n.)—yoke
Zacarías—Zechariah
Zaqueo—Zacchaeus

Answers

Chapter 1

Ejercicio-A

1. F; **2.**F; **3.**M; **4.**F; **5.**M; **6.** F; **7.** F; **8.** M; **9.** F; **10.** M; **11.** M; **12.** M; **13.** M; **14.** B; **15.** F

Ejercicio-B

el regalo	los regalos
la alabanza	las alabanzas
el voluntario	los voluntarios
el edificio	los edificios
la muchacha	las muchachas
el himno	los himnos
la virtud	las virtudes
la Biblia	las Biblias
el pacto	los pactos
el elogio	los elogios
la doctrina	las doctrinas
la cruz	las cruces
el sacramento	los sacramentos
el equipo	los equipos
el servicio	los servicios

Ejercicio-C

1. las Biblias azules, **2.** las iglesias viejas, **3.** los estudios bíblicos, **4.** las invitaciones nuevas, **5.** los servicios voluntarios, **6.** los pastores buenos, **7.** los testigos falsos, **8.** las doctrinas cristianas, **9.** las ofrendas grandes, **10.** las mujeres religiosas

Ejercicio-D

1. la iglesia Bautista; **2.** las misiones españolas; **3.** los cuatro ángeles; **4.** la oración nueva; **5.** la comunidad española; **6.** la misa católica

Scripture Passages

A. Dios, Cristo Jesús, Señor, gracia, misericordia, paz; **B.** Santo, santo, santo, Señor, Dios, todopoderoso

Names of the Holy Trinity

1	2	3	4	5
Jesús	Religión	Cruz	Escritura	Milagro
Elegido	Eterno	Resurrección	Sagrado	Eternidad
Honra	Dios	Inmortal	Paz	Salvador
Oración	Evangelio	Santo	Ídolo	Ídolo
Verdad	Nombre	Templo	Reino	Alabanza
Ángel	Trono	Oportunidad	Iglesia	Santo
	Ofrenda		Trinidad	
	Regalo		Ungido	
			Sacerdote	
			Alma	
			Nombre	
			Testigo	
			Ofrenda	

Chapter 2

Ejercicio-A

1. Yo prometo venir mañana. Tú prometes venir mañana. Ella promete venir mañana. María y yo prometemos venir mañana. El pastor promete venir mañana. **2.** Él cree en Jesucristo. Yo creo en Jesucristo. Nosotros creemos en Jesucristo. Los niños creen en Jesucristo. Tú crees en Jesucristo. **3.** La creyente ora en la iglesia. Usted ora en la iglesia. Ella ora en la iglesia. Nosotros oramos en la iglesia. Juan y Miguel oran en la iglesia.

Ejercicio-B

1. yo quiero, nosotras queremos, usted quiere; **2.** ella sabe, yo sé, María y yo sabemos; **3.** él viene, ellos vienen, nosotros venimos, yo vengo; **4.** ustedes dan, yo doy, tú das, Jesús da; **5.** yo digo, tú dices, Pedro y Mario dicen; **6.** usted tiene, ella tiene, yo tengo, tú tienes; **7.** Dios va, nosotros vamos, el pastor va

Word Scramble

1. cruz; **2.** gozo; **3.** boda; **4.** ángel; **5.** diablo; **6.** alma; **7.** Biblia; **8.** coro; **9.** trono; **10.** gracia; **11.** mucho; **12.** himno; **13.** ayuno; **14.** trabajo; **15.** santo

Ejercicio-C

1. La congregación sabe la doctrina. ¿Sabe la congregación la doctrina? No, la congregación no sabe la doctrina. **2.** María tiene el regalo. ¿Tiene María el regalo? No, María no tiene el regalo. **3.** Ustedes dicen la bendición. ¿Dicen ustedes la bendición? No, nosotros no decimos la bendición, (*or:* No, ustedes no dicen la bendición.) **4.** María quiere leer la Biblia. ¿ Quiere María leer la Biblia? No, María no quiere leer la Biblia.

Ejercicio-D

1. Él es pastor. **2.** Nosotros somos de Cuba. **3.** Carlota es madre. **4.** ¿Dónde está la iglesia? **5.** Ellas son misioneras. **6.** ¿Están en casa Luisa y Miguel? **7.** El libro es de él. **8.** La niña está triste. **9.** Los creyentes están en la iglesia. **10.** Es necesario leer las escrituras.

Ejercicio-E

1. un, unos; **2.** una, unas; **3.** una, unas; **4.** un, unos; **5.** una, unas; **6.** un, unos; **7.** un, unos; **8.** una, unas; **9.** una, unas; **10.** una, unas

Ejercicio-F

1. yo pido, tú pides, nosotros pedimos, ustedes piden; **2.** él confiesa, Miguel y yo confesamos, usted confiesa, ellas confiesan; **3.** Juan duerme, tú duermes, yo duermo, nosotros dormimos; **4.** ella muere, nosotros morimos, Juan y José mueren, él muere

Ejercicio-G

1. Yo soy de Chicago; **2.** Voy a la iglesia y después al bautizo; **3.** Los libros son del Pastor Denny.

Ejercicio-H

1. Miguel va a abrir esas puertas. Miguel va a abrir ese libro. Miguel va a abrir esa capilla. **2.** Nosotros conocemos bien aquellos edificios. Nosotros conocemos bien aquella comunidad. **3.** Yo quiero este himno. Yo quiero estas plumas. Yo quiero estos versículos.

Ejercicio-I

1. Hay lluvia en Chicago. **2.** Hay alabanza aquí. **3.** El Anticristo es muy malo. **4.** Hay amor en este sitio. **5.** Hay libertad en los Estados Unidos. **6.** Los niños hablan despacio (o lentamente). **7.** El servicio empieza tarde. **8.** Hay cristianos aquí. **9.** Hay sabiduría en las escrituras. **10.** Jesús y los apóstoles llegan despacio (o lentamente).

Words of Discernment
1. D, Holy Trinity; **2.** A, kingdom of God; **3.** D, characteristics of God

Virtues and Gifts of the Believer Puzzle
A. el ánimo; **B.** el perdón; **C.** la verdad; **D.** la humildad; **E.** la alabanza; **F.** la paz; **G.** el creyente; **H.** el examen; **I.** la fe; **J.** sagrado

A 24	H 25	O 7	R 20	A, 22	■	P 10	U 26	E 1	S, 55	■	P 10	E 8	R 20	M 6	A 31	N 36	E 8	C 44	E 11	N 36
E 8	S 55	T 49	A 35	S 55	■	T 49	R 45	E 19	S 55	■	V 18	I 5	R 12	T 49	U 26	D 21	E 8	S: 55	■	L 2	A 42
F 54	E, 8	■	L 9	A 38	■	E 43	S 55	P 41	E 19	R 20	A 40	N 4	Z 37	A, 34	■	Y 47		E 46	L 28
A 29	M 6	O 7	R. 12	■	P 41	E 19	R 12	O 14	■	L 16	A 53		M 27	Á 3	S 55
E 1	X 52	C 44	E 51	L 33	E 19	N 15	T 49	E 48	■	D 13	E 50	E 11	L 23	L 39	A 17	S 55	E 46	S 55
E 8	L 30	■	A 32	M 27	O 14	R. 20

Scripture Passage
fruto, Espíritu, amor, alegría, paz, paciencia, amabilidad, bondad, fidelidad, humildad, dominio propio

Chapter 3

Ejercicio-A
1. ayer; **2.** el año pasado; **3.** anoche; **4.** hoy; **5.** el mes pasado; **6.** mañana; **7.** el domingo; **8.** septiembre; **9.** mañana por la mañana; **10.** el próximo año

Ejercicio-B
1. comí, comió, comió, comieron; **2.** adoró, adoramos, adoraste, adoraron; **3.** creó, crearon, creaste, creó; **4.** prometí, prometió, prometieron, prometió; **5.** compartieron, compartió, compartimos, compartí

Ejercicio-C
1. di, dio, dimos, dieron; **2.** fuimos, fue, fue, fuiste; **3.** fueron, fue, fueron

Match Up

1. d; **2.** c; **3.** f; **4.**g; **5.**i; **6.** j; **7.** a; **8.** b,e; **9.** l; **10.** h; **11.** m; **12.** n; **13.** h; **14.** o; **15.** k

Ejercicio-D

1. perdonabas, perdonaba, perdonaban, perdonábamos; **2.** sufrían, sufría, sufrían, sufría; **3.** evangelizaba, evangelizaba, evangelizaban, evangelizábamos; **4.** iba, íbamos, iba, ibas

Ejercicio-E

1. Sí, preparo mi lección de la Biblia. **2.** Sí, leímos su carta. **3.** Sí, necesitamos su apoyo. **4.** Sí, Dios contesta nuestras oraciones. **5.** Sí, recibí su invitación de boda.

Ejercicio-F

1. d; **2.** f; **3.** a; **4.** g; **5.** k; **6.** b; **7.** i; **8.** c; **9.** j; **10.** e; **11.** l; **12.** h

Scripture Passage

Cristo, bautizar, predicar, evangelio

Crossword Puzzle

```
 ¹P  A  ²D  R  E  N  ³U  E  S  T  R  O      ⁴D
     E      O              S                     ⁵D  I  O  ⁶S
     C      ⁷S ⁸A  L  ⁹V  A ¹⁰D  O  R     ¹¹D      Á      O
     A      R      A      A      A          E     ¹²C  O  M  O
     R     ¹³C  R  E  Y  E  N  T     ¹⁴E    C      O      E
            E      A           O          S      I      N      T
 ¹⁵J         P              ¹⁶S  A  C  E  R  D  O  T  E     ¹⁷S
¹⁸B  E  N  D  E  C  I  R              R                     E
     S         N                     I        ¹⁹C               Ñ
²⁰R  U  T     ²¹T  R ²²E  S        ²³T  I  E  R  N ²⁴O        O
     C         I      S           U      I      Í      R
²⁵O  R  O     ²⁶M  A  T  E  O        R     ²⁷S  E  R
     I         U           ²⁸P  A  Z     T     ²⁹O
³⁰É  S  A     E      D     ³¹T        S      I      R
     T         N      I      R        ³²G  R  A  C  I  A
³³N  O         T      O      O              N      C
 A        ³⁴L  O  S  S  I  N  T  E ³⁵C  H  O      I
 V        ³⁶S         B      O        R     ³⁷A     Ó
³⁸I  R  A         Í                 U     ³⁹A  Y  U  N  O
 D      T     ⁴⁰B  A  U  T ⁴¹I  Z ⁴²O      E      R
 A     ⁴³Á  N  G ⁴⁴E  L        G      F      R
 D      N     ⁴⁵N  I  Ñ  O     L      R     ⁴⁶C
               C           ⁴⁷E  L  E  G ⁴⁸I  D  O
    ⁴⁹C  R  E ⁵⁰A  D  O  R     S      N      D      R
        M      S           I      D      E      O
⁵¹P  E  R  D  Ó  N        ⁵²A  L  A  B  A  R
```

Chapter 4

Beatitudes
Verses: 3. (*none*); 4. serán, **ser**-to be; 5. recibirán, **recibir**-to receive; 6. serán, **ser**-to be; 7.serán, **ser**-to be; 8. verán, **ver**-to see; 9. serán, **ser**-to be; 10. (*none*)

Ejercicio-A
1. Alberto irá a la comunidad de inmigrantes. Yo iré a la comunidad de inmigrantes. Nosotros iremos a la comunidad de inmigrantes. Mi pastor irá a la comunidad de inmigrantes; **2.** María y Miguel llegarán después del bautizo. Usted llegará después del bautizo. Tú llegarás después del bautizo. Nosotros llegaremos después del bautizo; **3.** Yo serviré con su predicador. Nosotros serviremos con su predicador. Ellos servirán con su predicador. Ustedes servirán con su predicador.

Ejercicio-B
1. Mi hermano buscaría a Jesús. Los niños buscarían a Jesús. El pecador buscaría a Jesús. Nosotros buscaríamos a Jesús. **2.** Nuestro pastor enseñaría los estudios bíblicos. Miguel y yo enseñaríamos los estudios bíblicos. Usted enseñaría los estudios bíblicos. Los Señores Rodríguez enseñarían los estudios bíblicos. **3.** Tú creerías en las Escrituras. Usted y yo creeríamos en las Escrituras. El apóstol creería en las Escrituras. Los ángeles creerían en las Escrituras.

Ejercicio-C
1. Los misioneros vendrán esta noche. La madrina vendrá esta noche. Nosotros vendremos esta noche. Anna vendrá esta noche. **2.** Ustedes podrían visitar el orfanato. El diácono podría visitar el orfanato. Usted y yo podríamos visitar el orfanato. Yo podría visitar el orfanato.

Fill in the Blanks
1. F-¿Quién; **2.** B-quiere; **3.** C-Ellos; **4.** H-son; **5.** G-unos; **6.** D-pluma; **7.** E-La; **8.** F-al; **9.** J-tendría; **10.** I-dinero

Words of Discernment
1. D, names of Christ; **2.** C, places of worship; **3.** D, fruits of the Spirit

Ejercicio-D

1. Entraron en aquél. **2.** El patrocinador prefiere ésta. **3.** No quiero leer ése. **4.** El pastor entraba en aquéllos. **5.** Mañana sabré éstos. **6.** ¿Dónde estaba aquélla?

Ejercicio-E

1. Lucas invita a los misioneros. Lucas, invite usted a los misioneros. Inviten ustedes a los misioneros. **2.** Rita lleva el himno. Rita, lleve usted el himno. Lleven ustedes el himno. **3.** Ana abre la Biblia. Ana, abra usted la Biblia. Abran ustedes la Biblia. **4.** Lupe viene al grupo de apoyo de matrimonios. Lupe, venga usted al grupo de apoyo de matrimonios. Vengan ustedes al grupo de apoyo de matrimonios. **5.** María hace una donación. María, haga usted una donación. Hagan ustedes una donación.

The Ten Commandments

tener-to have
1. No <u>tengas</u> otros dioses además de mí.

hacer-to make
2. No <u>hagas</u> ningún ídolo.

pronunciar-to pronounce
3. No <u>pronuncies</u> el nombre del Señor tu Dios a la ligera.

Observar-to observe   *consagrar-to consecrate*
4. <u>Observa</u> el día sábado, y <u>conságraselo</u> al Señor tu Dios.

Honrar-to honor
5. <u>Honra</u> a tu padre y a tu madre.

matar-to kill
6. No <u>mates</u>.

cometer-to commit
7. No <u>cometas</u> adulterio.

robar-to rob
8. No <u>robes</u>.

dar-to give
9. No <u>des</u> testimonio falso en contra de tu prójimo.

Codiciar-to covet
10. No <u>codicies</u> la mujer de tu prójimo, ni nada que le pertenezca.

Ejercicio-F

1. Quiero que usted lea las noticias. Quiero que usted hable con ellos. Quiero que usted estudie la Biblia.

2. Mi padrino prefiere que yo converse con mi pastor. Mi padrino prefiere que yo ayude a mi pastor. Mi padrino prefiere que yo viaje con mi pastor.

3. El misionero necesita un pastor que lea la Biblia. El misionero necesita un pastor que visite las viudas. El misionero necesita un pastor que interprete.

Ejercicio-G

1. Mis amigos la escuchan. **2.** Luis y yo la aceptamos. **3.** Yo no las conocí. **4.** Usted los obedece. **5.** Tomás lo escribe. **6.** ¿Quién los ayudó? **7.** El pecador la necesita. **8.** El apóstol Juan lo escribió. **9.** El maestro lo predica. **10.** La niña lo oraba.

Ejercicio-H

1. indirect; **2.** indirect, direct; **3.** indirect, direct; **4.** direct; **5.** direct; **6.** indirect

Ejercicio-I

1. de ella; **2.** contigo; **3.** conmigo; **4.** para ti, para ellas; **5.** conmigo, con él; **6.** con ellos, con ella; **7.** a ella; **8.** a él; **9.** conmigo; **10.** con nosotros

Ejercicio-J

1. reflexive; **2.** reflexive; **3.** reflexive, reflexive; **4.** not reflexive; **5.** reflexive; **6.** not reflexive

Ejercicio-K

1. llama; **2.** amo; **3.** baña; **4.** afeita

Match Up

1. G; **2.** A; **3.** C; **4.** D; **5.** B; **6.** H; **7.** E; **8.** I; **9.** F; **10.** J

Crucigrama

See answers on following page

Scripture Passage

Be, pray, give, will, Christ Jesus

Crucigrama

	¹P	A	²L	A	B	R	A	S	B	L	³A	S	F	⁴E	M	⁵A	S		⁶I	R	⁷A
		E		U								B			S		D					Ñ
		R		⁸J	U	R	A	⁹M	E	¹⁰N	T	O			C		I		¹¹P			O
		S		U				A		E	M				L		C		E		¹²H
¹³L	E	E	R			¹⁴R		L		C	I				A		C		R		O
	C		¹⁵I	D	O	L	O			I	N				V		I		D		M
	U			A		B			O		¹⁶A	L	C	O	H	Ó	L	I	C	O
	C			¹⁷L	A				S		C					N		D		S
¹⁸V	I	C	I	O		¹⁹E				I		²⁰I			²¹D	O	L	E	R
	Ó				X		²²H	I	P	Ó	C	R	I	T	²³A				X
²⁴E	N	²⁵E	²⁶M	I	G	O	S			N		A		Ú		²⁷F		U
N		²⁸S	E		R		²⁹N				³⁰M	E	N	T	I	R	A
O		³¹A	N	T	I	C	R	I	S	T	O		A			E	L
J		T			I		Ñ			³²A	F	L	I	G	I	R	I
³³A	F	L	I	G	E	S		O		³⁴S		M	D			A	D
R			R			³⁵T	E	S	T	I	G	O	F	A	L	S	O	A
	³⁶J	A	C	T	A			N			R		D			³⁷N	A	D	A

Chapter 5

Ejercicio-A

1. Favor de ir al aeropuerto. **2.** Favor de interpretar este versículo. **3.** Favor de aprender su lección. **4.** Favor de esperar aquí. **5.** Favor de apoyar su comunidad. **6.** Favor de cerrar la puerta. **7.** Favor de llevar mi maleta. **8.** Favor de traerme las toallas. **9.** Favor de obedecer a sus padres. **10.** Favor de regresar mañana. **11.** Favor de no virar aquí. **12.** Favor de usar el mapa.

¿Quién es?

1. C; **2.** G; **3.** H; **4.** A; **5.** B; **6.** E; **7.** D; **8.** F; **9.** J; **10.** I

Words of Discernment

1. D, crucifixion; **2.** B, Books of the Old Testament; **3.** D, apostles of Jesus Christ; **4.** D, Old Testament prophets

Books of the Bible Word Search

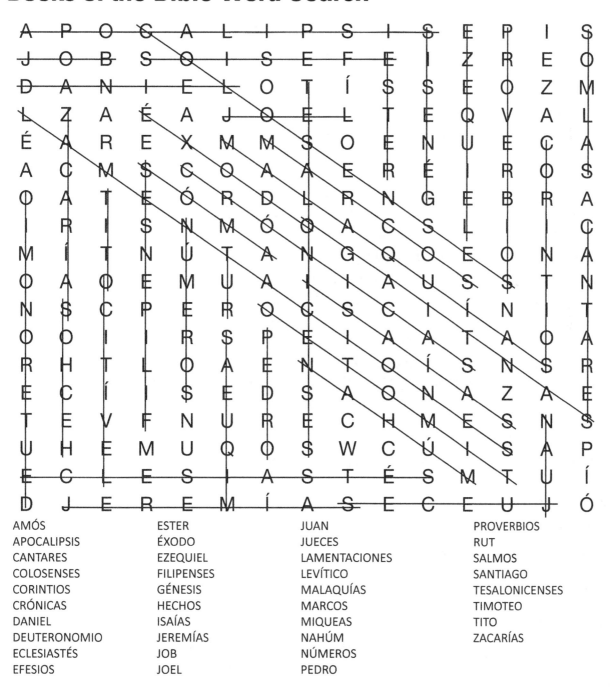

AMÓS	ESTER	JUAN	PROVERBIOS
APOCALIPSIS	ÉXODO	JUECES	RUT
CANTARES	EZEQUIEL	LAMENTACIONES	SALMOS
COLOSENSES	FILIPENSES	LEVÍTICO	SANTIAGO
CORINTIOS	GÉNESIS	MALAQUÍAS	TESALONICENSES
CRÓNICAS	HECHOS	MARCOS	TIMOTEO
DANIEL	ISAÍAS	MIQUEAS	TITO
DEUTERONOMIO	JEREMÍAS	NAHÚM	ZACARÍAS
ECLESIASTÉS	JOB	NÚMEROS	
EFESIOS	JOEL	PEDRO	

Ejercicio B

1. las invitaciones escritas; **2.** los regalos devueltos; **3.** una biblia cerrada; **4.** la comida preparada; **5.** los niños bautizados

Ejercicio C

1. Las invitaciones serán escritas por María. **2.** Ayer los regalos fueron devueltos por mi hermana. **3.** La ventana fue abierta por el ladrón. **4.** La comida fue preparada por mi madre. **5.** Nuestros niños serán bautizados por nuestro pastor.

Ejercicio D

1. hube abierto; **2.** has visto; **3.** hemos vivido; **4.** han hablado; **5.** habrá destruido

Scripture Passage

amado (loved), creído (believed), venido (came)

Ejercicio-E

Padre nuestro que estás en el (**CIELO** / iglesia / camino),
santificado sea tu (Biblia / hombre / **NOMBRE**),
venga tu (gloria / Dios / **REINO**),
hágase tu (servicio / **VOLUNTAD** / alma)
en la (cruz/ **TIERRA** / paz) como en el cielo.
Danos hoy nuestro (**PAN** / Mesías / ira) cotidiano.
Perdónanos nuestras (adicciones / **DEUDAS** / misas),
como (ninguno / nadie / **TAMBIÉN**) nosotros hemos
perdonado a nuestros (**DEUDORES** / lujurias / infierno).
Y no nos dejes caer en (**TENTACIÓN** / idolatría / Anticristo),
sino líbranos del (espíritu / **MALIGNO** / blasfemia).

Parables and Miracles

1. F; **2.** E; **3.** C; **4.** J; **5.** B; **6.** I; **7.** D; **8.** A; **9.** G; **10.** H

Scripture Passage

amado, complacido

Words of Discernment

1. A, Old Testament kings; **2.** A, special days of the year

Ejercicio-F

1. alabando; **2.** comiendo; **3.** comprando; **4.** aprendiendo; **5.** preparando; **6.** recibiendo; **7.** estudiando; **8.** saliendo; **9.** hablando; **10.** sufriendo

Visit us at www.SpanishForChristianService.com

Ejercicio-G

1. ellos están hablando; **2.** tú estás pensando; **3.** Marco y yo estamos escuchando; **4.** el misionero está viajando; **5.** el niño está llorando; **6.** yo estoy sirviendo; **7.** nosotros estamos comprando; **8.** Pedro está trayendo; **9.** el ladrón está huyendo; **10.** mis amigos están leyendo; **11.** los creyentes están alabando; **12.** los voluntarios están construyendo

Ecclesiastes 3: 1-8

verse 1 (no infinitives) **verse 2** nacer—to be born morir—to die plantar—to plant cosechar—to uproot **verse 3** matar—to kill sanar—to heal destruir—to destroy, tear down construir—to build **verse 4** llorar—to cry, weep reír—to laugh estar (de luto)—to mourn saltar (de gusto)—to dance, jump	**verse 5** esparcir—to scatter recoger(las)—to gather abrazarse—to embrace, hug despedirse—to say goodbye, refrain **verse 6** intentar—to attempt, search desistir—to desist, give up guardar—to keep desechar—to throw away **verse 7** rasgar—to tear coser—to sew, mend callar—to be silent hablar—to speak **verse 8** amar—to love odiar—to hate

Words of Discernment

1. D, sins   2. A, evil spirits   3. D, sexual sins

Selected Mystery Scriptures

2 John 3	Grace, mercy, peace, Jesus Christ, truth, love
1 Corin. 13:13	faith, hope, love, love
2 Tim. 1:2	Dios, Cristo Jesús, Señor
1 Thess. 1:5	gospel, power, Holy Spirit
John 3:16-18	God, only Son, eternal life, Son, world, condemn, world, save believes, condemned, believe, condemned, one & only (only begotten)
1 Thess. 5:16-18	Be, pray, give, will
Matt. 7:7-8	Ask, given, seek, find, knock, opened asks, receives, seeks, finds, knocks, opened
Psalms 46:10	Be, know
Prov. 3:5-6	Señor, corazón, caminos, sendas
Psalms 119:105	word, light
Matt. 7:21-23	Señor, Señor, reino, cielos, voluntad, Padre, cielo Señor, Señor, nombre, nombre, demonios, milagros hacedores, maldad
John 8:12	am, light, world, darkness, light, life
Phil. 4:19	Dios, todo, riquezas, Cristo Jesús
Matt. 11:28-30	Come, give, learn, am, heart, is
Phil. 1:6	buena obra, día, Cristo Jesús
Matt.11:25-26	Jesus, praise, Lord, heaven, earth, things, wise, children, Father, good
1 John 2:15	amen, mundo, ama, mundo, amor
Heb. 13:5-6	free, love, money, have, leave, forsake, confidence, Lord, afraid, do
Mark 8:36	mundo, entero

Heb. 4:12	word, living, soul, spirit, judges, heart
Col.3:23	trabajen, Señor
Jer. 29:11	have, Lord, hope, future
Matt. 19:17	Por qué, bueno, uno, bueno, vida, obedece, mandamientos
John 20:27-29	Thomas, Put, see, hand, Lord, God, Because, blessed, believed
John 10:27	voz, conozco
1 Corin. 2:9	However, no, no, no, God, love
Prov. 27:12	peligro, sufre
1 Thess 5:1-5	brothers, need, Day of the Lord, thief, night, Peace, safety, destruction, pains, escape, brothers, darkness, thief, sons, light, day, night, darkness
John 11:25-26	Jesús, resurrección, vida, cree, vivirá, vive, cree
Matt. 4:1-4	Jesus, Spirit, devil, forty days, forty nights, tempter, Son, God, Jesus, word, God
Matt.5:29-30	pecar, perder, infierno, pecar, perder, infierno
Phil. 4:13	can, Him (Christ)
Matt. 21:9	Hijo, Bendito, nombre del Señor, Hosanna
Matt 22:44	Lord, Lord, enemies
Phil. 1:3	gracias, Dios, vez, ustedes
Heb. 10:16	covenant, after, Lord, laws, heart (s), write
John 14:6	verdad, vida, Padre
James 4:7-8	God, devil, God, you
John 8:31-32	enseñas, discípulos, verdad, verdad
Rev. 1:8	Alpha, Omega, Lord God, is, was, come, Almighty
2 Tim. 1:7	Dios, espíritu, poder, amor
Prov. 27:1	boast, tomorrow, day
Psalm 8:4	hombre, que
Prov.15:1	answer, wrath

Workbook Review Answers

1. creador	**6.** bendecido	**11.** enseña	**16.** engaña
2. promete	**7.** perdonan	**12.** ayunó	**17.** blasfeman
3. redimió	**8.** debemos, ir	**13.** diezmo	**18.** adulteran
4. heredamos	**9.** somete	**14.** necesitan	**19.** sufrió
5. provee	**10.** invito	**15.** destrozado, apostó	**20.** enseñará

Translation Exercise Answers

1. Jesús me ama.
2. Gloria a Dios en el cielo.
3. Mi redentor vive.
4. Jesús hizo señales y maravillas/prodigios.
5. Rendí mi vida a Jesucristo.
6. Creo en milagros.
7. Nosotros perseveramos en nuestra fe Cristiana.
8. Nuestra esperanza está en Cristo.
9. Perdonamos con la gracia de Dios.
10. Él confía en la sabiduría del Espíritu Santo.
11. El evangelismo es un regalo del Espíritu.
12. Hoy ayunamos.
13. El grupo de compañerismo empieza el miércoles.
14. ¿Dónde está el servicio funerario?
15. Servimos la comunión el primer domingo de cada mes.
16. La asistencia de nuestra iglesia crece.
17. Tenemos la práctica de coro el martes.
18. ¿Le gustaría ser bautizado,-a?
19. Lloro la muerte de mi padre.
20. Los incrédulos sufrirán la tribulación.
21. Satanás acusa a los creyentes.
22. Ella es víctima de violación.
23. Él sufre de adicción y alcoholismo.
24. El juego es su debilidad.
25. Visitamos la cárcel de Florida los martes.

The Heavenly Minded

				[1] L		[2] S	[3] A	L	V	A	[4] C	I	Ó	N		[5] R	[6] A	P	T	[7] O
		[8] J		E			S				R						L			R
[9] E		[10] E	L	E	[11] S	P	Í	R	I	T	U	S	[12] A	N	T	[13] O				A
T		S			A						C		M			M			[14] S	R
E		U		[15] U	N	O	[16] S		[17] Á	N	I	M	O			[18] N	I	Ñ	O	
[19] R	I	C	O		T		A				F					I			B	
N		R		[20] C	I	E	L	O		[21] S	I	T	I	[22] O		[23] P	O	D	E	R
I		I			D		V		[24] P		X			R		O			R	
D		S			A		A		R		I		[25] S	A	N	T	I	D	A	D
A		T		[26] A	D	[27] O	R	N	O		Ó			R		E			N	
[28] D	I	O	S			M			[29] M	E	N	O	S		[30] U	N	O		O	
				[31] D		N		[32] D	E							T		[33] S		[34] H
[35] B	[36] E	[37] N	D	E	[38] C	I	R		[39] T	O	[40] D	[41] O	[42] P	O	D	E	R	O	S	O
	[43] L	O			O			[44] S	E		[45] I	R	A					L		N
	L		[46] M		[47] M	I	S	E	R	I	C	O	R	D	I	O	S	O		R
[48] C	A	R	I	Ñ	O			R			E		A							A

References

Chapter 1

1. "Spanish Pronto! New Spanish Alphabet," http://www.spanishpronto.com/spanishalphabet.html. last modified 4/2/11, accessed November 7, 2011.

2. "Principales novedades de la última edición de la lengua española (2010)," Real Academia Española, accessed October 24, 2011, http://www.rae.es/rae/gestores/gespub000018.nsf/ (voAnexos)/arch8100821B76809110C.

3. "Spanish Pronto! New Spanish Alphabet," http://www.spanishpronto.com/spanishalphabet.html.

4. "Spanish Pronto! New Spanish Alphabet," http://www.spanishpronto.com/spanishalphabet.html.

5. Turk, Laurel, Carlos Solé, and Aurelio Espinosa. *Foundation Course in Spanish* (Massachusetts: D.C Heath and Company, 1993), 4.

6. "Principales novedades de la última edición de la lengua española (2010)," Real Academia Española, accessed October 24, 2011, http://www.rae.es/rae/gestores/gespub000018.nsf/ (voAnexos)/arch8100821B76809110C.

7. Meizel, Janet. *Spanish for Medical Personnel* (Texas: Skidmore-Roth Publishing, 1993), X.

8. Turk, 395.

9. Ibid., 396.

10. Meizel, XIV.

11. Meizel, XV.

12. Meizel, XV.

13. Ibid., XV.

14. Ibid., XV.

15. Ibid., XVI.

16. Ibid., XVI.

17. Turk, 139.

18. Meizel, XVI.

19. Ibid., XVI.

20. Turk, 4.

21. Meizel, 1.

22. Turk, 17.

23. Meizel, 1.

24. Ibid., 1.

25. Turk, 18.
26. Meizel, 3.
27. Turk, 16.
28. Prado, Marcial. *Advanced Spanish Grammar, a Self Teaching Guide* (New York: John Wiley and Sons, 1984), 129.
29. Turk, 17.
30. Ibid., 17.
31. Zlotchew, Clark M. *Spanish at Your Fingertips* (New York: The Penguin Group, 2007), 71.
32. Turk, 31.
33. Zlotchew, 71-73.
34. Turk, 31-32.
35. Zlotchew, 75-76.
36. *Santa Biblia/Holy Bible, NVI/NIV Version* (Colorado: International Bible Society, 2007), 2Timothy 1:2, Revelation 4:8.

Chapter 2

1. Zlotchew, Clark M. *Spanish at Your Fingertips* (New York: The Penguin Group, 2007), 108-109.
2. Meizel, Janet. *Spanish for Medical Personnel* (Texas: Skidmore-Roth Publishing, 1993), 5.
3. Turk, Laurel, Carlos Solé, and Aurelio Espinosa. *Foundation Course in Spanish* (Massachusetts: D.C Heath and Company, 1993), 14.
4. Ibid., 55.
5. Turk, 28, 104.
6. Ibid., 18.
7. Ibid., 19.
8. Ibid., 19.
9. Ibid., 141-142.
10. Ibid., 29, 59-60.
11. Ibid., 70, 71.
12. Ibid., 30.
13. Ibid., 30.
14. Ibid., 30.
15. Renjilian-Burgy, Joy, Ana Beatriz Chiquito, and Susan M. Mraz. *Caminos* (Boston, Ma: Houghton Mifflin Company, 1999), 103.
16. Ibid., 103.
17. Ibid., 103.
18. Zlotchew, 91.
19. Turk, 45-46.
20. Zlotchew, 91-92.

21. Turk, 45.
22. Zlotchew, 94.
23. Turk, 46.
24. Ibid., 93.
25. Zlotchew, 311.
26. Ibid., 86-87.
27. Turk, 29.
28. Ibid., 162.
29. *Santa Biblia/Holy Bible, NVI/NIV Version* (Colorado: International Bible Society, 2007), Galatians 5:22.

Chapter 3

1. Turk, Laurel, Carlos Solé, and Aurelio Espinosa. *Foundation Course in Spanish* (Massachusetts: D.C Heath and Company, 1993), 47.
2. Zlotchew, Clark M. *Spanish at Your Fingertips* (New York:The Penguin Group, 2007), 33-34.
3. Turk, 46-47.
4. Ibid., 74.
5. Renjilian-Burgy, Joy, Ana Beatriz Chiquito, and Susan M. Mraz. *Caminos* (Boston, Ma: Houghton Mifflin Company, 1999), 174.
6. Turk, 139, 140.
7. Ibid., 140.
8. Ibid., 159.
9. Zlotchew, 146.
10. Turk, 158.
11. Ibid., 160-163.
12. Ibid., 57.
13. Ríos, Joanna, and Jóse Fernandez Torres. *McGraw-Hill's Complete Medical Spanish.* New York: McGraw-Hill, 2004, 57.
14. Ibid., 55.
15. Ibid., 144.
16. Ibid., 144.
17. Ibid., 96.
18. Ibid., 96.
19. Ibid., 144.
20. Ibid., 143.
21. Ibid., 163.
22. Prado, Marcial. *Advanced Spanish Grammar, a Self Teaching Guide* (New York: John Wiley and Sons, 1984), 83.
23. *Santa Biblia/Holy Bible, NVI/NIV Version* (Colorado: International Bible Society, 2007), 1Corinthians 1:17.

Chapter 4

1. Turk, Laurel, Carlos Solé, and Aurelio Espinosa. *Foundation Course in Spanish* (Massachusetts: D.C Heath and Company, 1993), 247-249.
2. *Santa Biblia/Holy Bible, NVI/NIV Version* (Colorado: International Bible Society, 2007), Mateo 5:3-10.
3. Ibid., Matthew 5:3-10.
4. Rios, Joanna, and Jóse Fernandez Torres. *McGraw-Hill's Complete Medical Spanish.* New York: McGraw-Hill, 2004, 95.
5. Zlotchew, Clark M. *Spanish at Your Fingertips* (New York:The Penguin Group, 2007), 158.
6. Ibid., 158.
7. Turk, 249.
8. Turk, 248.
9. Zlotchew 154, 155.
10. Turk, 211.
11. Ibid., 212.
12. Renjilian-Burgy, Joy, Ana Beatriz Chiquito, and Susan M. Mraz. *Caminos* (Boston, Ma: Houghton Mifflin Company, 1999), 124.
13. Zlotchew, 308-309.
14. Ibid., 249-250.
15. Turk, 56.
16. Ibid., 175.
17. Ibid., 266.
18. Ibid., 175.
19. Ibid., 175.
20. *Santa Biblia/Holy Bible, NVI/NIV Version* (Colorado: International Bible Society, 2007), Deuteronomio 5:6-21.
21. Zlotchew, 228.
22. Turk, 287-289.
23. Ibid., 287-288.
24. Prado, Marcial. *Advanced Spanish Grammar, a Self Teaching Guide* (New York: John Wiley and Sons, 1984), 209.
25. Turk, 289.
26. Prado, 209.
27. Zlotchew, 58.
28. Turk, 92.
29. Zlotchew, 60.
30. Turk, 105.
31. Ibid., 104-105.
32. Zlotchew, 60-62.

33. Ibid., 58.
34. Ibid., 61.
35. Turk, 105, 210.
36. Zlotchew, 65.
37. Turk, 192.
38. Ibid., 192.
39. Ibid., 192.
40. Ibid., 121.
41. Ibid., 122.
42. Zlotchew, 214, 217.
43. *Santa Biblia/Holy Bible, NVI/NIV Version* (Colorado: International Bible Society, 2007), 1 Thessalonians 5:16-18.

Chapter 5

1. Ríos, Joanna, and Jóse Fernandez Torres. *McGraw-Hill's Complete Medical Spanish.* New York: McGraw-Hill, 2004, 155.
2. *Santa Biblia/Holy Bible, NVI/NIV Version* (Colorado: International Bible Society, 2007).
3. Ibid.
4. Ibid.
5. Turk, Laurel, Carlos Solé, and Aurelio Espinosa. *Foundation Course in Spanish* (Massachusetts: D.C Heath and Company, 1993), 227.
6. Zlotchew, Clark M. *Spanish at Your Fingertips* (New York:The Penguin Group, 2007), 192.
7. Ibid, 193-195.
8. Ibid, 201.
9. Turk, 406.
10. Ibid., 406.
11. *Santa Biblia/Holy Bible, NVI/NIV Version* (Colorado: International Bible Society, 2007), John 16:27.
12. *Santa Biblia/Holy Bible, NVI/NIV Version,* Matthew 6:9-13.
13. *Santa Biblia/Holy Bible, Versión Reina Valera 1960/King James Version.* (Nashville: Broadman and Holman Publishers, 1988). Matthew 6:9-13.
14. *Santa Biblia/Holy Bible, Versión Reina Valera 1960/King James Version.*
15. Ibid.
16. *Santa Biblia/Holy Bible, NVI/NIV Version* (Colorado: International Bible Society, 2007), Matthew 3:17.
17. *Santa Biblia/Holy Bible, NVI/NIV Version,* Psalm 23:1-6.
18. Turk, 71.
19. Kendris, Christopher. *501 Spanish Verbs* (New York: Barron's Educational

Series), 1990, XI.
20. Zlotchew, 176.
21. Turk, 71.
22. Ibid., 190.
23. Ibid., 190.
24. Kendris, XI.
25. *Santa Biblia/Holy Bible, NVI/NIV Version,* Ecclesiastes 3:1-8.
26. *Santa Biblia/Holy Bible, NVI/NIV Version,* sources listed in individual selections.
27. Harvey, William. *Spanish for Health Care Professionals* (New York: Barron's Educational Series, 2008), 287-288.

Appendix

1. Turk, Laurel, Carlos Solé, and Aurelio Espinosa. *Foundation Course in Spanish* (Massachusetts: D.C Heath and Company, 1993), 92, 104.
2. Zlotchew, Clark M. *Spanish at Your Fingertips* (New York:The Penguin Group, 2007), 59-60.
3. Turk, 43, 95, 193.
4. Ibid., 194.
5. Kendris, Christopher. *501 Spanish Verbs* (New York: Barron's Educational Series), 1990, XXI-XXX.
6. Turk, 211, 323.
7. Ibid., 121, 142, 344.
8. Ibid., 28, 122, 159-161, 249-250, 289.
9. Kendris, XXI-XXX.
10. Devney, Dorothy. *Guide to Spanish Suffixes* (Illinois: Passport Books, 1992), 4, 30, 36, 57, 66, 73, 77, 82, 130, 132, 143, 165, 168, 171, 186, 187, 209, 213, 215.
11. Kendris, 130, 148, 157, 160, 228, 256, 259, 280, 366, 367, 392, 423, 426, 438, 469, 489, and 490.

Bibliography

Devney, Dorothy. *Guide to Spanish Suffixes*. Illinois: Passport Books, 1992.

Gold, David L. *Random House Latin-American Spanish Dictionary: Spanish-English, English-Spanish.* New York: Random House Publishing Group, 1996.

____. *Harrap's Concise Spanish, English-Spanish Español-English.* New York: Harrap Books Limited, 1991.

Harvey, William. *Spanish for Health Care Professionals*. New York: Barron's Educational Series, 2008.

Kendris, Christopher. *501 Spanish Verbs.* New York: Barron's Educational Series, 1990.

Meizel, Janet. *Spanish for Medical Personnel*. Texas: Skidmore-Roth Publishing, 1993.

Prado, Marcial. *Advanced Spanish Grammar, a Self Teaching Guide.* New York: John Wiley and Sons, 1984.

"Principales novedades de la última edición de la lengua española (2010)," Real Academia Española, accessed October 24, 2011, http://www.rae.es/rae/gestores/gespub000018.nsf/ (voAnexos)/arch8100821B76809110C.

Renjilian-Burgy, Joy, Ana Beatriz Chiquito, and Susan M. Mraz. *Caminos.* Boston, Ma: Houghton Mifflin Company, 1999.

Ríos, Joanna, and Jóse Fernandez Torres. *McGraw-Hill's Complete Medical Spanish.* New York: McGraw-Hill, 2004.

Santa Biblia/Holy Bible, NVI/NIV Version. Colorado: International Bible Society, 2007.

Santa Biblia/Holy Bible, Versión Reina Valera 1960/ King James Version. Nashville: Broadman and Holman Publishers,1988.

"Spanish Pronto! New Spanish Alphabet," http://www.spanishpronto.com/spanishalphabet.html. last modified 4/2/11, accessed November 7, 2011.

Turk, Laurel, Carlos Solé, and Aurelio Espinosa. *Foundation Course in Spanish.* Massachusetts: D.C Heath and Company, 1993.

Zlotchew, Clark M. *Spanish at Your Fingertips.* New York: The Penguin Group, 2007.

Index

F

favor de
    with infinitives, 117
Fill in the Blanks, 87
future action words, 82
future tense. *See* verbs: future tense

G

gerunds, 141

H

haber, *184*
    as a helping verb, 127
    subjunctive mood, 96
    uses with past participles, 127
hacer, *185*
    command form, 91
    past participle, 124
hay, 49
    with nouns, 50
Heavenly Minded Crossword, 162
huir
    present participle, 139

I

-ido endings, 124
imperfect tense. *See* verbs:imperfect tense
indefinite articles. *See* articles, indefinite
indefinite pronouns. *See* pronouns, indefinite
indirect object pronouns. *See* pronouns, indirect
    object
infinitive verb forms
    English to Spanish, 204
    Spanish to English, 209
infinitive verbs. *See* verbs: infinitive
interrogative pronouns. *See* pronouns, interrogative
ir, *186*
    command form, 92
    imperfect tense, 64
    past participle, 124
    past tense, 61
    present participle, 139
    present tense, 33
    subjunctive mood, 96
    with infinitives, 71
    with nouns, 71

L

la, 97, 167
language
    definite articles, 15
    definite articles before *hablar*, *en* or *de*, 16
las, 97, 167
le, 99, 167
leer
    present participle, 139
    with indirect object pronouns, 100
les, 99, 167
llegar
    use of prepositions with, 43
lo, 97, 167
location adverbs. *See* adverbs, location
Lord's Prayer
    NVI/NIV, 129
    Reina Valera/KJV, 130
los, 97, 167

M

mandar
    with indirect object pronouns, 100
Match Up, 62, 109
me, 97, 99, 103, 167, 175
mentir
    present participle, 139
mi, 66
mí, 101
mío, 175
mis, 66
morir
    past participle, 124
    present participle, 139
Mystery Scriptures, 146

N

nada, 35
nadie, 35
Names of the Holy Trinity, 24
-ndo endings, 138, 141
necesitar
    with infinitives, 71
    with nouns, 71
negative sentences
    double negatives, 35
negative sentences, forming, 35

Page Index of Scripture Verses

Pathway to Salvation

Dear God,	Amado Dios,
I believe that I am a sinner, and I repent of my sins. I believe in my heart that Jesus died for my sins, and now my sins are forgiven. I recognize Jesus as my Lord and Savior of my life. I ask that He may come into my life and be my Savior. Thank you, God Most High, for this precious gift of Salvation, in Jesus' name. Amen	Creo que soy pecador, y me arrepiento de mis pecados. Creo en mi corazón que Jesucristo murió por mis pecados, y ahora mis pecados son perdonados. Yo reconozco a Jesucristo como mi Señor y Salvador de mi vida. Yo le pido a Jesus que entre en mi vida y sea mi Salvador. Gracias, Dios Altísimo, por el regalo precioso de Salvación, en el nombre de Jesús. Amen.
Dear God,	Amado Dios,
I believe that I am a sinner, and I repent of my sins. I believe in my heart that Jesus died for my sins, and now my sins are forgiven. I recognize Jesus as my Lord and Savior of my life. I ask that He may come into my life and be my Savior. Thank you, God Most High, for this precious gift of Salvation, in Jesus' name. Amen	Creo que soy pecador, y me arrepiento de mis pecados. Creo en mi corazón que Jesucristo murió por mis pecados, y ahora mis pecados son perdonados. Yo reconozco a Jesucristo como mi Señor y Salvador de mi vida. Yo le pido a Jesus que entre en mi vida y sea mi Salvador. Gracias, Dios Altísimo, por el regalo precioso de Salvación, en el nombre de Jesús. Amen.

Travel and Everyday Encounters

I would like a roundtrip ticket.	*Quisiera un boleto de ida y vuelta.*
Where is the departure/arrival?	*¿Dónde está la salida/llegada?*
Here is my passport/document.	*Aquí está mi pasaporte/mi documento.*
I do not have anything to declare.	*No tengo nada declarar.*
Here are my suitcases.	*Aquí están mis maletas.*
I am staying for a few days/ weeks/months/ year.	*Me quedaré por unos días/unas semanas/unos meses/un año.*
Where is the exit/ entrance?	*¿Dónde está la salida/ entrada?*
Do you go to...?	*¿Va usted a...?*
How far is it from here?	*¿Cuántos lejos está de aquí?*
Do you have a map?	*¿Tiene usted un mapa?*
Is it north/south/east/west of here?	*¿Está al norte/sur/este/oeste de aquí?*
Where is the boat/bus/motor taxi/taxi/train/?	*¿Dónde está el bote/autobús/mototaxi/ taxi/ tren/?*
When does the train leave/arrive?	*¿Cuándo sale/llega el tren?*
Where is the airport/bank/ hotel/post office/restaurant/ restroom?	*¿Dónde está el aeropuerto/banco/ hotel/correo/restaurante/ cuarto de baño?*
Where is a church/ drugstore/ gas station/ grocery store?	*¿Dónde está una iglesia/ farmacia/ gasolinera/ tienda de comestibles?*
What time do they open/ close?	*¿A qué hora se abren/se cierran?*
Can you please help me?	*¿Por favor, puede ayudarme?*
Do you speak English?	*¿Habla inglés?*
We are lost.	*Estamos perdidos.*
Go straight ahead.	*Siga derecho.*
Turn around.	*Dé vuelta.*
Turn to the left/ right.	*Doble a la izquierda/derecha.*
Hello. Goodbye.	*Hola. Adios.*
Good morning/afternoon/ night.	*Buenos días/buenas tardes/ buenas noches.*
My name is... What is your name?	*Me llamo... ¿Cómo se llama?*
See you later.	*Hasta luego.*

What time is it?	*¿Qué hora es?*
How much does it cost?	*¿Cuánto cuesta?*
Excuse me. I am sorry.	*Con permiso. Lo siento.*
Please. Thank you.	*Por favor. Gracias.*
You are welcome.	*De nada.*
I do not understand.	*No lo comprendo.*
Please repeat that.	*Repítalo, por favor.*
Please speak slowly.	*Hable despacio, por favor.*
I need an interpreter.	*Necesito un intérprete.*
The bill please.	*La cuenta, por favor.*
Do you take credit cards/ traveler's checks?	*¿Se aceptan tarjetas de crédito/cheques de viajero?*
I want to pay in cash.	*Quiero pagar en efectivo.*
I need to make a phone call/ call collect.	*Necesito llamar por teléfono/ llamar a cobro revertido.*
I want to send an email.	*Quiero enviarle un mensaje electrónico.*
I need to go to the doctor/ hospital.	*Necesito ir al doctor/ hospital.*
I am sick.	*Estoy enfermo-/a.*
I have a backache/ headache/ stomach ache/ cramps/ chest pain.	*Tengo dolor de espalda/ dolor de cabeza/dolor de estómago/ calambres/ dolor de pecho.*
I feel nauseous/ dizzy.	*Tengo náusea/ mareos.*
I am allergic to ...	*Soy alérgico/-a a...*
I have the flu.	*Tengo gripe.*
I have a fever/diarrhea/ vomiting.	*Tengo fiebre/diarrea/vómito..*
Help!	*¡Ayúdeme!*
It is an emergency.	*Es una emergencia.*
No smoking.	*No fumar/ se prohíbe fumar.*
No parking.	*No estacionar /no aparcar.*
Danger!	*¡Peligro!*
Stop!	*¡Alto! ¡Pare!*
Police!	*¡Policía!*
Be careful!	*¡Cuidado!*

CPSIA information can be obtained at www.ICGtesting.com
Printed in the USA
LVOW021731230413

330561LV00011B/337/P